Notebook Leaflets from the Elmshaven Library Vol. 1

Ellen G. White

1945

Contents

Christian Experience 13
  Chapter 1—The Loving Watchcare of Jesus 14
    The Outward Adorning 14
    Self an Idol 15
    A Great Surprise 15
    Left Behind 16
    The Self-Deceived 16
    God's Purpose For His People 17
  Chapter 2—Christ Holds Control 18
    We Need More Faith 18
    Funds Needed 19
    Arise, Shine 19
    Awake! Awake! 20
    Never Be Discouraged 20
    Humility and Faith 21
  Chapter 3—Willing to Spend and Be Spent 22
    Help in Every Time of Need 23
  Chapter 4—How to Deal With Error 25
    Sanctifying Truth 25
    Bible Piety 26
    Artificial Lights 27
    Angels Looking for Co-operation 27
  Chapter 5—How to Be Preserved From Deceptive Influences 29
    Take Heed How Ye Hear 30
    Thousands of Streams 31
  Chapter 6—By Faith See Jesus 32
    Behold the Mighty Healer 33
    Choose! Oh, Choose! 34
  Chapter 7—Unity and Devotion 35
    The Ministry of Trials 37
  Chapter 8—In Every Place 38
  Chapter 9—Fortitude in Affliction 41
    Parents and Children 42

Chapter 10—Our Duty to the Missionary Work 44
   Jealousy Would Cease 45
   Our Message World Wide 45
   A Safe Investment 46
   Louder Than Words 47
   A Time for Economy 47
   Care in Benevolence 48
   Spiritual Awakening Called For 49
   Laborers with God 50
Chapter 11—A Deeper Experience 51
   Clasp the Hand of Christ 51
   The Life of Faith 52
   Looking Unto Jesus 53
   Look Up 53
Chapter 12—Examine Yourselves 54
   Serving in Meekness 54
   The Highest Service 55
   The Unnamed Multitudes 56
   Our Responsibilities 56
   What Are We Doing? 57
   A Great Awakening 57
   Warnings to Be Given 57
   Arise, Shine 58
   Daily Surrender 58
   Our Message 58
   Receiving and Giving 59
   In Hard Places 60
   Walk in the Light 60
Chapter 13—"No Other Gods Before Me" 62
   A Caution Regarding Extreme Positions 63
   One-Idea Men 63
   Pictures Used by God 64
Chapter 14—Be of Good Cheer 66
   Words of Encouragement 67
   Perplexities 67
   Present Duty 68
   The Final Triumph of Truth 70
Chapter 15—Good Angels More Powerful Than Evil 72

Power of Satan Limited	72
Chapter 16—Our Duty to Represent the Master	75
Bring Forth Good Fruit	75
Christ Judged by His Followers	76
When the Church Awakes	77
The Passive Graces	78
A Quick Work	79
Signs of Christ's Coming	79
At the End of the Conflict	80
The Keeping Power of God	80
The Church	83
Chapter 17—Babylon and the Remnant Church	84
The Church the Light of the World	84
A Work of Tearing Down	85
A Divinely Appointed Ministry	86
The Time of Celestial Glory	86
Miracles Not the Sign	87
Beware of False Teachers	87
Walk in Unity	88
Chosen Watchmen	88
No New Organization	88
What Constitutes Babylon	89
Poisonous Doctrines	89
Following Rome	89
Call to Come Out	89
The Sins of Babylon	90
The Doctrine of Eternal Torment	90
Alliance with the World	90
Chapter 18—Restlessness and Accusation	91
The Accuser Rebuked	91
The Encouraging Word	91
Words of Accusation Not of God	92
False Messages Will Come	92
A Work of Deception	93
The Need of Men and Means	93
Preparing a People to Stand	94
Restless Minds	94
Spurious Gifts	95

A Sound Work 96
Fruits of Inconsistency 97
Bibliography 97
Chapter 19—Apostasies 99
Charmed by Spurious Holiness 99
False Prophets 100
Rebellion and Apostasy 101
Voicing the Dragon's Words 101
The Shadows of Satan 102
Difficulties Lead to Prayer 102
Behold the Light 103
Growth in Grace 103
An Active Conflict 104
Deceived Men Oppose God's Law 104
Satan's Wiles 105
Denying Christ 105
Chapter 20—The Pillars of Our Faith 106
Prophecy Fulfilled 106
Confidence Assailed 107
Instruction Given the Redeemed 108
Christ's Abiding Presence 108
Work of Minister and Doctor 108
Chapter 21—Relation of Faith and Works 110
No Compromise With Sin 112
No Short Route to Holiness 113
Co-operation with God 113
Repentance the Gift of God 113
From First to Last, A Laborer Together With God 114
Effort and Labor Required 114
How Daniel Overcame 115
While Submitting to the Holy Spirit 115
He Becomes Our Righteousness 115
Chapter 22—Doubting the Testimonies 116
Error's Bewitching Power 117
Importance of Heeding Testimonies 117
A Partial Acceptance 118
The Cost of Rejection 118
What Are We Worth? 119

Chapter 23—What Are We Worth?	120
A Hypocritical Fast	120
The Acceptable Fast	121
The Reward	121
What Are We Worth?	121
Personal Experience	122
Our Privilege	123
In God Is Our Strength	123
Helping Establish A School	124
Opportunities for Service	124
Is Sister White Getting Rich?	125
A Gift to Our Schools	125
Perseverance Under Affliction	126
A Pioneer	126
Earnest, Untiring Activity	127
Simple Agencies Will Be Used	127
Chapter 24—An Earnest Appeal	129
Christ the Pattern Man	130
Hasty Decisions	131
The Influence of Doubt	132
A Commission from the King of Kings	133
Reward of Fidelity	134
The Two Paths	135
Exalting Christ	136
Education	137
Chapter 25—The Church School Question	138
The Home A School	138
Influence of the Home	138
Companionship of Angels	139
Miracle-Working Powers	139
Not Allowed to Drift	140
Politeness and Courtesy	140
Faith to Be Exercised	141
Lessons in Fellowship	142
Children to be Shielded From Contaminating Influences	142
Evils of Newspapers	143
An Unmistakable Distinction	143
A Lesson from Israel	143

Bible Principles Diligently Taught 144
A Reformation Necessary 144
Regarding Children 145
Chapter 26—Appeal to Young Men 147
The Expectation of Friends 147
Sympathy with Teachers 148
Fun and Lawlessness 149
Agents of Righteousness 150
Choosing a Leader 150
Help-One-Another Societies 151
Be Helpers 151
A Right Choice 152
Evil Associations to be Shunned 154
Chapter 27—Parents and Children 155
Converted Parents 156
A Training for Eternity 157
Co-Operation 157
Kindness and Patience 158
A Blessed Work 159
Arouse, Arouse, Arouse! 159
Chapter 28—A Work of Co-operation 161
A Divine Relationship 163
Perfection of Character 163
Words to Parents 164
Cultivate the Soil of the Heart 165
Why God Chose Abraham 165
The Harvest 166
Chapter 29—Home Training 167
Working in Unity 167
Govern with Wisdom 168
Vigilance 169
Effects of Misrule 170
Educate for the Master 170
A Sacred Circle 171
Husband the Time 172
Why Men are Condemned 173
Chapter 30—Useful Occupation Better Than Games 174
The Danger in Sports 174

The More Excellent Way	175
Missionary Work for Students	176
Beneficial Methods of Exercise	176
The Dangers to Spirituality	177
Need of Self-Sacrificing Effort	177
A Gracious Invitation	178
Example of Faithfulness	179
Methods	**181**
Chapter 31—Admonition Will Be Heard	182
Dangers of the Last Days	182
An Unflinching Testimony	182
Heard by All Classes	183
Nineveh an Example	183
False Hopes Exposed	184
What Shall We Do?	184
The Sword of Truth at Work	185
Repent! Repent!	185
The Message for Today	185
Stern Rebuke Called For	186
Earnestness is Necessary	187
Chapter 32—How to Present Truth	189
Creating A False Appetite	189
Works of Healing	189
Christ's Work Our Example	190
Best Methods for Large Cities	190
Avoid Peculiar Ideas	191
How to Shine	191
Chapter 33—Deeper Consecration	192
A Real Conversion Needed	192
An Inspiring Message	193
A Timely Warning	194
Working Together	194
Chapter 34—The Teaching of Extreme Views	195
Dwell on Essential Themes	195
Differing Experiences in Conversion	196
Leave Christ Room to Work	197
Idolizing Fine-Drawn Theories	197
Detached Sentences	198

Truth Mingled with Supposition	198
Straining for Originality	199
Talk Not of Divisions	200
Walk Day by Day with God	201
Harmonize with Your Brethren	201
Avoid Foolish Contentions	201
God's Way of Winning Souls	202
Chapter 35—Appeal to a Popular Evangelist	204
To Reach Thousands	204
Cultivate Gentleness	205
The Use of Flesh Meats	205
Our Relation to Health Reform	206
Be Like Minded	207
Divine and Human Agencies in the Work of Saving Souls	208
Messengers of Mercy	208
Chapter 36—Christ's Lifework and Ours	211
Christ the Pattern	212
Chapter 37—The Attitude in Prayer	214
To Bow Down	215
A Growing Laxness	216
A Token of Complete Subjection	217
On Bended Knee	218
Witnesses for God	218
Prayer Never Inappropriate	219
Chapter 38—Be Earnest and Steadfast	221
The Conflict of Two Leaders	221
Fanciful Theories Regarding God	222
Distinct Personalities	223
New Glories of the Word of God	223
Chapter 39—Brace Your Souls for Action	225
Work in the Cities	226
Barriers Broken Down	226
Work for Laymen in Cities	227
Growing in Grace	227
Chapter 40—A Variety of Gifts	229
"Have Root in Yourselves"	229
Pray for the Laborers	230
In Humanity and Weakness	231

Call for Action	231
Religion in the Home	232
Workers in Many Lines to Blend	232
By the Power of the Spirit	233
Begin at the Heart	233
God Honors the Humble Worker	234
Chapter 41—A Perfect Service Required By God	236
Proper Use of the Voice	236
Seek for Perfection	237
An Increase of Vitality	237
Counsel Regarding Prayer	238
Importunate, Prevailing Prayer	239
Angels Are Amazed	239
Spasmodic Repentance	240
As Morning Dew	241
Chapter 42—Give the Medical Missionary Work Its Place	243
The Call for Reform	244
Teaching Health Principles	244
A Pioneer Work	245
Each Member to Work	246
Practical Missionary Work	247
Come Into Line	247
No Better Way	248
Chapter 43—How to Open Closed Doors	249
No Other Work So Successful	249
A Revelation of Christ's Compassion	250
Brings Rays of Heavenly Brightness	251
This is True Ministry	251
The Right Hand of the Gospel	251
Preparing for Service	252
The Divine Plan	253
Christ's Instruction	253
In Time of Persecution	254
Zeal and Perseverance In Medical Missionary Work	255

Christian Experience

Chapter 1—The Loving Watchcare of Jesus[*]

By Ellen G. White

As I write I have a deep sense of gratitude for the loving watchcare of our Saviour over us all. As I read the Word of God and kneel in prayer, I am so impressed with the goodness and mercy of God that I cannot offer my petition without weeping. My heart is subdued and broken as I think of my heavenly Father's goodness and love. I hunger and thirst for more and still more of Jesus in *this* life. Christ was crucified for me, and shall I complain if I am crucified with Christ? ...

We know not what is before us, and our only safety is in walking with Christ, our hand in His, our hearts filled with perfect trust. Has He not said, "Let him take hold of My strength, that he may make peace with Me; and he shall make peace with Me"? Let us keep close to the Saviour. Let us walk humbly with Him, filled with His meekness. Let self be hid with Him in God....

The Outward Adorning

Those who cherish and flatter self, fostering pride and vanity, giving to dress and appearance the time and attention that ought to be given to the Master's work, are incurring a fearful loss. Many who are clothed in beautiful outward garments know nothing of the inward adorning that is in the sight of God of great price. Their fine clothing covers a heart that is sinful and diseased, full of vanity and pride. They know not what it means to "seek those things which are above, where Christ sitteth on the right hand of God."

I long to be filled day by day with the Spirit of Christ. The treasure of His grace is of more value to me than gold or silver or costly array. I never felt a more earnest longing for righteousness than at the present time.

---
[*]Portion of letter written February 18, 1904.

Self an Idol

When my sisters catch a glimpse of what Christ has suffered in their behalf, that they might become children of God by adoption, they will no longer be satisfied with worldly pride and self-love. No longer will they worship self. God will be the object of their supreme regard.

My heart aches as I am shown how many there are who make self their idol. Christ has paid the redemption price for them. To Him belongs the service of all their powers. But their hearts are filled with self-love, and the desire for self-adorning. They give no thought to the words, "Whosoever will come after Me, let him deny himself, and take up his cross, and follow Me." Self-gratification is hiding Christ from their view. They have no desire to walk before God in meekness and lowliness. They are not looking to Jesus. They are not praying that they may be changed into His likeness. Their cases are represented by the man who came to the king's banquet clothed in his common citizen dress. He had refused to make the preparation required by the king. The garment provided for him at great cost he disdained to wear. To the king's demand, "How camest thou in hither not having a wedding garment?" he could answer nothing. He was speechless; for he was self-condemned.

Many who profess to be Christians are such only in name. They are not converted. They keep self prominent. They do not sit at the feet of Jesus, as Mary did, to learn of Him. They are not ready for Christ's coming.

A Great Surprise

In the night season I was in a company of people whose hearts were filled with vanity and conceit. Christ was hid from their eyes. Suddenly in loud, clear accents, the words were heard, "Jesus is coming to take to Himself those who on this earth have loved and served Him, to be with Him in His kingdom forever." Many of those in the company went forth in their costly apparel to meet Him. They kept looking at their dress. But when they saw His glory, and realized that their estimation of one another had been so largely measured by outward appearance, they knew that they were without the robe of Christ's righteousness, and that the blood of souls was on their garments.

Left Behind

When Christ took His chosen ones, they were left; for they were not ready. In their lives self had been given the first place, and when the Saviour came, they were not prepared to meet Him.

I awoke with the picture of their agonized countenances stamped on my mind. I cannot efface the impression. I wish I could describe the scene as it was presented to me. Oh, how sad was the disappointment of those who had not learned by experience the meaning of the words, "Ye are dead, and your life is hid with Christ in God."

There are many professing Christians who know not Christ by an experimental knowledge. Oh, how my heart aches for these poor, deceived, unprepared souls! As I stand before congregations, and see the self-sufficient, self-righteous ones, and know that they are not preparing themselves to do acceptable work for Christ, and to meet Him in peace, I am so burdened that I cannot sleep. I ask myself, What can I say to these souls that will arouse them to a sense of their true condition? Self is the all-absorbing theme of their life. I long to reveal Christ so plainly that they will behold *Him*, and cease to center their attention on self....

The Self-Deceived

Among those to whom bitter disappointment will come at the day of final reckoning will be some who have been outwardly religious, and who apparently have lived Christian lives. But self is woven into all they do. They pride themselves on their morality, their influence, their ability to stand in a higher position than others, [and] their knowledge of the truth, for they think that these will win for them the commendation of Christ. "Lord," they plead, "we have eaten and drunk in Thy presence, and Thou hast taught in our streets." "Have we not prophesied in Thy name? and in Thy name have cast out devils? and in Thy name done many wonderful works?"

But Christ says, "I tell you, I know you not whence ye are; depart from Me." "Not every one that saith unto Me, Lord, Lord, shall enter into the kingdom of heaven; but he that doeth the will of My Father which is in heaven."

There is no discussion; the time for that is past. The irrevocable sentence has been pronounced. They are shut out from heaven by their own unfitness for its companionship. (Read Matthew 7:24-27.)—Letter 91, 1904.

* * * * *

Through the plan of redemption, God has provided means for subduing every sinful trait, and resisting every temptation, however strong.—The Review and Herald, December 22, 1885.

* * * * *

God's Purpose For His People

God has in store love, joy, peace, and glorious triumph for all who serve Him in spirit and in truth. His commandment-keeping people are to stand constantly in readiness for service. They are to receive increased grace and power, and increased knowledge of the Holy Spirit's working. But many are not ready to receive the precious gifts of the Spirit which God is waiting to bestow on them. They are not reaching higher and still higher for power from above, that, through the gifts bestowed, they may be recognized as God's peculiar people, zealous of good works.—Testimonies for the Church 8:247, 248.

* * * * *

If God's people had the love of Christ in the heart; if every church member were thoroughly imbued with the spirit of self-denial; if all manifested thorough earnestness, there would be no lack of funds for home and foreign missions; our resources would be multiplied; a thousand doors of usefulness would be opened, and we would be invited to enter. Had the purpose of God been carried out by His people in giving the message of mercy to the world, Christ would have come to the earth, and the saints would ere this have received their welcome into the city of God.—*Union Conference Record (Australasian), Oct. 15, 1898.*

Chapter 2—Christ Holds Control

By Ellen G. White

The Gergesenes desired Christ to depart. They of Capernaum received Him, and among them He wrought wonderful miracles.

Christ has all power in heaven and in earth. He is the great Physician, upon whom we are to call when suffering from physical or spiritual disease. Over the winds and the waves and over men possessed with demons, He showed that He possessed absolute control. To Him have been given the keys of death and of hell. Principalities and powers were made subject to Him, even while in His humiliation....

We Need More Faith

Why do we not exercise greater faith in the divine Physician? As He worked for the man with the palsy, so He will work today for those who come to Him for healing. We have great need of more faith. I am alarmed as I see the lack of faith among our people. We need to come right into the presence of Christ, believing that He will heal our physical and spiritual infirmities.

We are too faithless. Oh, how I wish that I could lead our people to have faith in God! They need not feel that in order to exercise faith, they must be wrought up into a high state of excitement. All they have to do is to believe God's Word, just as they believe one another's word. "He hath said it, and He will perform His Word." Calmly rely on His promise, because He means all that He says. Say, He has spoken to me in His Word, and He will fulfill every promise that He has made. Do not become restless. Be trustful. God's Word is true. Act as if your heavenly Father could be trusted....

Funds Needed

Men are appointed to proclaim the truth in new places. These men must have funds for their support. And they must have a fund to draw upon for the help of the poor and needy whom they meet in their work. The benevolence that they show toward the poor gives influences to their efforts to proclaim the truth. Their willingness to help those in need gains for them the gratitude of those they help, and the approval of Heaven.

These faithful workers should have the sympathies of the church. The Lord will hear prayer in their behalf. And the church should not fail to show a practical interest in their work.

No one lives to himself. In God's work each one is assigned a post of duty. The union of all strengthens the work of each. As the faith and love and unity of the church grow stronger, their circle of influence enlarges, and ever they are to reach to the farthest limit of this influence, constantly extending the triumphs of the cross.

Arise, Shine

God calls upon us to burst the bands of our precise, indoor service. The message of the gospel is to be borne in the cities and outside of the cities. We are to call upon all to rally around the banner of the cross. When this work is done as it should be, when we labor with divine zeal to add converts to the truth, the world will see that a power attends the message of truth. The unity of the believers bears testimony to the power of the truth that can bring into perfect harmony men of different dispositions, making their interests one.

[12]

The prayers and offerings of the believers are combined with earnest, self-sacrificing efforts, and they are indeed a spectacle to the world, to angels and to men. Men are converted anew. The hand that once grasped for recompense in higher wages has become the helping hand of God. The believers are united by one interest—the desire to make centers of truth where God shall be exalted. Christ joins them together in holy bonds of union and love, bonds which have irresistible power.

It was for this unity that Jesus prayed just before His trial, standing but a step from the cross. "That they all may be one," He said, "as Thou, Father, art in Me, and I in Thee, that they also may be one in us: that the world may believe that Thou hast sent Me."

Awake! Awake!

God calls upon those who are half awake to arouse, and engage in earnest labor, praying to Him for strength for service. Workers are needed. It is not necessary to follow rules of exact precision. Receive the Holy Spirit, and your efforts will be successful. Christ's presence is that which gives power. Let all dissension and strife cease. Let love and unity prevail. Let all move under the guidance of the Holy Spirit. If God's people will give themselves wholly to Him, He will restore to them the power they have lost by division. May God help us all to realize that disunion is weakness and that union is strength.—Letter 32, 1903.

* * * * *

Never Be Discouraged

Whatever may arise, never be discouraged. The Lord loves us, and He will perform His Word. Try to encourage in the patients a trust in God. Bid them be of good courage. Talk hope, even to the last. If they are to die, let them die praising the Lord. He ever lives; and though some of His faithful followers may fall in death, their works will follow them, and theirs will be a joyous awakening in the resurrection morning.

Let us not be discouraged. Let us not talk doubt, but faith; for faith brings infinite power. If we lay hold upon this power, and do not trust in our own human strength, we shall see the salvation of God. There are many who are hungering and thirsting for a better knowledge of spiritual truths, and it is the privilege of those in this institution to impart to them that which will satisfy their longing.—The Review and Herald, December 30, 1909.

* * * * *

Humility and Faith

In the work for this time, it is not money or talent or learning or eloquence that are needed so much as faith graced with humility. No opposition can prevail against truth presented in faith and humility, by workers who willingly bear toil and sacrifice and reproach for the Master's sake. We must be co-workers with Christ if we would see our efforts crowned with success. We must weep as He wept for those who will not weep for themselves, and plead as He pleaded for those who will not plead for themselves.—Manuscript 24, 1903.

Chapter 3—Willing to Spend and Be Spent

By Ellen G. White

He who loves God supremely and his neighbor as himself will work with the constant realization that he is a spectacle to the world, to angels, and to men. Making God's will his will, he will reveal in his life the transforming power of the grace of Christ. In all the circumstances of life, he will take Christ's example as his guide.

Every true, self-sacrificing worker for God is willing to spend and be spent for the sake of others. Christ says, "He that loveth his life shall lose it; and he that hateth his life in this world shall keep it unto life eternal." By earnest, thoughtful efforts to help where help is needed, the true Christian shows his love for God and for his fellow beings. He may lose his life in service. But when Christ comes to gather His jewels to Himself, he will find it again.

My brethren and sisters, do not spend a large amount of time and money on self, for the sake of appearance. Those who do this are obliged to leave undone many things that would have comforted others, sending a warm glow to their weary spirits. We all need to learn how to improve more faithfully the opportunities that so often come to us to bring light and hope into the lives of others. How can we improve these opportunities if our thoughts are centered upon self? He who is self-centered loses countless opportunities for doing that which would have brought blessing to others and to himself. It is the duty of the servant of Christ, under every circumstance, to ask himself, "What can I do to help others?" Having done his best, he is to leave the consequences with God.

I desire so to live that in the future life I can feel that during this life I did what I could. God has provided for every one pleasure that may be enjoyed by rich and poor alike—the pleasure found in cultivating pureness of thought and unselfishness of action, the pleasure that comes from speaking sympathizing words and doing kindly deeds. From those who perform such service the light of Christ shines to brighten lives darkened by many shadows.

God is dishonored when we fail to speak the truth plainly to one another. But we are to speak the truth in love, bringing tenderness and sympathy into our voices.

The perils of the last days are upon us. Those who live to please and gratify self are dishonoring the Lord. He cannot work through them, for they would misrepresent Him before those who are ignorant of the truth. Be very careful not to hinder, by an unwise expenditure of means, the work that the Lord would have done in proclaiming the warning message to a world lying in wickedness. Study economy, cutting down your personal expense to the lowest possible figure. On every hand the necessities of the cause of God are calling for help. God may see that you are fostering pride. He may see that it is necessary to remove from you blessings which, instead of improving, you have used for the gratification of selfish pride. The truth that we hear will save us only as we gladly accept it, showing in our lives the result of its working, growing in grace and in a knowledge of God.

Help in Every Time of Need

Those who are laboring in places where the work has not long been started, will often find themselves in great need of better facilities. Their work will seem to be hindered for lack of these facilities; but let them not worry. Let them take the whole matter to the Lord in prayer. When trying to build up the work in new territory, we have often gone to the limit of our resources. At times it seemed as if we could not advance farther. But we kept our petitions ascending to the heavenly courts, all the time denying self; and God heard and answered our prayers, sending us means for the advancement of the work.

Lay every care at the feet of the Redeemer. "Ask, and ye shall receive." Work, and pray, and believe with the whole heart. Do not wait until the money is in your hands, before doing anything. Walk out by faith. God has declared that the standard of truth is to be planted in many places. Learn to believe, as you pray to God for help. Practice self-denial; for Christ's whole life on this earth was one of self-denial. He came to show us what we must be and do in order to gain eternal life.

Do your best, and then wait, patiently, hopefully, rejoicingly, because the promise of God cannot fail. Failure comes because many who could put their means into circulation for the advancement of God's work are lacking in faith. The longer they withhold their means, the less faith they will have. They are barrier builders, who fearfully retard the work of God.

My dear fellow workers, be true, hopeful, heroic. Let every blow be made in faith. As you do your best, the Lord will reward your faithfulness. From the life-giving fountain draw physical, mental, and spiritual energy. Manliness, womanliness—sanctified, purified, refined, ennobled—we have the promise of receiving. We need that faith which will enable us to endure the seeing of Him who is invisible. As you fix your eyes upon Him, you will be filled with a deep love for the souls for whom He died, and will receive strength for renewed effort.

Christ is our only hope. Come to God in the name of Him who gave His life for the world. Rely upon the efficacy of His sacrifice. Show that His love, His joy, is in your soul, and that because of this your joy is full. Cease to talk unbelief. In God is our strength. Pray much. Prayer is the life of the soul. The prayer of faith is the weapon by which we may successfully resist every assault of the enemy.—Manuscript 24, 1904.

*****

If we will restrain the expression of unbelief, and by hopeful words and prompt movements strengthen our own faith and the faith of others, our vision will grow clearer. The pure atmosphere of heaven will surround our souls.—Testimonies for the Church 6:462.

Chapter 4—How to Deal With Error

By Ellen G. White

When errors come into our ranks, we are not to enter into controversy over them. We are to present the message of reproof and then lead the minds of the people away from fanciful, erroneous ideas, presenting the truth in contrast with error. Presenting heavenly scenes will open up principles that rest upon a foundation as enduring as eternity.

Christ is the root, His people are the branches. This makes a perfect whole. Those people are most serviceable to the Master whose Christian convictions are so consistent and so commendable that their characters are of solid worth. Nothing can move them from the faith. Truth is to them a precious treasure. The truth of God is found in His Word, and those who feel that they must seek elsewhere for present truth need to be converted anew. They have habits to mend, evil ways to be abandoned. They need to seek anew the truth as it is in Jesus, that their character building may be in harmony with the lessons of Christ. As they abandon their human ideas and take up their duties, beholding Christ and becoming conformed to His image, they say, "Nearer, my God, to Thee, nearer to Thee, e'en though it be a cross that raiseth me."

Sanctifying Truth

With the Word of God in hand, we may draw nearer, step by step, in consecrated love, to Jesus Christ. Let those who have been deluded give up all their fallacies. The love of Jesus will not endure such rivals. As the Spirit of God becomes better known, the Bible will be received as the only foundation of faith. God's people will receive the Word as the leaves of the tree of life, more precious than fine gold purified in the fire and more powerful to sanctify than any other agency. To talk of Christ without the Word leads to sentimentalism. And to receive the theory of the Word, without accepting and appreciating the Author, makes men legal formalists. But Christ and His precious Word are in perfect harmony. Received and obeyed, they open a sure path for the feet of all who are willing to walk in the light as Christ is in the light.

If the people of God would appreciate His Word, what a heaven we should have here below in the church. Christians would be eager, hungry to search the Word. They would be anxious for time to compare scripture with scripture and to meditate upon the Word. They would be more eager for the light of the Word than for the morning papers, magazines, or novels. Their greatest desire would be to eat the flesh and drink the blood of the Son of God.

And as a result their lives would be conformed to the principles and promises of His Word. Its instruction would be to them as the leaves of the tree of life. It would be in them a well of water, springing up unto everlasting life. Refreshing showers of grace would refresh and revive the soul, causing them to forget all weariness and toil. They would be strengthened and encouraged by the words of inspiration.

[16] Then the ministers would be inspired by divine truth. Their prayers would be characterized by earnestness, filled with the divine assurance of truth. Weariness would be forgotten as the soul basks in the sunlight from the heavenly atmosphere. Truth would be interwoven with their lives, and its heavenly principles would be as a fresh running stream, continually satisfying the soul. "And thou shalt be like a watered garden, and like a spring of water, whose waters fail not....

Bible Piety

The Lord's philosophy is the rule of the Christian's life. The entire being is imbued with the life-giving principles of heaven. The busy nothings which consume the time of so many shrink into their proper subordinate position before a healthy, sanctifying, Bible piety. The Bible, and the Bible alone, can produce this good fruit. It is the wisdom of God and the power of God, and it works with all power in the receptive heart. Oh, what might we not reach if we would conform our wills to the will of God. Oh, it is the power of God we need, my dear brother and sister, wherever we are. The mass of frivolity that cumbers the church makes it weak and inefficient. The Father, the Son, and the Holy Spirit are seeking and longing for channels through which to communicate the divine principles of truth to the world.

Artificial Lights

Artificial lights may appear, claiming to come from heaven, but they cannot shine forth as the star of holiness, the star of heavenly brightness, to guide the feet of the pilgrim and the stranger into the city of our God. Shall we allow heaven's bright beams to be eclipsed by artificial lights? False lights will take the place of the true, and many souls will be for a time deceived. God forbid that it should be so with us. The true light now shineth, and will light up the windows of the soul that are opened heavenward.—Letter 43, 1901.

* * * * *

Angels Looking for Co-operation

Satan uses human agents to bring the soul under the power of temptation, but the angels of God are searching for human agents through whom they may co-operate to save the tempted ones. Angels are looking for those who will work in Christ's lines, who will be moved by the realization that they belong to Christ. They are looking for those who will feel that those who fall under temptation, whether high or low, are the ones who need their special labors, and that Christ looks on those who are passed by, neglected, wounded, and bruised by the enemy, and ready to die, and is grieved at the hardness of men, who refuse to exercise the faith that works by love, which will purify the soul.

Angels of God will work with, and through, and by those who will co-operate with the heavenly agencies for the saving of a soul from death, and the hiding of a multitude of sins, that will lead them to consider themselves, lest they also be tempted.

It is the sick that need a physician, not those who are whole. When you expend labor on those who do not need it, and take no notice of the very ones whom your words and actions could bless, you are forming a character that is not after the likeness of Christ—Letter 70, 1894.

Chapter 5—How to Be Preserved From Deceptive Influences

By Ellen G. White

Satan often finds a powerful agency for evil in the power which one human mind is capable of exerting on another human mind. This influence is so seductive that the person who is being molded by it is often unconscious of its power. God has bidden me speak warning against this evil, that His servants may not come under the deceptive power of Satan. The enemy is a master worker, and if God's people are not constantly led by the Spirit of God, they will be snared and taken.

For thousands of years Satan has been experimenting upon the properties of the human mind, and he has learned to know it well. By his subtle workings in these last days, he is linking the human mind with his own, imbuing it with his thoughts; and he is doing this work in so deceptive a manner that those who accept his guidance know not that they are being led by him at his will: The great deceiver hopes so to confuse the minds of men and women, that none but his voice will be heard.

When Christ revealed to Peter the time of trial and suffering that was just before Him, and Peter replied, "Be it far from Thee, Lord: this shall not be unto Thee," the Saviour commanded, "Get thee behind Me, Satan." Satan was speaking through Peter, making him act the part of the tempter. Satan's presence was unsuspected by Peter, but Christ could detect the presence of the deceiver, and in His rebuke to Peter He addressed the real foe.

On one occasion, speaking to the twelve, and referring to Judas, Christ declared, "One of you is a devil." Often in the days of His earthly ministry the Saviour met His adversary in human form, when Satan as an unclean spirit took possession of men. Satan takes possession of the minds of men today. In my labors in the cause of

God, I have again and again met those who have been thus possessed, and in the name of the Lord I have rebuked the evil spirit.

It is not by force that Satan takes possession of the human mind. While men sleep, the enemy sows tares in the church. While men are spiritually sleeping, the enemy accomplishes his work of iniquity. It is when his subject "understandeth it not" that he catcheth away the good seed sown in the heart. When men and women are in this condition, when their spiritual life is not being constantly fed by the Spirit of God, Satan can imbue them with his spirit, and lead them to work his works....

I entreat that there may be a putting away from the life every action which does not bear the approval of God. We are drawing near to the close of earth's history; the battle is growing daily more fierce. There is a day appointed when men who have bowed to the mandates of Satan will find themselves the subjects of the wrath of God, when the Judge of all the earth shall pronounce the sentence against Satan and his adherents, "Depart from Me, ye cursed, into everlasting fire, prepared for the devil and his angels."—Letter 244, 1907.

[18] ## Take Heed How Ye Hear

From time to time we need unitedly to examine the reasons of our faith. It is essential that we study carefully the truths of God's Word; for we read that "some shall depart from the faith, giving heed to seducing spirits, and doctrines of devils." We are in grave danger when we lightly regard any truth; for then the mind is opened to error. We must take heed how and what we hear. We need not seek to understand the arguments that men offer in support of their theories, when it may be readily discerned that these theories are not in harmony with the Scriptures. Some who think that they have scientific knowledge are by their interpretations giving wrong ideas both of science and of the Bible. Let the Bible decide every question that is essential to man's salvation....

Only by accepting Christ as a personal Saviour, can human beings be uplifted. Beware of any theory that would lead men to look for salvation from any other source than that pointed out in the Word. Only through Christ can men sunken in sin and degradation be led to a higher life. Theories that do not recognize the atonement that has been made for sin, and the work that the Holy Spirit is to do in the hearts of human beings, are powerless to save.

Man's pride would lead him to seek for salvation in some other way than that pointed out in the Scriptures. He is unwilling to be accounted as nothing, unwilling to recognize Christ as the only One who can save to the uttermost. To this pride Satan appealed in the temptation that he brought to our first parents. "Ye shall be as gods"; "ye shall not surely die," he said. And by a belief of his words, they placed themselves on his side.—Letter 25, 1904.

* * * * *

Thousands of Streams

When our churches will fulfill the duty resting upon them, they will be living, working agencies for the Master. The manifestation of Christian love will fill the soul with a deeper, more earnest fervor to work for Him who gave His life to save the world. By being good and doing good Christ's followers expel selfishness from the soul. To them the most costly sacrifice seems too cheap to give. They see a large vineyard to be worked, and they realize that they must be prepared by divine grace to labor patiently, earnestly, in season and out of season, in a sphere which knows no boundaries. They obtain victory after victory, increasing in experience and efficiency, extending on all sides their earnest efforts to win souls for Christ. They use to the best advantage their increasing experience; their hearts are melted by the love of Christ.

We shall see the medical missionary work broadening and deepening at every point of its progress, because of the inflowing of hundreds and thousands of streams, until the whole earth is covered as the waters cover the sea.—Manuscript 32, 1901.

Chapter 6—By Faith See Jesus

By Ellen G. White

I am pleased that the Lord is in mercy again visiting the church. My heart trembles as I think of the many times He has come in and His Holy Spirit has worked in the church; but after the immediate effort was over, the merciful dealings of God were forgotten. Pride, spiritual indifference, was the record made in heaven. Those who were visited by the rich mercy and grace of God, dishonored their Redeemer by their unbelief.

When Christ was upon the earth, He used every means possible to gain admission to the hearts of those whose doors should have been thrown open to receive Him. He came to His vineyard seeking fruit. He dug about the vine He had planted. He pruned it and dressed it. But when He looked for grapes, behold, only wild grapes rewarded His care. The people disappointed their Saviour.

How earnestly and untiringly Christ labored to reach the most lowly, as well as those who occupied higher positions. Hear Him saying to His disciples, "Sit ye here, while I go and pray yonder." What an example He gave them of His prayers in their behalf, that their faith should not fail, but increase.

Christ's heart was ever touched by human woe. He walked and worked in the streets of the cities, teaching the weary, inviting them to come to Him, crying, "Come unto Me, all ye that labor and are heavy laden, and I will give you rest. Take My yoke upon you, and learn of Me; for I am meek and lowly in heart: and ye shall find rest unto your souls. For My yoke is easy, and my burden is light." Christ employed every means to arrest the attention of the impenitent. How tender and considerate were His dealings with all. He longed to break the spell of infatuation upon those who were deceived and deluded by satanic agencies. He longed to give the sin-polluted soul pardon and peace.

Behold the Mighty Healer

Christ was the mighty Healer of all spiritual and physical maladies. Look, oh, look upon the sympathetic Redeemer. With the eye of faith behold Him walking in the streets of the cities, gathering the weak and weary to Himself. Helpless, sinful human beings crowd about Him. See the mothers with their sick and dying little ones in their arms pressing through the crowd that they may get within reach of His notice and touch. Let the eye of faith take in the scene. Watch these mothers pressing their way to Him, pale, weary, almost despairing, yet determined and persevering, bearing their burden of suffering in their arms.

As these anxious ones are being crowded back, Christ makes His way to them step by step, until He is close by their sides. Tears of gladness and hope fall freely as they catch His attention, and look into the eyes expressing such tender pity and love, for the weary mother as well as for the suffering child. He invites her confidence, saying, What shall I do for you? She sobs out her great want, Master, that Thou wouldest heal my child. She has shown her faith in urging her way to Him, though she did not know that He was making His way to her; and Christ takes the child from her arms. He speaks the word, and disease flees at His touch. The pallor of death is gone; the life-giving current flows through the veins; the muscles receive strength.

[20]

Words of comfort and peace are spoken to the mother, and then another case just as urgent is presented. The mother asks help for herself and her children; for they are all sufferers. With willingness and joy Christ exercises His life-giving power, and they give praise and honor and glory to His name who doeth wonderful things.

No frown on Christ's countenance spurned the humble suppliant from His presence. The priests and rulers sought to discourage the suffering and needy, saying that Christ healed the sick by the power of the devil. But His way could not be hedged up. He was determined not to fail or become discouraged. Suffering privation Himself, He traversed the country that was the scene of His labor, scattering His blessings, and seeking to reach obdurate hearts.

That Saviour has oft visited you in -----. Just as verily as He walked the streets of Jerusalem, longing to breathe the breath of spiritual life into the hearts of those discouraged and ready to die, has He come to you. The cities that were so greatly blessed by His presence, His pardon, His gifts of healing, rejected Him....

Jerusalem is a representation of what the church will be if it refuses to receive and walk in the light that God had given. Jerusalem was favored of God as the depository of sacred trusts. But her people perverted the truth, and despised all entreaties and warnings. They would not respect His counsels. The temple courts were perverted with merchandise and robbery. Selfishness and love of mammon, envy and strife, were cherished. Everyone sought for gain from his quarter. Christ turned from them, saying, O Jerusalem, Jerusalem, how can I give thee up? "How often would I have gathered thy children together, even as a hen gathereth her chickens under her wings, and ye would not." So Christ sorrows and weeps over our churches, over our institutions of learning, that have failed to meet the demand of God....

Choose! Oh, Choose!

Those who receive Christ by faith as their personal Saviour cannot be in harmony with the world. There are two distinct classes. One is loyal to God, keeping His commandments, while the other talks and acts like the world, casting away the Word of God, which is truth, and accepting the words of the apostate, who rejected Jesus.

On whose side are we? The world cast Christ out; the heavens received Him. Man, finite man, rejected the Prince of life; God, our Sovereign Ruler, received Him into the heavens. God has exalted Him. Man crowned Him with a crown of thorns; God has crowned Him with a crown of royal majesty. We must all think candidly. Will you have this man Christ Jesus to rule over you, or will you have Barabbas? The death of Christ brings to the rejecter of His mercy the wrath and judgments of God, unmixed with mercy. This is the wrath of the Lamb. But the death of Christ is hope and eternal life to all who receive Him and believe in Him.—Letter 31, 1898.

Chapter 7—Unity and Devotion

By Ellen G. White

The Lord has appointed His work to go forward in missionary lines in such a way as to extend the knowledge of the truth for these last days. A deception has certainly been on those who ought to have been wide awake to see the great, grand work to be done by the people who bear God's sign as represented in Exodus 31:12-18.

The Lord desires faithful stewards to measure the fields to be worked, and then use wisely His means in advancing the work in these fields. God has a people, and a ministry, who are to co-operate with Him....

The Lord will work for His people if they will submit to be worked by the Holy Spirit, not thinking that they must work the Spirit. "And now, Israel, what doth the Lord thy God require of thee, but to fear the Lord thy God, to walk in all His ways, and to love Him, and to serve the Lord thy God with all thy heart and with all thy soul, to keep the commandments of the Lord, and His statutes, which I command thee this day for thy good?" ...

God's ministers have a most solemn, sacred work to do in our world. The end is near. The message of truth must go. As faithful shepherds of the flock, God's servants are to bear a clear, sharp testimony. There is to be no perverting of the truth. Divine grace never leads away from mercy and the love of God. It is the power of Satan that does this. When Christ preached, His message was like a sharp, two-edged sword, piercing the consciences of men and revealing their inmost thoughts. The work that Christ did His faithful messengers will have to do. In simplicity, purity, and the strictest integrity they are to preach the Word. Those who labor in word or doctrine are to be faithful to their charge. They are to watch for souls as they that must give an account. Never are they to clothe a "Thus saith the Lord" with enticing words of man's wisdom. Thus they destroy its living energy, making it weak and powerless, so that it fails to convict of sin. Every word spoken by the direction of the Holy Spirit will be full of the deepest solicitude for the salvation of souls.

The minister's acceptance with God depends not on outward show, but on his faithful discharge of duty. Christ's road to exaltation lay through the deepest humiliation. Those who are partakers with Christ in His sufferings, who follow cheerfully in His footsteps, will be partakers with Him in His glory.

It has been the continual endeavor of the enemy to introduce into the church persons who assent to much that is truth, but who are not converted. Professed Christians who are false to their trust are channels through whom Satan works. He can use unconverted church members to advance his own ideas and retard the work of God. Their influence is always on the side of wrong. They place criticism and doubt as stumbling blocks in the way of reform. They introduce unbelief because they have closed their eyes to the righteousness of Christ and have not the glory of the Lord as their rereward.

[22] Unity is the strength of the church. Satan knows this, and he employs his whole force to bring in dissension. He desires to see a lack of harmony among the members of the church of God. Greater attention should be given to the subject of unity. What is the recipe for the cure of the leprosy of strife and dissension? Obedience to the commandments of God.

God has been teaching me that we are not to dwell upon the differences which weaken the church. He prescribes a remedy for strife. By keeping His Sabbath holy we are to show that we are His people. His Word declares the Sabbath to be a sign by which to distinguish the commandment-keeping people. Thus God's people are to preserve among them a knowledge of Him as their Creator. Those who keep the law of God will be one with Him in the great controversy commenced in heaven between Satan and God. Disloyalty to God means contention and strife against the principles of God's law.

Everything connected with the cause of God is sacred, and is to be thus regarded by His people. The counsels that have any reference to the cause of God are sacred. Christ gave His life to bring a sinful world to repentance. Those who are imbued with the spirit that dwelt in Christ will work as God's husbandmen in caring for His vineyard. They will not merely work in spots which they may choose. They are to be wise managers and faithful workers, making it their highest aim to fulfill the commission which Christ has given. Just before His ascension the Saviour told His disciples that beginning at Jerusalem they must go to all nations, kindreds, tongues, and peoples; and He added, "Lo, I am with you always, even unto the end of the world."—Manuscript 14, 1901.

* * * * *

The Ministry of Trials

In Christian experience, the Lord permits trials of various kinds to call men and women to a higher order of living and to a more sanctified service. Without these trials there would be a continual falling away from the likeness of Christ, and men would become imbued with a spirit of scientific, fanciful, human philosophy, which would lead them to unite with Satan's followers.

In the providence of God, every good and great enterprise is subjected to trials, to test the purity and the strength of the principles of those who are standing in positions of responsibility, and to mold and substantiate the individual human character after God's model. This is the highest order of education.

Perfection of character is attained through exercise of the faculties of the mind, in times of supreme test, by obedience to every requirement of God's law. Men in positions of trust are to be instrumentalities in the hands of God for promoting His glory, and in performing their duties with the utmost faithfulness, they may attain perfection of character.

In the lives of those who are true to right principles, there will be a continual growth in knowledge. They will have the privilege of being acknowledged as colaborers with the great Master Worker in behalf of the human family, and will act a glorious part in carrying out the purposes of God. Thus, by precept and example, as laborers together with God, they will glorify their Creator.—Manuscript 85, 1906.

Chapter 8—In Every Place

By Ellen G. White

Christ was the great Medical Missionary to our world. He calls for volunteers who will co-operate with Him in the great work of sowing the world with truth. God's workers are to plant the standards of truth in every place to which they can gain access. The world needs restoring. It is lying in wickedness and the greatest peril. God's work for those out of Christ should broaden and extend. God calls upon His people to labor diligently for Him, so that Christian efficiency shall become widespread. His kingdom is to be enlarged. Memorials for Him are to be raised in America and in foreign countries.

The work of health reform connected with the present truth for this time, is a power for good. It is the right hand of the gospel, and often opens fields for the entrance of the gospel. But let it ever be remembered that the work must move solidly and in complete harmony with God's plan of organization. Churches are to be organized, and in no case are these churches to divorce themselves from the medical missionary work. Neither is the medical missionary work to be divorced from the gospel ministry. When this is done, both are one-sided. Neither is a complete whole.

The work for this time is to appeal to the Christian's mind as the most important work that can be done. It is the question of cultivating the Lord's vineyard. In this vineyard every man has a lot and a place, which the Lord has assigned him. And the success of each depends on his individual relationship to the one Divine Head.

The grace and love of our Lord Jesus Christ and His tender relationship to His church on earth are to be revealed by the growth of His work and the evangelization of people in many places. The heavenly principles of truths and righteousness are to be seen more and still more plainly in the lives of Christ's followers. More unselfishness and uncovetousness is to be seen in business transactions than has been seen in the churches since the pouring out of the Holy Spirit on the day of Pentecost. Not a vestige of the influence of selfish, worldly monopolies is to make the slightest impression on the people who are watching and working and praying for the second coming of our Lord and Saviour Jesus Christ in the clouds of heaven with power and great glory.

As a people we are not ready for the Lord's appearing. If we would close the windows of the soul earthward and open them heavenward, every institution established would be a bright and shining light in the world. Each member of the church, if he lived the great, elevated, ennobling truths for this time, would be a bright shining light. God's people cannot please Him unless they are surcharged with the Holy Spirit's efficiency. So pure and true is to be their relationship to one another that by their words, their affections, their attributes, they will show that they are one with Christ. They are to be as signs and wonders in our world, carrying forward intelligently every line of the work. And the different parts of the work are to be so harmoniously related to one another that all will move like well-regulated machinery. Then will the joy of Christ's salvation be understood. There will then be none of the representation now made by those who have been given the light of truth to communicate, but who have not revealed the principles of truth in their association with one another, who have not done the Lord's work in a way that glorifies Him....

After Christ rose from the dead, He proclaimed over the sepulcher, "I am the resurrection and the life." Christ, the risen Saviour, is our life. As Christ becomes the life of the soul, the change is felt, but language cannot describe it. All claims to knowledge, to influence, to power, are worthless without the perfume of Christ's character. Christ must be the very life of the soul, as the blood is the life of the body....

Those who are connected with the service of God must be purified from every thread of selfishness. All is to be done in accordance with the injunction, "Whatsoever ye do, in word or deed, do all to the glory of God." God's laws of justice and equity must be strictly obeyed in the transactions between neighbor and neighbor, brother and brother. We are to seek for perfect order and perfect righteous-

[24]

ness, after God's own similitude. On these grounds alone will our works bear the test of the judgment....

Christianity is the revealing of the tenderest affection for one another. The Christian life is made up of Christian duties and Christian privileges. Christ in His wisdom gave to His church in its infancy a system of sacrifices and offerings, of which He Himself was the foundation, and by which His death was prefigured. Every sacrifice pointed to Him as the Lamb slain from the foundation of the world, that all might understand that the wages of sin is death. In Him was no sin, yet He died for our sins.

The symbolic system of ceremonies worked to one end—the vindication of the law of God, that all who believe in Christ might come "in the unity of the faith, and of the knowledge of the Son of God, unto a perfect man, until the measure of the stature of the fullness of Christ." In Christian work there is ample room for the activity of all the gifts God has given. All are to be united in carrying out God's requirements, revealing at every advance step that faith which works by love and purifies the soul.

Christ is to receive supreme love from the beings He has created. And He requires also that man shall cherish a sacred regard for his fellow beings. Every soul saved will be saved through love, which begins with God. True conversion is a change from selfishness to sanctified affection for God and for one another. Will Seventh-day Adventists now make a thorough reformation, that their sin-stained souls may be cleansed from the leprosy of selfishness?

I must speak the truth to all. Those who have accepted the light from God's Word are never, never to leave an impression upon human minds that God will serve with their sins. His Word defines sin as the transgression of the law.—Manuscript 16, 1901.

Chapter 9—Fortitude in Affliction

By Ellen G. White

Dear Brother and Sister,

When the last mail was enveloped and sent to the office, I had six pages written that, by some mistake of mine, were left out of the envelope....

You will not forget that I am doing considerable writing. Every mail has taken from one to two hundred pages from my hand, and most of it has been written either as I am now propped up on the bed by pillows, half lying or half sitting, or bolstered up sitting in an uncomfortable chair.

It is very painful to my hip and to the lower part of my spine to sit up. If such easy chairs were to be found in this country as you have at the Sanitarium, one would be readily purchased by me, if it cost thirty dollars.... It is with great weariness that I can sit erect and hold up my head. I must rest it against the back of the chair on the pillows, half reclining. This is my condition just now.

But I am not at all discouraged. I feel that I am sustained daily. In the long weary hours of the night when sleep has been out of the question, I have devoted much time to prayer; and when every nerve seemed to be shrieking with pain, when if I considered myself, it seemed I should go frantic, the peace of Christ has come into my heart in such measure that I have been filled with gratitude and thanksgiving. I know that Jesus loves me and I love Jesus. Some nights I have slept three hours; a few nights four hours and much of the time only two, and yet in these long, Australian nights, in the darkness, all seems light about me, and I enjoy sweet communion with God.

When I first found myself in a state of helplessness I deeply regretted having crossed the broad waters. Why was I not in America? Why at such expense was I in this country? Time and again I could have buried my face in the bed quilts and had a good cry. But I did not long indulge in the luxury of tears. I said to myself, "Ellen G. White, what do you mean? Have you not come to Australia because you felt that it was your duty to go where the Conference judged it best for you to go? Has not this been your practice?" I said, "Yes." "Then why do you feel almost forsaken and discouraged? Is not this the enemy's work?" I said, "I believe it is." I dried my tears as quickly as possible and said, "It is enough; I will not look on the dark side any more. Live or die, I commit the keeping of my soul to Him who died for me."

I then believed that the Lord would do all things well, and during this eight months of helplessness, I have not had any despondency or doubt. I now look at this matter as a part of the Lord's great plan, for the good of His people here in this country, and for those in America, and for my good. I cannot explain why or how, but I believe it. And I am happy in my affliction. I can trust my heavenly Father. I will not doubt His love. I have an ever-watchful guardian day and night, and I will praise the Lord; for His praise is upon my lips because it comes from a heart full of gratitude.—Letter 18a, 1892.

Parents and Children

Many parents who have believed the truth for years have failed to train their children in the way they should go. Notwithstanding all the light that has shone on them, they have indulged their children, making them mere household pets, mere idols....

Too often parents allow their children to grow up in ignorance of household labor. To save their children the least discomfort, the father and the mother make themselves the household drudges. They get up early in the morning to build a fire and cook breakfast. While they are busy with their daily cares, they allow their dear, lazy children to lie in bed, calling them only in time to eat that which has been prepared by the labor of others. They consult the wishes of their children and excuse them if they are not up early.

What a delusion parents must be under who pursue so unwise a course in training children! In thus making everything secondary to the supposed comfort of their children, unwise parents deprive them of the capacity for enjoying even this life. Parents should train their daughters to bear life's burdens, that they may be well qualified to act their part as faithful, judicious, ingenious, economical housekeepers. In afterlife they will appreciate the training that taught them to bear burdens.

Many girls from sixteen to twenty years of age are unskilled in cookery or in any other kind of domestic labor. These girls can eat, sleep, and dress; they can use their fingers in doing fancy-work; but they claim that labor over a washtub makes them sick. Cooking they do not understand. "Mother prefers to cook," they say. Why does she?—Because her daughters have not chosen to help her. They have not been trained to enjoy the doing of home duties and are as unfitted to become wives as are babies.

Among us are hard-working men, men who earn large wages, but who are always financially cramped and often in debt. What is the cause?—Nothing more, nothing less, than this: Their wives are not practical housekeepers. In their youth they did not gain the experience that they should have gained. They are not skilled cooks. They waste much—enough to supply another family. Yet their own families are not half provided with nourishing food. They think they must use canned meat, or something else already prepared. If in their girlhood such wives had been taught how to make a little go as far as possible, they could prepare palatable, nourishing food from simple, inexpensive ingredients.

Such girls seldom realize and remedy their deficiencies, and therefore, when they become mothers, they are unprepared to educate their children aright. They cannot give to others the knowledge that they themselves do not possess. Because of a lack of care, skill, economy, and experience in household matters, both mothers and children waste much. Thus they spend all that the father earns. The hard-working husband and father is always cramped financially. Because he never has at his command means to aid the cause of God, he is discouraged.

These cases are not rare. On every hand they are to be found. And many an honest, truehearted man has become so discouraged and desperate that in order to lighten his load he has been led to practice dishonesty.—Manuscript 21, 1902.

Chapter 10—Our Duty to the Missionary Work*

By Ellen G. White

The members of the church are not all called to labor in foreign lands, but all have a part to act in the great work of giving light to the world. The gospel of Christ is aggressive and diffusive. In the day of God not one will be excused for having been shut up to his own selfish interests. There is work for every mind and for every hand. There is a variety of work, adapted to different minds and varied capabilities. Everyone who is connected with God will impart light to others. If there are any who have no light to give, it is because they have no connection with the Source of light.

Ministers should not do the work which belongs to the church, thus wearying themselves, and preventing others from performing their duty. They should teach the members how to labor in the church and in the community. There is work for all to do in their own borders, to build up the church, to make the social meetings interesting, and to train the youth of ability to become missionaries. All should cultivate spirituality and self-sacrifice, and by their means and their earnest prayers assist those who enter new and difficult fields. They should co-operate actively with the minister in his labors, making the section of country around them their field of missionary effort; and the larger churches should labor to build up and encourage those that are weak or few in numbers.

This work has been neglected. Is it any marvel that God does not visit the churches with greater manifestations of His power, when so large a number are shut in to themselves, engrossed in their own interests? It is thus that their piety becomes tame and weak, and they grow bigoted and self-caring. It is in working for others that they will keep their own souls alive. If they will become co-laborers with Jesus, we shall see the light in our churches steadily burning

---
*A appeal written in 1886 from Basel, Switzerland.

brighter and brighter, sending forth its rays to penetrate the darkness beyond their own borders.

Jealousy Would Cease

A close sympathy with Christ in His mission of love and mercy would bring the workers into sympathy with one another, and there would be no disposition to cherish the evils, which, if indulged, are the curse of the churches. The jealousy and fault finding, the heartburnings, the envy and dissension, the strife for the supremacy, would cease. The attention given to the work of saving souls would stimulate the workers themselves to greater piety and purity. There would be with them a unity of purpose, and the salvation of the soul would be felt to be of so great importance that all little differences would be lost sight of....

Heaven is indignant at the ease of men and women in Zion, while souls are going down to ruin in their ignorance and their sins. If the members of the church were to see themselves as God sees them, they would be overwhelmed with self-reproach. They could not endure to look their responsibilities and delinquencies in the face.

Our Message World Wide

If we indeed have the truth for these last days, it must be carried to every nation, kindred, tongue, and people. Erelong the living and the dead are to be judged according to the deeds done in the body, and the law of God is the standard by which they are to be tested. Then they must now be warned; God's holy law must be vindicated, and held up before them as a mirror. To accomplish this work, means is needed. I know that times are hard, money is not plenty; but the truth must be spread, and money to spread it must be placed in the treasury....

Our message is world wide; yet many are doing literally nothing, many more so very little, with so great a want of faith, that it is next to nothing. Shall we abandon the fields we have already opened in foreign countries? Shall we drop part of the work in our home missions? Shall we grow pale at a debt of a few thousand dollars? Shall we falter and become laggards now, in the very last scenes of this earth's history? My heart says, No, no. I cannot contemplate this question without a burning zeal to have the work go. We would not deny our faith, we would not deny Christ, yet we shall do this unless we move forward as the providence of God opens the way.

A Safe Investment

The work must not stop for want of means. More means must be invested in it. Brethren in America, in the name of my Master I bid you wake up! You that are placing your talents of means in a napkin and hiding them in the earth, who are building houses and adding land to land, God calls upon you, "Sell that ye have, and give alms." There is a time coming when commandment keepers can neither buy nor sell. Make haste to dig out your buried talents. If God has entrusted you with money, show yourselves faithful to your trust; unwrap your napkin, and send your talents to the exchangers, that when Christ shall come, He may receive His own with interest.

In the last extremity, before this work shall close, thousands will be cheerfully laid upon the altar. Men and women will feel it a blessed privilege to share in the work of preparing souls to stand in the great day of God, and they will give hundreds as readily as dollars are given now. If the love of Christ were burning in the hearts of His professed people, we would see the same spirit manifested today. Did they but realize how near is the end of all work for the salvation of souls, they would sacrifice their possessions as freely as did the members of the early church. They would work for the advancement of God's cause as earnestly as worldly men labor to acquire riches. Tact and skill would be exercised, and earnest and unselfish labor put forth to acquire means, not to hoard, but to pour into the treasury of the Lord.

What if some become poor in investing their means in the work? Christ for your sakes became poor; but you are securing for yourselves eternal riches, a treasure in heaven that faileth not. Your means is far safer there than if deposited in the bank, or invested in houses and lands. It is laid up in bags that wax not old. No thief can approach it, no fire consume it.

Some have selfishly retained their means during their lifetime, trusting to make up for their neglect by remembering the cause in their wills; but not one half the means thus bestowed in legacies ever comes to the objects specified. Brethren and sisters, invest in the bank of heaven yourselves, and do not leave your stewardship upon another.

Louder Than Words

In obeying the Saviour's injunction, our example will preach louder than words. The highest display of the power of truth is seen when those who profess to believe it give evidence of their faith by their works. Those who believe this solemn truth should possess such a spirit of self-sacrifice as will rebuke the worldly ambition of the money worshiper.

My soul is burdened as I look over the destitute fields here in Europe, and see the poverty of many, and the difficulties they must meet in keeping the Sabbath, and then think how the way to reach souls is blocked up for want of means. The Lord has made provision that all may be reached by the message of truth, but the means placed in the hands of His stewards for this very purpose has been selfishly devoted to their own gratification.

How much has been thoughtlessly wasted by our youth, spent for self-indulgence and display, for that which they would have been just as happy without. Every dollar which we possess is the Lord's. Instead of spending means for needless things, we should invest it in answering the calls of missionary work.

A Time for Economy

As new fields are opened, the calls for means are constantly increasing. If ever we needed to exercise economy it is now. All who labor in the cause should realize the importance of closely following the Saviour's example of self-denial and economy. They should see in the means they handle a trust which God has committed to them, and they should feel under obligation to exercise tact and financial ability in the use of their Lord's money. Every penny should be carefully treasured. A cent seems like a trifle, but a hundred cents make a dollar, and rightly spent may be the means of saving a soul from death. If all the means which has been wasted by our own people in self-gratification had been devoted to the cause of God, there would be no empty treasuries, and missions could be established in all parts of the world.

Let the members of the church now put away their pride and lay off their ornaments. Each should keep a missionary box at hand, and drop into it every penny he is tempted to waste in self-indulgence. But something more must be done than merely to dispense with superfluities. Self-denial must be practiced. Some of our comfortable and desirable things must be sacrificed. The preachers must sharpen up their message, not merely assailing self-indulgence, and pride in dress, but presenting Jesus, His life of self-denial and sacrifice. Let love, piety, faith be cherished in the heart, and the precious fruits will appear in the life.

Care in Benevolence

In many cases means which should be devoted to the missionary work is diverted into other channels, from mistaken ideas of benevolence. We may err in making gifts to the poor which are not a blessing to them, leading them to feel that they need not exert themselves and practice economy, for others will not permit them to suffer. We should not give countenance to indolence, or encourage habits of self-gratification by affording means for indulgence. While the worthy poor are not to be neglected, all should be taught, so far as possible, to help themselves. The salvation of souls is the burden of our work. It was for this that Christ made the great sacrifice, and it is this that specially demands our beneficence.

We shall be brought into strait places in our work. Trials will come. God will test the strength of our faith; He will prove us to see if we will trust Him under difficulties. The silver and gold are the Lord's, and when His stewards have done their duty fully, and can do no more, they are not to sit down at ease, let things take their course, and let the missionary work come to a standstill. It is then that they should cry to God for help. Let those who have faith seek the Lord earnestly, remembering that "the kingdom of heaven suffereth violence, and the violent taketh it by force."

There are those in the church who have with open hand and heart come forward to the work hitherto, and they will not be behind now. We have confidence in their integrity. But the offerings of the church have been in many instances more numerous than her prayers. The missionary *movement* is far in advance of the missionary *spirit*. Earnest prayers have not, like sharp sickles, followed the workers into the harvest field. It is true there is an interest to see success attend the efforts to unfurl the banner of truth in foreign lands, but there has been a lack of heartfelt sympathy with the laborers, and real burden of soul that the means invested may do its work.

Spiritual Awakening Called For

This is the ground of our difficulties; this is the reason for the pressure for means. The people must be called to reflection. There must be a spiritual awakening. They must have a personal interest, a burden of soul, to watch and pray for the success of the work. Let every one who gives of his means also send up his prayers daily that it may bring souls to the foot of the cross. In every church there should be stated seasons for united prayer for the advancement of this work. Let all be united, having a specific object for their faith and entreaties. Brethren, move high heaven with your prayers for God to work with the efforts of His servants.

We need to cry to God as did Jacob for a fuller baptism of the Holy Spirit. The time for labor is short. Let there be much praying. Let the soul yearn after God. Let the secret places of prayer be often visited. Let there be a taking hold of the strength of the Mighty One of Israel. Let the ministers walk humbly before the Lord, weeping between the porch and the altar, and crying, "Spare Thy people, O Lord, and give not Thine heritage to reproach."

Let none indulge the thought that we have attempted too much. No, no; we have attempted too little. The work which we are now doing ought to have been done years ago. Our plans must enlarge, our operations must be extended. What is needed now is a church whose individual members shall be awake and active to do all that is possible for them to accomplish.

Laborers with God

We are not left alone in this work. We are laborers together with God, in partnership with divine resources. The Lord has agencies that He will put in operation in answer to the importunate prayer of faith. He will fulfill His word, "Lo, I am with you alway, even unto the end of the world." The Captain of our salvation is on every field of battle where truth is waging war against error. The truth which we profess offers the highest encouragement to the most devoted self-denial and persevering effort that mortal energies can bestow. We should have the courage of heroes and the faith of martyrs.—*Historical Sketches of S.D.A. Foreign Missions, pp. 290-294.*

Chapter 11—A Deeper Experience

By Ellen G. White

Dear Brother and Sister Haskell,

Never did I see as now the necessity of thorough sanctification to God. We teach the truth, but do we practice it? Is the Word of God eaten by us? Do we drink the water of life in the rich current of love? Do we practice the Word of God by seeking for that perfect unity that should exist? "Sanctify them through Thy truth: Thy Word is truth." We must have a deeper experience, which will lead us to let go self and hold fast to Christ.

If we keep a firm hold of self, we cannot possibly get hold of Christ. Let us now who believe that the end of all things is at hand, seek the Lord most earnestly. It is no time to be depressed. There is no safety in trusting in self. We must educate our souls to trust in God. I see that Satan will contest every step of progress we may make. There is no safety for us only as we walk with our hands in the hand of Christ. Our feet will sometimes slip upon the supposed safest path. But the only safe path is to be sure we love God supremely and our neighbor as ourself.

Clasp the Hand of Christ

Not one thread of selfishness must be drawn into the fabric of character we are weaving. To go on without fear we must know that an almighty hand will hold us up, and an infinite humanity in Christ pities us. But do not let us pity ourselves, for this is not the thing to do. It is not enough for us to have faith in law and force, things which have no pity, and never hear the cry for help. We need to clasp a hand that is warm, and trust in a heart full of love and tenderness. We are never to feel that there is no danger, thinking, "I have a large experience; I shall never fall." God permits the wisest to be brought into circumstances which reveal their human weakness. We shall meet with obstacles all along the path heavenward, but if we abide in Christ, self will not appear in so many ways.

"As ye have therefore received Christ Jesus the Lord, so walk ye in Him, rooted and built up in Him, and stablished in the faith, as ye have been taught." Through faith we receive the Lord Jesus. Through faith we are united to Him. Through faith we are rooted and established in Him. We are united with Christ. We are not to lose our first love. He will each day do for us who are repenting, believing sinners just as much as He did when we first surrendered our hearts to Him.

The Life of Faith

We are to live a life of faith in Jesus Christ. That love that He has manifested for us is to be an increasing love. Self must die. We find that this is hard; for self dies hard. It is not our work to uphold self. "Without Me," Christ says, "ye can do nothing." The life of grace is always a life of faith. Without faith it is impossible to please God.

My brother, might you not better look to the source of your strength, and take Christ at His word? Feeling is nothing; praise of men, good or bad, is nothing. Whatever men may say or think of me, it cannot make me white or black. I am not changed in character at all by what others think of me. Looking unto Jesus, who is the Author and Finisher of my faith, I can overcome all things. My guilt in the past He has forgiven. Saying the words in faith, I am in Christ. He is the parent stock. According to my faith I unite fiber to fiber with the living Vine. The parent stock bears me, not I the parent stock.

All things are possible to him that believeth. We need not try to lead ourselves. He leads, He guides, He sanctifies through the truth. We need now, just now, to surrender self, and all its worries and perplexities. If we live by every word that proceeds from the mouth of God, we possess the richest grace mortals can have. But if we look on the dark side, and talk unbelief, we shall have plenty of unbelief. Throw this rubbish overboard, and taking the oars of faith, row as for your life. Do not think of self, but of Christ. Draw nigh to God, and then you will draw nigh to one another. You will love as brethren. Remember that Jesus intercedes for erring souls.

Looking Unto Jesus

You need not be surprised if everything in the journey heavenward is not pleasant. There is no use in looking to our own defects. Looking unto Jesus, the darkness passes away, and the true light shineth. Go forth daily, expressing the prayer of David, "Hold up my goings in Thy paths, that my footsteps slip not." All the paths of life are beset with peril, but we are safe if we follow where the Master leads the way, trusting the One whose voice we hear saying, "Follow Me." "He that followeth Me shall not walk in darkness, but shall have the light of life." Let your heart repose in His love. We need sanctification, soul, body, and spirit. This we must seek for....

Look Up

We must do our work purely and faithfully even though there is no one in the world to say, "It is well done." Our lives must be just what God designs they shall be, faithful in good words, in kind and thoughtful deeds, in the expression of meekness, purity, and love. Thus we represent Christ to the world. On our own peculiar phase of character, whatever it may be, Christ can imprint His own image, if we will allow Him to do this. The toil-worn men, who are now first and foremost in the great work of saving souls, are the ones whom God will honor. They have wrought righteousness and subdued their own hearts. They have learned the sacredness of work and the joy of self-denial and self-sacrifice, and this knowledge brings an eternal reward.

Look up, look up, not down, for guidance and protection. You will find it.—Letter 120, 1898.

Chapter 12—Examine Yourselves

By Ellen G. White

"Examine yourselves, whether ye be in the faith; prove your own selves." Closely criticize the temper, the disposition, the thoughts, words, inclinations, purposes, and deeds. How can we ask intelligently for the things we need unless we prove by the Scriptures the condition of our spiritual health?

Many in their religious life are making crooked paths for their feet. Their prayers are offered in a loose, haphazard manner. He who is placed in a position of responsibility should remember that of himself he is not able to do that which is required of him. Every day he should remember that he is a spectacle unto the world, to angels, and to men.

No one is to wait to be borne to fields of labor and provided with costly facilities for doing good. He who serves must cheerfully take up his work, however humble it is, and wherever he may be placed. Christ, our example in all things, was poor, that through His poverty He might make many rich.

Serving in Meekness

He whose heart is filled with the grace of God and love for his perishing fellow men will find opportunity, wherever he may be placed, to speak a word in season to those who are weary. Christians are to work for their Master in meekness and lowliness, holding fast to their integrity amid the noise and bustle of life.

God calls upon men to serve Him in every transaction of life. Business is a snare when the law of God is not made the law of the daily life. He who has anything to do with the Master's work is to maintain unswerving integrity. In all business transactions, as verily as when on bended knees he seeks help from on high, God's will is to be his will. He is to keep the Lord ever before him, constantly studying the subjects about which the Holy Word speaks. Thus, though living amid that which would debase a man of lax principles, the man of piety and stern integrity preserves his Christianity.

The world is no more favorable today for the development of Christian character than in Noah's day. Then wickedness was so widespread that God said, "I will destroy man whom I have created from the face of the earth; both man, and beast, and the creeping thing, and the fowls of the air; for it repenteth Me that I have made them. But Noah found grace in the eyes of the Lord.... Noah was a just man and perfect in his generations, and Noah walked with God." Yes, amid the corruption of that degenerate age, Noah was a pleasure to his Creator.

We are living in the last days of this earth's history, in an age of sin and corruption, and like Noah we are to so live that we shall be a pleasure to God, showing forth the praises of Him "who hath called you out of darkness into His marvelous light." In the prayer which Christ offered to His Father just before His crucifixion, He said, "I pray not that Thou shouldest take them out of the world, but that Thou shouldest keep them from the evil."

The Highest Service

When men and women have formed characters which God can endorse, when their self-denial and self-sacrifice have been fully made, when they are ready for the final test, ready to be introduced into God's family, what service will stand highest in the estimation of Him who gave Himself a willing offering to save a guilty race? What enterprise will be most dear to the heart of infinite love? What work will bring the greatest satisfaction and joy to the Father and the Son?—The salvation of perishing souls. Christ died to bring to men the saving power of the gospel. Those who co-operate with Him in carrying forward His great enterprise of mercy, laboring with all the strength God has given them to save those nigh and afar off, will share in the joy of the Redeemer when the redeemed host stand around the throne of God.

God has entrusted means and capabilities to His servants for the doing of a work far higher than that which today He looks upon.

"O," said the heavenly messenger, "the Lord's institutions are terribly behind the greatness of the truths which are being fulfilled at the present time. There is a fearful misconception of the claims of duty. The frosty atmosphere in which believers are content to live retards the self-sacrificing movements which should be made to warn the world and save souls.

The Unnamed Multitudes

"The powers of darkness are working with an intensity of effort, and year by year thousands of people, from all kindreds, nations, and tongues, pass into eternity, unwarned and unready. Our faith must mean something more definite, more decided, more important.

"Ask my institutions and churches, 'Do you believe the Word of God? What then are you doing in missionary lines? Are you working with self-denial and self-sacrifice? Do you believe that the Word of God means what it says? Your actions show that you do not. How will you meet at the bar of God the countless millions who, unwarned, are passing into eternity? Will there be a second probation? No, no. This fallacy might just as well be given up at once. The present probation is all that we shall have. Do you realize that the salvation of fallen human beings must be secured in this present life, or they will be forever lost?'"

Our Responsibilities

The Laodicean message is applicable to the church at this time. Do you believe this message? Have you hearts that feel? Or are you constantly saying, We are rich and increased in goods, and have need of nothing? Is it in vain that the declaration of eternal truth has been given to this nation to be carried to all the nations of the world? God has chosen a people and made them the repositories of truth weighty with eternal results. To them has been given the light that must illuminate the world. Has God made a mistake? Are we indeed His chosen instrumentalities? Are we the men and women who are to bear to the world the messages of Revelation fourteen, to proclaim the message of salvation to those who are standing on the brink of ruin? Do we act as if we were?

What Are We Doing?

In a clear, determined voice the messenger said, "I ask you what you are doing? O that you could comprehend! O that you could understand the importance of the warning and what it means to you and to the world! If you did understand, if you were filled with the spirit of the One who gave His life for the life of the world, you would co-operate with Him, making earnest, self-sacrificing efforts to save sinners."

A Great Awakening

"He that saith, I know Him, and keepeth not His commandments, is a liar, and the truth is not in him." A great awakening must come to the church. If we only knew, if we only understood, how quickly the spirit of the message would go from church to church. How willingly would the possessions of believers be given to support the work of God. God calls upon us to pray and watch unto prayer. Cleanse your homes of the picture-idols which have consumed the money that ought to have flowed into the Lord's treasury. The light must go forth as a lamp that burneth. Those who bear the message to the world should seek the Lord earnestly, that His Holy Spirit may be abundantly showered upon them. You have no time to lose. Pray for the power of God, that you may work with success for those nigh and afar off.

Warnings to Be Given

We must have genuine faith. As yet we scarcely grasp the reality of the truth. We only half believe the Word of God. A man will act out all the faith he has. Notwithstanding that the signs of the times are fulfilling all over the world, faith in the Lord's coming has been growing feeble. Clear, distinct, certain, the warnings are to be given. At the peril of our souls we are to learn the prescribed conditions under which we are to work out our own salvation, remembering that it is God which worketh in us, both to will and to do of His good pleasure.

It will not do for us to float along with the current, guided by tradition and presumptuous fallacies. We are called laborers together with God. Then let us arise and shine. There is no time to spend in controversy. Those who have a knowledge of the truth as it is in Jesus must now become one in heart and purpose. All differences must be swept away. The members of the church must work unitedly under the great Head of the church.

Arise, Shine

Let those who have a knowledge of the truth arise and shine. "Cry aloud, spare not, lift up thy voice like a trumpet." No longer mutilate the truth. Let the soul cry out for the living God. Cease ye from man, whose breath is in his nostrils. The Comforter will come to you, if you will open the door to Him. "Seeing then that we have a great high priest, that is passed into the heavens, Jesus the Son of God, let us hold fast our profession. For we have not an high priest which cannot be touched with the feelings of our infirmities; but was in all points tempted like as we are, yet without sin. Let us therefore come boldly unto the throne of grace, that we may obtain mercy, and find grace to help in every time of need."—Manuscript 51, 1901.

* * * * *

Daily Surrender

I arise this morning at one o'clock A.M. I have tried to sleep, but cannot

I am feeling deeply over the work which is to be done all around us. Whichever way we may turn we find temporal and spiritual poverty. Sometimes my spirit is weighed down, but although I see the great need soliciting our attention at every place we go, we need not feel that the burden rests upon us. There is One who is our burden bearer. Neither are we capable of bearing the sins of others.

Our Message

We have always a decided message to bear, "Behold the Lamb of God, which taketh away the sin of the world." Satan will cast his hellish shadow athwart our pathway, and if we allow our eyes to rest on this shadow, we cannot discern the light which is beyond. Whatever discouragement may appear to our human sight, we must ever remember that there is infinity beyond the darkness. Our faith cannot, must not, for a moment sink in that dark shadow. Light beyond is shining for every soul of us. Our voice, our words, must testify of that light.

If the life we live in this world is wholly and entirely for Christ, it is a life of daily surrender. He has the freewill service, and each soul is His own jewel. If we can impress upon the minds of our sisters the good which it is in their power to do through the Lord Jesus Christ, we shall see a large work accomplished. But this work can be done only through the Holy Spirit.

If we can arouse the mind and heart to co-operate with the great Worker, we shall gain through the work they may accomplish great victories. But self must be hidden. Christ must appear as the worker. Christ invites us, Abide in Me, and I in you. Cannot we bring these souls to understand without a moment's delay that every day is the ever-present *now*?

Receiving and Giving

There must ever be an interchange of taking in and giving out, receiving and restoring. This links us up as laborers together with God. Not one expression of unbelief is to come from our lips under the hardest trial. Heaven is much nearer to earth when every soul who knows the truth, expresses it in word and action. The giving out ever expresses the truth, and increases the power of taking in. This is the lifework of the Christian. He that will lose his life will find it.

The capacity for receiving the holy oil from the two olive trees which empty themselves, is by the receiver emptying that holy oil out of himself in word and in action to supply the necessities of other souls. Work, precious, satisfying work—to be constantly receiving and constantly imparting! The capacity for receiving is only kept up by imparting. Isaiah 58 explains the matter: "Thy righteousness shall go before thee; the glory of the Lord shall be thy rereward."

We need and must have fresh supplies every day. And how many souls we may help by communicating to them. All heaven is waiting for channels through whom can be poured the holy oil to be a joy and refreshing to others. We may work continuously and solidly, so that our work may abide, if Christ is abiding with us. I have no fears of any person making blundering work, if he will only become one with Christ. The divine fullness will flow through the consecrated human agent, to be given forth to others. Linked with the unchanging Jesus Himself, there is a representation of Christ in character. Truth, our Saviour continually insisted upon, must be sought after, found, and given to others. He, our Lord and Saviour, insisted that we should sell all to secure the treasure. Self-sacrifice must be seen in this path at every step. There is to be no lifting up of self, not a thread of self-seeking; for this always separates from Christ....

When we feel oppressed, as we often will, I find it is my best remedy to talk of the light and love of God. My soul is strengthened and blessed; for I draw nigh unto God, and He draws nigh to me, and lifts up for me a standard against the enemy.—Letter 119, 1898.

In Hard Places

Often God's soldiers find themselves brought into hard and difficult places, they know not why. But are they to relax their hold because difficulties arise? Is their faith to diminish because they cannot see their way through the darkness? God forbid. They are to cherish an abiding sense of God's power to uphold them in their work. They cannot perish, neither can they lose their way if they will follow His guidance, and strive to uphold His law.—Manuscript 69, 1896.

* * * * *

Walk in the Light

I was shown that God's people dwell too much under a cloud. It is not His will that they should live in unbelief. Jesus is light, and in Him is no darkness at all. His children are the children of light. They are renewed in His image, and called out of darkness into His marvelous light. He is the light of the world, and so also are they that follow Him. They shall not walk in darkness, but shall have the light of life. The more closely the people of God strive to imitate

Christ, the more perseveringly will they be pursued by the enemy; but their nearness to Christ strengthens them to resist the efforts of our wily foe to draw them from Christ.—Testimonies for the Church 1:405, 406.

Chapter 13—"No Other Gods Before Me"

By Ellen G. White

Every true child of God will be sifted as wheat, and in the sifting process every cherished pleasure which diverts the mind from God must be sacrificed. In many families the mantel shelves, stands, and tables are filled with ornaments and pictures. Albums filled with photographs of the family and their friends are placed where they will attract the attention of visitors. Thus the thoughts, which should be upon God and heavenly interests, are brought down to common things. Is not this a species of idolatry? Should not the money thus spent have been used to bless humanity, to relieve the suffering, to clothe the naked, and to feed the hungry? Should it not be placed in the Lord's treasury to advance His cause and build up His kingdom in the earth?

This matter is of great importance, and it is urged upon you to save you from the sin of idolatry. Blessing would come to your souls if you would obey the word spoken by the Holy One of Israel, "Thou shalt have no other gods before Me." Many are creating unnecessary cares and anxieties for themselves by devoting time and thought to the unnecessary ornaments with which their houses are filled. The power of God is needed to arouse them from this devotion; for to all intents and purposes it is idolatry.

He who searches the heart, desires to win His people from every species of idolatry. Let the Word of God, the blessed book of life, occupy the tables now filled with useless ornaments. Spend your money in buying books that will be the means of enlightening the mind in regard to present truth. The time you waste in moving and dusting the multitudinous ornaments in your house, spend in writing a few lines to your friends, in sending papers or leaflets or little books to someone who knows not the truth. Grasp the word of the Lord as the treasure of infinite wisdom and love; this is the Guidebook that points out the path to heaven. It points us to the sin-pardoning Saviour, saying, "Behold the Lamb of God, which taketh away the sin of the world."

O that you would search the Scriptures with prayerful hearts, and a spirit of surrender to God! O that you would search your hearts as with a lighted candle, and discover and break the finest thread that binds you to worldly habits, which divert the mind from God! Plead with God to show you every practice that draws your thoughts and affections from Him. God has given His holy law to man as His measure of character. By this law you may see and overcome every defect in your character. You may sever yourself from every idol, and link yourself to the throne of God by the golden chain of grace and truth.—The Review and Herald, May 14, 1901.

* * * * *

A Caution Regarding Extreme Positions

There were some who had capabilities to help the church, but who needed first to set their own hearts in order. Some had been bringing in false tests, and had made their own ideas and notions a criterion, magnifying matters of little importance into tests of Christian fellowship, and binding heavy burdens upon others. Thus a spirit of criticism, faultfinding, and dissension had come in, which had been a great injury to the church. And the impression was given to unbelievers that Sabbath-keeping Adventists were a set of fanatics and extremists, and that their peculiar faith rendered them unkind, uncourteous, and really unchristian in character. Thus the course of a few extremists prevented the influence of the truth from reaching the people.

Some were making the matter of dress of first importance, criticizing articles of dress worn by others, and standing ready to condemn everyone who did not exactly meet their ideas. A few condemned pictures, urging that they are prohibited by the second commandment, and that everything of this kind should be destroyed.

One-Idea Men

These one-idea men can see nothing except to press the one thing that presents itself to their minds. Years ago we had to meet this same spirit and work. Men arose claiming to have been sent with a message condemning pictures, and urging that every likeness of anything should be destroyed. They went to such lengths as even to condemn clocks which had figures, or "pictures," upon them.

Now we read in the Bible of a good conscience; and there are not only good but bad consciences. There is a conscientiousness that will carry everything to extremes, and make Christian duties as burdensome as the Jews made the observance of the Sabbath. The rebuke which Jesus gave to the scribes and Pharisees applies to this class as well: "Ye tithe mint and rue and all manner of herbs, and pass over judgment and the love of God." One fanatic, with his strong spirit and radical ideas, who will oppress the conscience of those who want to be right, will do great harm. The church needs to be purified from all such influences.

Pictures Used by God

The second commandment prohibits image worship; but God Himself employed pictures and symbols to represent to His prophets lessons which He would have them give to the people, and which could thus be better understood than if given in any other way. He appealed to the understanding through the sense of sight. Prophetic history was presented to Daniel and John in symbols, and these were to be represented plainly upon tables, that he who read might understand.

It is true that altogether too much money is expended upon pictures; not a little means which should flow into the treasury of God is paid to the artist. But the evil that will result to the church from the course of these extremists is far greater than that which they are trying to correct. It is sometimes a difficult matter to tell just where the line is, where picturemaking becomes a sin. But those who love God and desire with all their hearts to keep His commandments, will be directed by Him. God would not have them depend on any man to be conscience for them. He who accepts all the ideas and impressions of unbalanced minds will become confused and bewildered. It is Satan's object to divert the attention from the third angel's message to side issues, that minds and hearts that should be growing in grace and in the knowledge of the truth, may be dwarfed and enfeebled, so that God may not be glorified by them.—*Historical Sketches of S.D.A. Foreign Missions, pp. 211, 212.*

Chapter 14—Be of Good Cheer[*]

By Ellen G. White

I feel very thankful that it is our privilege to believe in God, and to walk carefully in accordance with the instruction He has given us in His Word. If we do this, our hearts will respond to the impressions of the Spirit of God, and we shall follow on to know the Lord, whose going forth is prepared as the morning. And let us always remember that just as His going forth is prepared as the morning, so we are to expect the revelations of His grace as we advance.

But if we keep silent, if we do not feel the importance of moving in harmony with His will, we shall not have His blessing attending us. We cannot afford, brethren and sisters, to be without His help and guidance. We need to be in a position where we can talk with God. We are to commune with Him. He who is our sanctification, our righteousness, has given us the privilege of being in a position where we may have a continually increasing faith. We must ever live by faith, and follow on to know the Lord.

God's promises to us are so rich, so full, that we need never hesitate or doubt; we need never waver or backslide. In view of the encouragements that are found all through the Word of God, we have no right to be gloomy or despondent. We may have weakness of body; but the compassionate Saviour says: "Ask, and it shall be given you; seek, and ye shall find; knock, and it shall be opened unto you: for every one that asketh receiveth; and he that seeketh findeth; and to him that knocketh it shall be opened."

Will you believe these assurances? Will you say, "Yes, Lord, I take Thee at Thy word. I will begin where I am, to talk an increase of faith; I will take hold of the promises; they are for me"? O brethren and sisters, what we want is a living, striving, growing faith in the promises of God, which are indeed for you and for me.

---

[*]Words addressed to board of directors of the College of Medical Evangelists, Loma Linda, California, November 9, 1912.

Words of Encouragement

Many, many times I have been instructed by the Lord to speak words of courage to His people. We are to put our trust in God, and believe in Him, and act in accordance with His will. We must ever remain in a position where we can praise the Lord and magnify His name. Then we shall see light in His Word, and follow on to know Him, whose going forth is prepared as the morning. Read 1 Peter 1:1-5.

These words are all-sufficient evidence that God desires us to receive great blessings. His promises are so clearly stated that there is no cause for uncertainty. He desires us to take Him at His word. At times we shall be in great perplexity, and not know just what to do. But at such times it is our privilege to take our Bibles, and read the messages He has given us; and then get down on our knees, and ask Him to help us. Over and over again He has given evidence that He is a prayer-hearing and a prayer-answering God. He fulfills His promises in far greater measure than we expect to receive help.

Perplexities

So long as Satan continues to live, we shall have perplexity; and if we choose to follow the counsel of the enemy, we shall have constant difficulty; but if we refuse to yield to satanic influences, choosing rather to lay hold on God and on the promises of His Word, we shall be able to help and strengthen and uphold one another. Thus we shall bring into the work with which we are connected a spirit of courage.

Never are we to utter a word that would arouse doubt or fear, or that would cast a shadow over the minds of others. I am determined not to permit myself to speak discouraging words; and when I hear criticism and complaint, or an expression of doubt and fear, I know that he who thus speaks has his eyes turned away from the Saviour. I know every such person does not appreciate Him who at infinite sacrifice left the royal courts and came down into the world that was lost, and lived among the children of men in order that He might speak words of hope and good cheer to the discouraged and the desponding.

Wherever we are, we are under obligation, as disciples of our Lord and Master, to anchor our faith in the promises of God. Individually we are to believe. We are not to cast about for a possible doubt, or imagine that sometime we may have to stand beneath the shadow of a cloud that seems to be gathering. We are chosen of God to be His children. We have been bought with an infinite price, and we have no occasion for placing the suggestions of the enemy before the assurances of the Lord Jesus Christ.

The Lord desires us to act sensibly. We shall have trials; we need never expect anything else; for the time has not yet come when Satan is to be bound. Wherever we may be, we shall continue to have trials. But if we give up to the suggestions of the enemy, we lose the battle. Can we afford to yield to the arch-deceiver? Oh, no! We are to turn for help and deliverance to Him who "according to His abundant mercy hath begotten us again unto a lively hope by the resurrection of Jesus Christ," even the hope of an eternal inheritance reserved for those "who are kept by the power of God through faith unto salvation." ...

If unbelievers come in and talk their doubts and fears, remember that Satan is not dead. He has agencies through whom he works. But shall we become discouraged because of this? Oh, no! Christ, our Saviour, lives and reigns. Let us not look on the dark side. As soon as we yield to the temptation to do this, we shall have plenty of company. But there is nothing to be gained by looking on the dark side. What we want is courage in the Lord; and we want to follow on to know the Lord, that we may know that His going forth is prepared as the morning. This is not going back into darkness. You know how the morning is prepared. If you follow on to know the Lord every day, you will increase in brightness, in courage, in faith, and the Lord Jesus will be to you a present help in every time of need.—Manuscript 71, 1912.

* * * * *

Present Duty

We must seek to become a united people. Every phase of our work is to bear the signature of God. Those who have not placed themselves on the Lord's side are becoming more bold and more defiant. He calls upon His people to take their stand firmly on the platform of eternal truth. To His true and loyal subjects He has given the words of eternal life. It is for them to obey His Word and do His work, in accordance with His instructions.

God sends His Holy Spirit to kindle in the hearts of His followers a desire to open the Word to those who sit in darkness, that they may come to the light of the knowledge of God.

[41]

We are to carry forward in our world gospel medical missionary work. This work means far more than many comprehend. The one great work of medical missionaries is to be to fulfill the commission to carry the gospel of salvation to all parts of the world.

Medical missionary workers must be set apart by God Himself for His work. If they consecrate themselves to God, and are by Him sanctified, body, soul, and spirit; if they walk and work as men called to exalt Christ, they will be recognized as God's appointed agencies. But they need to study carefully the life and character of their divine Example, that all their work may be done after the divine similitude. They need to be humble. Then the language of their hearts will be, "Who is sufficient for these things?" Their success depends upon co-operation with Christ.

Who can say where Seventh-day Adventists might be standing today, had they fully carried out the instruction given in the sixth chapter of John, had they received the words which, Christ declares, are spirit and life to the receiver? I hope and pray that we may now seek to understand these words; for they mean much to every soul.

Many do not earnestly seek to understand the lessons found in God's Word. They lay aside the Bible, and allow their minds to become engrossed with the cheap reading found in books of fiction, newspapers, and magazines.

"Search the Scriptures," said Christ, "for in them ye think ye have eternal life: and they are they which testify of Me." The Lord calls for workers whose motives are pure and sincere. He calls upon His people to arouse, and consecrate their capabilities to Him. He will lead all who are willing to be led by Him.

Will not all now make a resolute determination to exclude from the life all unprofitable reading, and to feed upon the Word, which, if received, is eternal life? At this time there needs to be a close searching of the heart. To become members of the royal family, children of the heavenly King, is of far greater value than treasures of gold and silver and precious stones.—Manuscript 146, 1903.

* * * * *

The Final Triumph of Truth

Ages before His incarnation, Christ distinctly chose His position. He foresaw His life of humiliation, His rejection and crucifixion, His victory over satanic agencies, His victory over death and the grave. He saw the world flooded with light and life, and heard the song of triumph sung by the millions rescued from the hold of Satan.

Christ is our Deliverer. He exclaims, "I will ransom them from the power of the grave; I will redeem them from death: O death, I will be thy plagues; O grave, I will be thy destruction." Thrice in rapid succession He exclaimed, "I will raise him up at the last day."

"Enoch also, the seventh from Adam, prophesied of these, saying, Behold, the Lord cometh with ten thousands of His saints, to execute judgment upon all." And Solomon, when in the capacity of a preacher tried to present the strongest motive to holy obedience—the motive that was above all estimate in view of the judgment to come—said, "Let us hear the conclusion of the whole matter: Fear God, and keep His commandments: for this is the whole duty of man. For God shall bring every work into judgment, with every secret thing, whether it be good, or whether it be evil."

God places every action in the scale. What a scene it will be! What impressions will be made regarding the holy character of God and the terrible enormity of sin, when the judgment, based on the law, is carried forward in the presence of all the worlds. Then before the mind of the unrepentant sinner there will be opened all the sins that he has committed, and he will see and understand the aggregate of sin and his own guilt.

When the loyal overcomers are crowned, God would have present all who have transgressed His law and broken their covenant with Him. And not one of the righteous will be absent. They see, in the Judge, Christ Jesus, the one whom every sinner has crucified. The Son of man shall come in His glory, and before Him shall be gathered all nations. The Father judgeth no man, but hath committed all judgment to the Son.

But the trumpet is waxing louder and louder, and the wicked dead come forth to confront Christ. When the multitude of the lost, those whom God has favored with great light, shall look upon the goodness, mercy, and love of Jesus, when those who might have been saved if they had accepted the light and the blessings of God's Word, but who refused to obey His law, see the great sacrifice made in their behalf, they understand the unmeasured love of the Redeemer; they understand His incarnation, the sweatdrops of blood, the marks of the nails in His hands and feet, the pierced side; and they ask to be hidden from the face of Him that sitteth on the throne, and from the wrath of the Lamb. They see as in reality the condemnation of Christ, they hear the loud cry, "Release unto us Barabbas." They hear the question, "What shall I do then with Jesus?" and the answer, "Crucify Him, crucify Him."

The reign of appearance and pretense is over. The voice of the righteous Judge speaks with awful emphasis, as He utters the sentence, "Depart from Me: I never knew you."

The division of the whole multitude will be made. "When the Son of man shall come in His glory, and all the holy angels with Him, then shall He sit upon the throne of His glory: and before Him shall be gathered all nations: and He shall separate them one from another, as a shepherd divideth his sheep from the goats; and He shall set the sheep on His right hand, but the goats on the left." Those who have done good and those who have done evil will receive a reward according to their works. Then shall Jesus say to those on His right hand, "Come, ye blessed of My Father, inherit the kingdom prepared for you from the foundation of the world." Thus He welcomes them, to live hereafter in eternal communion with Himself. Every voice in the mansions of heaven echoes the welcome, "Come, ye blessed of My Father; inherit the kingdom prepared for you from the foundation of the world."—Manuscript 77, 1906.

Chapter 15—Good Angels More Powerful Than Evil

By Ellen G. White

It is expressly stated that Satan works in the children of disobedience, not merely having access to their minds, but working through their influence, conscious and unconscious, to draw others into the same disobedience. If evil angels have such power over the children of men in their disobedience, how much greater power the good angels have over those who are striving to be obedient. When we put our trust in Jesus Christ, working obedience unto righteousness, angels of God work in our hearts unto righteousness....

Power of Satan Limited

Angels came and ministered to our Lord in the wilderness of temptation. Heavenly angels were with Him during all the period in which He was exposed to the assaults of satanic agencies. These assaults were more severe than man has ever passed through. Everything was at stake in behalf of the human family. In this conflict Christ did not frame His words even. He depended upon "It is written." In this conflict the humanity of Christ was taxed as none of us will ever know. The Prince of life and the prince of darkness met in terrible conflict, but Satan was unable to gain the least advantage in word or in action. These were real temptations, no pretense. Christ "suffered being tempted." Angels of heaven were on the scene on that occasion, and kept the standard uplifted, that Satan should not exceed his bounds and overpower the human nature of Christ.

In the last temptation Satan presented to Christ the prospect of gaining the whole world with all its glory if He would only worship him who claimed to be sent of God. Christ must then issue His command. He must then exercise authority above all satanic agencies. Divinity flashed through humanity, and Satan was pre-emptorily repulsed. "Get thee hence, Satan," Christ said, "for it is written, Thou shalt worship the Lord thy God, and Him only shalt thou serve." It was enough. Satan could go no farther. Angels ministered to the Saviour. Angels brought Him food. The severity of this conflict no human mind can compass. The welfare of the whole human family and of Christ Himself was at stake. One admission from Christ, one word of concession, and the world would be claimed by Satan as his; and he, the prince of the power of darkness, would, he supposed, commence his rule. There appeared unto Christ an angel from heaven; for the conflict ended. Human power was ready to fail. But all heaven sang the song of eternal victory.

The human family have all the help that Christ had in their conflicts with Satan. They need not be overcome. They may be more than conquerors through Him who has loved them and given His life for them. "Ye are bought with a price." And what a price! The Son of God in His humanity wrestled with the very same fierce, apparently overwhelming temptations that assail men—temptations to indulgence of appetite, to presumptuous venturing where God has not led them, and to the worship of the god of this world, to sacrifice an eternity of bliss for the fascinating pleasures of this life. Everyone will be tempted, but the Word declares that we shall not be tempted above our ability to bear. We may resent and defeat the wily foe.

Every soul has a heaven to win, and a hell to shun. And the angelic agencies are all ready to come to the help of the tried and tempted soul. He the Son of the infinite God endured the test and trial in our behalf. The cross of Calvary stands vividly before every soul. When the cases of all are judged, and they are delivered to suffer for their contempt for God and their disregard of His honor in their disobedience, not one will have an excuse, not one will need to have perished. It was left to their own choice who should be their prince, Christ or Satan. All the help Christ received, every man may receive in the great trial. The cross stands as a pledge that not one need be lost, that abundant help is provided for every soul. We can conquer the satanic agencies, or we can join ourselves with the powers that seek to counterwork the work of God in our world....

We have an Advocate pleading in our behalf. The Holy Ghost is continually engaged in beholding our course of action. We need now keen perception, that by our own practical godliness the truth may be made to appear truth as it is in Jesus. The angelic agencies are messengers from heaven, actually ascending and descending, keeping earth in constant connection with the heaven above. These angel messengers are observing all our course of action. They are ready to help all in their weakness, guarding all from moral and physical danger according to the providence of God. And whenever souls yield to the softening, subduing influence of the Spirit of God under these angel ministrations, there is joy in heaven; the Lord Himself rejoices with singing.

Men take altogether too much glory to themselves. It is the work of heavenly agencies co-operating with human agencies according to God's plan that brings the result in the conversion and sanctification of the human character. We cannot see and could not endure the glory of angelic ministrations if their glory was not veiled in condescension to the weakness of our human nature. The blaze of the heavenly glory, as seen in the angels of light, would extinguish earthly mortals. Angels are working upon human minds just as these minds are given to their charge; they bring precious remembrances fresh before the mind as they did to the women about the sepulcher.

A created instrumentality is used in heaven's organized plan for the renewing of our nature, working in the children of disobedience obedience unto God. The guardianship of the heavenly host is granted to all who will work in God's ways and follow His plans. We may in earnest, contrite prayer call the heavenly helpers to our side. Invisible armies of light and power will work with the humble, meek, and lowly one....

"Thus saith the high and lofty One that inhabiteth eternity, whose name is Holy: I dwell in the high and holy place, with him also that is of a contrite and humble spirit, to revive the spirit of the humble, and to revive the heart of the contrite ones." Isaiah 57:15. [Read also verses 16-19.]—Letter 116, 1899.

Chapter 16—Our Duty to Represent the Master*

By Ellen G. White

We are usually well, and are seeking to put our entire dependence in the Lord. I have been looking over a large amount of matter. My head was tired on Sabbath and I had to keep quiet.

We are having most beautiful weather. It is almost like summer. The light of the moon makes the nights almost as light as day.

I have received a letter from Elder Haskell. They are on their way to Loma Linda, and they expect to meet me there. But I do not really see it to be my duty to leave my workers and break up just at this critical time. We need every jot of ability we have.

I have to work carefully and not feel too deeply over the known position of our brethren who are not disentangling themselves from erroneous science and making sure that they are on the firm foundation. I carry a burden continually because of the souls who know the truth, but have not manifested its sanctifying power in their lives and characters. I should suffer much if I could not lay my burden upon the great Burden Bearer.

Bring Forth Good Fruit

We must keep before the people veracity, justice, love, goodness, and every virtue that comes to us through the Lord Jesus Christ. In all the lowliness, meekness, and gentleness of Christ, His love is expressed to us. His spiritual life energy we must have if we are daily overcomers. All our power is derived from Him. Of His fullness we have all received, and grace for grace. The prayer of Christ to His Father is a representation of what we must be if we are working to be overcomers; and if we meet this representation we shall certainly bring forth good fruits. [John 17:17-26.]

---

*Portion of a Letter written from St. Helena, California, December 10, 1905.

As Christ came to the world to seek and to save perishing souls, that they should have the light of truth, so also hath He committed the same work to all who receive Him as their Saviour. "And for their sakes I sanctify Myself, that they also might be sanctified through the truth."

How important that we should be rooted and grounded in the truth! No falsehood is of the truth. The Lord Jesus has promised that if we receive Him by faith and believe in Him as our pattern He will give us "power to become the sons of God." The gospel of Jesus Christ contains the grand principles of all truth, expressed in a life of purity. In love and true righteousness these principles are to be proclaimed to the world. In all our dealings with one another we are to obey the precepts of the law of God. "I sanctify Myself, that they also might be sanctified through the truth. Neither pray I for these alone, but for them also which shall believe on Me through their word."

Christ Judged by His Followers

From these words we see how much is dependent on the character of all those who claim to believe the gospel of Jesus Christ. By the lives of Christ's followers the world will judge the Saviour. If anyone, in word or deed, departs from the living principles of the truth, he dishonors his Saviour and puts Christ to open shame. Let every soul believe in Christ, and receive the power that Christ has promised, that he may be a child of God, holding the truth conscientiously, its principles interwoven with his words, his spirit, and all his works. Thus Christians may become a refining, purifying influence, working against false religion and infidelity. Their presence brings with it the grand influence of heavenly principles, making them, through Christ, an honor to the gospel. They increase in power to communicate the sanctifying grace of heaven, gaining continually in influence through their increasing reverence for the truth. Their hearts are filled with the peace of Christ.

A true Christian feels daily that his lifework should be to represent the untiring earnestness that was shown in the life of Christ. Every soul should feel under sacred obligation to represent Christ to the world. All are to remember that they are in the presence of

Christ, and in no case are they to utter a word that will grieve the Holy Spirit. They must show to the world that they are sons of God, that because they have chosen and believed on Christ, He has given them power to become the sons of God. In every business deal, in every act, they must honor Him who has given them this power.

I am instructed to present these principles, the message to which I have listened in the night season. I am to present the underlying principles of the Christian warfare. All who truly love the Lord Jesus will accept His yoke and learn of Him. "Learn of Me," said the holy, sanctified Teacher, "for I am meek and lowly in heart: and ye shall find rest unto your souls."

The Christian life is a warfare, not against believing brethren, but against the seducing spirit of the enemy, against the subtle, deceiving influence of the serpent, which creeps into our thoughts and minds. "Resist the devil, and he will flee from you." Make no provision for the flesh, to deceive, to falsify, to work just as Satan worked in Eden. He is watching his chance to develop if he can only have an opportunity. Give him no foothold. There is something we are charged to do: "Resist the devil," and the promise is, "he will flee from you." Why? Because the angel of God lifts up for you a standard against the enemy, and he flees.—Letter 327, 1905.

* * * * *

When the Church Awakes

Prayer is needed in the home life, in the church life, in the missionary life. The efficiency of earnest prayer is but feebly understood. Were the church faithful in prayer, she would not be found remiss in so many things; for faithfulness in calling upon God will bring rich returns.

When the church awakes to the sense of her holy calling, many more fervent and effective prayers will ascend to heaven for the Holy Spirit to point out the work and duty of God's people regarding the salvation of souls. We have a standing promise that God will draw near to every seeking soul.

The church needs to be begotten again unto a lively hope "by the resurrection of Jesus from the dead, to an inheritance incorruptible, and undefiled, and that fadeth not away." When the church awakes to a sense of what must be done in our world, the members will have travail of soul for those who know not God and who in their spiritual ignorance, cannot understand the truth for this time. Self-denial, self-sacrifice, is to be woven into all our experience. We are to pray and watch unto prayer, that there may be no inconsistency in our lives. We must not fail to show others that we understand that watching unto prayer means living our prayers before God, that He may answer them.

[47]

The church will not retrograde while the members seek help from the throne of grace, that they may not fail to co-operate in the great work of saving the souls that are on the brink of ruin. The members of a church that is an active, working church, will have a realization that they are wearing Christ's yoke, and drawing with Him.

The heavenly universe is waiting for consecrated channels, through which God can communicate with His people, and through them with the world. God will work through a consecrated, self-denying church, and He will reveal His Spirit in a visible and glorious manner, especially in this time, when Satan is working in a masterly manner to deceive the souls of both ministers and people. If God's ministers will co-operate with Him, He will be with them in a remarkable manner, even as He was with His disciples of old.

Will not the church awake to her responsibility? God is waiting to impart the spirit of the greatest missionary the world has ever known to those who will work with self-denying, self-sacrificing consecration. When God's people receive this Spirit, power will go forth from them.—Manuscript 59, 1898.

* * * * *

The Passive Graces

The Lord permits circumstances to come that call for the exercise of the passive graces, which increase in purity and efficiency as we endeavor to give back to the Lord His own in tithes and offerings. You know something of what it means to pass through trials. These have given you the opportunity of trusting in God, of seeking Him in earnest prayer, that you may believe in Him, and rely upon Him with simple faith. It is by suffering that our virtues are tested, and our faith tried. It is in the day of trouble that we feel the preciousness of Jesus. You will be given opportunity to say, "Though He slay me, yet will I trust in Him." O, it is so precious to think that opportunities are afforded us to confess our faith in the face of danger, and amid sorrow, sickness, pain, and death....

With us, everything depends on how we accept the Lord's terms. As is our spirit, so will be the moral result upon our future life and character. Each individual soul has victories to gain, but he must realize that he cannot have things just as he wants them. We are to observe carefully every lesson Christ has given throughout His life and teaching. He does not destroy; He improves whatever He touches.—Letter 135, 1897.

* * * * *

A Quick Work

When divine power is combined with human effort, the work will spread like fire in the stubble. God will employ agencies whose origin man will be unable to discern; angels will do a work which men might have had the blessing of accomplishing, had they not neglected to answer the claims of God.—The Review and Herald, December 15, 1885.

* * * * *

Signs of Christ's Coming

Satan now knows that his time has come. He has deceived the world until his image and superscription is stamped upon all their ambitious projects. Whatever their object for wishing to gain the supremacy, men are willing to sell their souls to Satan in order to obtain the highest place.

Christ sees the termination of the conflict. The battle is waging more and more fiercely. Soon He will come whose right it is, and will take possession of all earthly things. All the confusion in our world, all the violence and crime, are a fulfillment of the words of

Christ. They are signs of the nearness of His coming.—Letter 264, 1903.

* * * * *

At the End of the Conflict

As Noah proclaimed his warning message, some listened, and worked with him in building the ark. But they did not endure. Evil influences prevailed. They turned away from the truth to become scoffers.

Thus it will be in the last days of this earth's history. Those who today hear the message of truth, but do not believe, will fall amid the moral infidelity, even as in Noah's day those who were not firmly grounded failed to stand till the end of their probation. When the Lord rewards every man according to his deeds, these men will understand that God is truth, and that His message would have been their life and salvation if they had accepted the evidence given, and practiced the conditions laid down. Then they will see that they might have been saved had they not rejected the only means of salvation.

The trials of God's people may be long and severe, but the Lord never forgets them. Those who believe the truth and obey the commandments will find refuge in Christ. They will have the effectual protection of His ever-loving care as long as they take their position on the side of God and His law, which ever has governed and ever will govern His kingdom. Those who hold fast the beginning of their confidence firm unto the end will find that God is faithful and that He will fulfill His covenant to His commandment-keeping people.—Manuscript 42, 1900.

* * * * *

The Keeping Power of God

We are not kept by our intelligence, by our words, or by our riches. In these we find no safety. We are kept only by the power of God through faith unto salvation. We are living in a period of time during which we must by faith be allied with an infinite God, or else we cannot overcome the strong powers of darkness seeking to destroy us. The Holy Spirit is as a light shining on our pathway. Let us put our trust in Christ, who is ever at our right hand to help us. Let us take courage, placing our confidence and our trust in Him. He has not left us destitute.—Manuscript 110, 1901.

The Church

Chapter 17—Babylon and the Remnant Church

The Contrast as Shown In the Writings of Ellen G. White

The Church the Light of the World

Although there are evils existing in the church, and will be until the end of the world, the church in these last days is to be the light of the world that is polluted and demoralized by sin. The church, enfeebled and defective, needing to be reproved, warned, and counseled, is the only object upon earth upon which Christ bestows His supreme regard. The world is a workshop in which, through the co-operation of human and divine agencies, Jesus is making experiments by His grace and divine mercy upon human hearts.

Angels are amazed as they behold the transformation of character brought about in those who yield themselves to God, and they express their joy in songs of rapturous praise to God and to the Lamb. They see those who are by nature the children of wrath, converted, and becoming laborers together with Christ in drawing souls to God. They see those who were in darkness becoming lights to shine amid the moral night of this wicked and perverse generation. They see them becoming prepared by a Christlike experience to suffer with their Lord, and afterward to be partakers with Him in His glory in heaven above.

God has a church on earth who are lifting up the downtrodden law, and presenting to the world the Lamb of God that taketh away the sins of the world. The church is the depositary of the wealth of the riches of the grace of Christ, and through the church eventually will be made manifest the final and full display of the love of God to the world that is to be lightened with its glory. The prayer of Christ that His church may be one as He was one with His Father, will finally be answered. The rich dowry of the Holy Spirit will be given, and through its constant supply to the people of God, they will become witnesses in the world of the power of God unto salvation.

A Work of Tearing Down

There is but one church in the world who are at the present time standing in the breach, and making up the hedge, building up the old waste places; and for any man to call the attention of the world and other churches to this church, denouncing her as Babylon, is to do a work in harmony with him who is the accuser of the brethren. Is it possible that men will arise from among us, who speak perverse things, and give voice to the very sentiments that Satan would have disseminated in the world in regard to those who keep the commandments of God, and have the faith of Jesus? Is there not work enough to satisfy your zeal in presenting the truth to those who are in the darkness of error?

As those who have been made stewards of means and ability, you have been misapplying your Lord's goods in disseminating error. The whole world is filled with hatred of those who proclaim the binding claims of the law of God, and the church who are loyal to Jehovah must engage in no ordinary conflict. "We wrestle not against flesh and blood, but against principalities, against powers, against the rulers of the darkness of this world, against spiritual wickedness in high places." Those who have any realization of what this warfare means, will not turn their weapons against the church militant, but with all their powers will wrestle with the people of God against the confederacy of evil.

Those who start up to proclaim a message on their own individual responsibility, who, while claiming to be taught and led of God, still make it their special work to tear down that which God has been for years building up, are not doing the will of God. Be it known that these men are on the side of the great deceiver. Believe them not. They are allying themselves with the enemies of God and the truth. They will deride the order of the ministry as a system of priestcraft. From such turn away, have no fellowship with their message, however much they may quote the Testimonies and seek to intrench themselves behind them. Receive them not; for God has not given them this work to do. The result of such work will be unbelief

[50]

in the Testimonies, and as far as possible, they will make of none effect the work that I have for years been doing.

Almost my whole lifetime has been devoted to this work, but my burden has often been made heavier by the arising of men who went forth to proclaim a message that God had not given them. This class of evil workers have selected portions of the Testimonies and have placed them in the framework of error, in order by this setting to give influence to their false testimonies. When it is made manifest that their message is error, then the Testimonies brought into the companionship of error, share the same condemnation; and people of the world, who do not know that the Testimonies quoted are extracts from private letters used without my consent, present these matters as evidence that my work is not of God, or of truth, but falsehood. Those who thus bring the work of God into disrepute will have to answer before God for the work they are doing.

A Divinely Appointed Ministry

God has a church, and she has a divinely appointed ministry. "And He gave some apostles; and some, prophets; and some, evangelists; and some, pastors and teachers; for the perfecting of the saints; for the work of the ministry, for the edifying of the body of Christ: till we all come in the unity of the faith, and of the knowledge of the Son of God, unto a perfect man, unto the measure of the stature of the fullness of Christ: that we henceforth be no more children tossed to and fro, and carried about with every wind of doctrine, by the sleight of men, and cunning craftiness, whereby they lie in wait to deceive; but speaking the truth in love, may grow up into Him in all things, which is the head, even Christ."—Testimonies to Ministers and Gospel Workers, 49-52.

The Time of Celestial Glory

Satan is a diligent Bible student. He knows that his time is short, and he seeks at every point to counterwork the work of the Lord upon this earth. It is impossible to give any idea of the experience of the people of God who shall be alive upon the earth when celestial glory and a repetition of the persecutions of the past are blended. They will walk in the light proceeding from the throne of God. By means of the angels, there will be constant communication between heaven and earth. And Satan, surrounded by evil angels, and claiming to be God, will work miracles of all kinds, to deceive, if possible, the very elect.

Miracles Not the Sign

God's people will not find their safety in working miracles; for Satan will counterfeit the miracles that will be wrought. God's tried and tested people will find their power in the sign spoken of in Exodus 31:12-18. They are to take their stand on the living word, "It is written." This is the only foundation upon which they can stand securely. Those who have broken their covenant with God will in that day be without God and without hope.—Testimonies for the Church 9:16.

[51]

Beware of False Teachers

Those who have proclaimed the Seventh-day Adventist Church as Babylon, have made use of the Testimonies in giving their position a seeming support; but why is it that they did not present that which for years has been the burden of my message—the unity of the church? Why did they not quote the words of the angel, "Press together, press together, press together"? Why did they not repeat the admonition and state the principle, that "in union there is strength, in division there is weakness"?

It is such messages as these men have borne, that divide the church, and put us to shame before the enemies of truth, and in such messages is plainly revealed the specious working of the great deceiver, who would hinder the church from attaining unto perfection in unity. These teachers follow the sparks of their own kindling, move according to their own independent judgment, and cumber the truth with false notions and theories. They refuse the counsel of their brethren, and press on in their own way, until they become just what Satan would desire to have them—unbalanced in mind.—Testimonies to Ministers and Gospel Workers, 56.

Walk in Unity

I urge those who claim to believe the truth, to walk in unity with their brethren. Do not seek to give to the world occasion to say that we are extremists, that we are disunited, that one teaches one thing, and one another. Avoid dissension. Let every one be on guard, and be careful to be found standing in the gap to make up the breach, in place of standing at the wall seeking to make a breach.

Let all be careful not to make an outcry against the only people who are fulfilling the description given of the remnant people, who keep the commandments of God, and have faith in Jesus, who are exalting the standard of righteousness in these last days.—Testimonies to Ministers and Gospel Workers, 57, 58.

Chosen Watchmen

In a special sense Seventh-day Adventists have been set in the world as watchmen and light bearers. To them has been entrusted the last warning for a perishing world. On them is shining wonderful light from the Word of God. They have been given a work of the most solemn import—the proclamation of the first, second, and third angels' messages. There is no other work of so great importance. They are to allow nothing else to absorb their attention.

The most solemn truths ever entrusted to mortals have been given us to proclaim to the world. The proclamation of these truths is to be our work. The world is to be warned, and God's people are to be true to the trust committed to them.—Testimonies for the Church 9:19.

* * * * *

No New Organization

The Lord has declared that the history of the past shall be rehearsed as we enter upon the closing work. Every truth that He has given for these last days is to be proclaimed to the world. Every pillar that He has established is to be strengthened. We cannot now step off the foundation that God has established. We cannot now enter into any new organization; for this would mean apostasy from the truth.—Manuscript 129, 1890.

What Constitutes Babylon

Poisonous Doctrines

It is our individual duty to walk humbly with God. We are not to seek any strange, new message. We are not to think that the chosen ones of God who are trying to walk in the light, compose Babylon.

The fallen denominational churches are Babylon. Babylon has been fostering poisonous doctrines, the wine of error. This wine of error is made up of false doctrines, such as the natural immortality of the soul, the eternal torment of the wicked, the denial of the preexistence of Christ prior to His birth in Bethlehem, and advocating and exalting the first day of the week above God's holy and sanctified day.—Testimonies to Ministers and Gospel Workers, 61.

Following Rome

Many of the Protestant churches are following Rome's example of iniquitous connection with "the kings of the earth"—the state churches, by their relation to secular governments; and other denominations, by seeking the favor of the world. And the term "Babylon"—confusion—may be appropriately applied to these bodies, all professing to derive their doctrines from the Bible, yet divided into almost innumerable sects, with widely conflicting creeds and theories.—The Great Controversy, 383.

Call to Come Out

God's word to His people is: "Come out from among them, and be ye separate, and touch not the unclean thing; and I will receive you, and will be a Father unto you, and ye shall be My sons and daughters." 2 Corinthians 6:17, 18.... God's people are to be distinguished as a people who serve Him fully, wholeheartedly, taking no honor to themselves, and remembering that by a most solemn covenant they have bound themselves to serve the Lord, and Him only.—Testimonies for the Church 9:17.

The Sins of Babylon

The great sin charged against Babylon is, that she "made all nations drink of the wine of the wrath of her fornication." This cup of intoxication which she presents to the world, represents the false doctrines that she has accepted as the result of her unlawful connection with the great ones of the earth. Friendship with the world corrupts her faith, and in her turn she exerts a corrupting influence upon the world by teaching doctrines which are opposed to the plainest statements of Holy Writ.—The Great Controversy, 388.

The Doctrine of Eternal Torment

The theory of eternal torment is one of the false doctrines that constitute the wine of the abominations of Babylon, of which she makes all nations drink. That ministers of Christ should have accepted this heresy and proclaimed it from the sacred desk, is indeed a mystery. They received it from Rome, as they received the false sabbath. True, it has been taught by great and good men; but the light on this subject had not come to them as it has come to us.—The Great Controversy, 536.

Alliance with the World

Babylon is also charged with the sin of unlawful connection with "the kings of the earth." It was by departure from the Lord, and alliance with the heathen, that the Jewish church became a harlot; and Rome, corrupting herself in like manner by seeking the support of worldly powers, receives a like condemnation.—The Great Controversy, 382.

Chapter 18—Restlessness and Accusation [53]

By Ellen G. White

The Accuser Rebuked

Satan stands at the head of all the accusers of the brethren; but when he presents the sins of the people of God, what does the Lord answer? He says, "The Lord rebuke [not Joshua, who is a representative of the tried and chosen people of God, but] thee, O Satan; even the Lord that hath chosen Jerusalem rebuke thee: is not this a brand plucked out of the fire? Now Joshua was clothed with filthy garments, and stood before the angel." Satan had represented the chosen and loyal people of God as being full of defilement and sin. He could depict the particular sins of which they had been guilty. Had he not set the whole confederacy of evil at work to lead them, through his seductive arts, into these very sins?

But they had repented, they had accepted the righteousness of Christ. They were therefore standing before God clothed with the garments of Christ's righteousness, and "He answered and spake unto those that stood before him, saying, Take away the filthy garments from him. And unto him he said, Behold, I have caused thine iniquity to pass from thee, and I will clothe thee with change of raiment." Every sin of which they had been guilty was forgiven, and they stood before God as chosen and true, as innocent, as perfect, as though they had never sinned.

The Encouraging Word

"And I said, Let them set a fair miter upon his head. So they [the angels of God] set a fair miter upon his head, and clothed him with garments. And the angel of the Lord stood by [Jesus their Redeemer]. And the angel of the Lord protested unto Joshua, saying, Thus saith the Lord of hosts: If thou wilt walk in My ways, and if thou wilt keep My charge, then thou shalt also judge My house, and shalt also keep My courts, and I will give thee places to walk among these that stand by." I wish that all who claim to believe present truth, would think seriously of the wonderful things presented in this chapter. However weak and compassed with infirmity the people of God may be, those who turn from disloyalty to God in this wicked and perverse generation, and come back to their allegiance, standing to vindicate the holy law of God, making up the breach made by the man of sin under the direction of Satan, will be accounted the children of God, and through the righteousness of Christ will stand perfect before God.

Truth will not always lie in the dust to be trampled underfoot of men. It will be magnified and made honorable; it will yet arise and shine forth in all its natural luster, and will stand fast forever and ever.

Words of Accusation Not of God

God has a people in which all heaven is interested, and they are the one object on earth dear to the heart of God. Let every one who reads these words give them thorough consideration; for in the name of Jesus I would press them home upon every soul. When anyone arises, either among us or outside of us, who is burdened with a message which declares that the people of God are numbered with Babylon, and claims that the loud cry is a call to come out of her, you may know that he is not bearing the message of truth. Receive him not, nor bid him Godspeed; for God has not spoken by him, neither has He given a message to him, but he has run before he was sent.

False Messages Will Come

The message contained in the pamphlet called the *Loud Cry*, is a deception. Such messages will come, and it will be claimed for them that they are sent of God, but the claim will be false; for they are not filled with light, but with darkness. There will be messages of accusation against the people of God, similar to the work done by Satan in accusing God's people, and these messages will be sounding at the very time when God is saying to His people, "Arise, shine; for thy light is come, and the glory of the Lord is risen upon thee. For, behold, the darkness shall cover the earth, and gross darkness the people: but the Lord shall arise upon thee, and His glory shall be seen upon thee."

A Work of Deception

It will be found that those who bear false messages will not have a high sense of honor and integrity. They will deceive the people, and mix up with their error the Testimonies of Sister White, and use her name to give influence to their work. They make such selections from the Testimonies as they think they can twist to support their positions, and place them in a setting of falsehood, so that their error may have weight, and be accepted by the people. They misinterpret and misapply that which God has given to the church to warn, counsel, reprove, comfort, and encourage those who shall make up the remnant people of God.

Those who receive the Testimonies as the message of God, will be helped and blessed thereby; but those who take them in parts, simply to support some theory or idea of their own, to vindicate themselves in a course of error, will not be blessed and benefited by what they teach.

To claim that the Seventh-day Adventist Church is Babylon, is to make the same claim as does Satan, who is an accuser of the brethren, who accuses them before God night and day. By this misusing of the Testimonies, souls are placed in perplexity, because they cannot understand the relation of the Testimonies to such a position as is taken by those in error; for God intended that the Testimonies should always have a setting in the framework of truth.

The Need of Men and Means

Those who advocate error, will say, "The Lord saith," "when the Lord hath not spoken." They testify to falsehood, and not to truth. If those who have been proclaiming the message that the church is Babylon, had used the money expended in publishing and circulating this error, in building up instead of tearing down, they would have made it evident that they were the people whom God is leading.

[55] There is a great work to be done in the world, a great work to be done in foreign lands. Schools must be established in order that youth, children, and those of more mature age may be educated as rapidly as possible to enter the missionary field. There is need not only of ministers for foreign fields, but of wise, judicious laborers of all kinds. The Macedonian cry is sounding from all parts of the world, "Come over and help us." With all the responsibility upon us to go and preach the gospel to every creature, there is great need of men and means, and Satan is at work in every conceivable way to tie up means, and to hinder men from engaging in the very work that they should be doing.

The money that should be used in doing the good work of building houses of worship, of establishing schools for the purpose of educating laborers for the missionary field, of drilling young men and women so that they may go forth and labor patiently, intelligently, and with all perseverance, that they may be agents through whom a people may be prepared to stand in the great day of God, is diverted from a channel of usefulness and blessing, into a channel of evil and cursing.—Testimonies to Ministers and Gospel Workers, 40-43.

* * * * *

Preparing a People to Stand

God is bringing out a people and preparing them to stand as one, united, to speak the same things, and thus carry out the prayer of Christ for His disciples. "Neither pray I for these alone, but for them also which shall believe on Me through their word; that they all may be one, as Thou, Father, art in Me, and I in Thee, that they also may be one in us; that the world may believe that Thou hast sent Me."

Restless Minds

There are little companies continually arising who believe that God is only with the very few, the very scattered, and their influence is to tear down and scatter that which God's servants build up. Restless minds who want to be seeing and believing something new continually, are constantly arising, some in one place and some in another, all doing a special work for the enemy, yet claiming to have the truth.

They stand separate from the people whom God is leading out and prospering, and through whom He is to do His great work. They are continually expressing their fears that the body of Sabbathkeepers are becoming like the world; but there are scarcely two of these whose views are in harmony.

They are scattered and confused, and yet deceive themselves so much as to think that God is especially with them. Some of these profess to have the gifts among them; but are led by the influence and teachings of these gifts to hold in doubt those upon whom God has laid the special burden of His work, and to lead off a class from the body. The people who, in accordance with God's Word, are putting forth every effort to be one, who are established in the message of the third angel, are looked upon with suspicion, for the reason that they are extending their labor, and are gathering souls into the truth.

They are considered worldly, because they have an influence in the world, and their acts testify that they expect God yet to do a special and great work upon the earth, to bring out a people and fit them for Christ's appearing.

This class do not know what they really believe, or the reasons of their belief. They are ever learning, and never able to come to the knowledge of the truth. One man arises with wild, erroneous views, and claims that God has sent him with new and glorious light, and all must believe what he brings. Some who have no established faith, who are not subject to the body, but are drifting about without an anchor to hold them, receive that wind of doctrine. His light shines in such a manner as to cause the world to turn from him in disgust and to hate him. Then he blasphemously places himself by the side of Christ, and claims that the world hate him for the same reason that they hated Christ....

Spurious Gifts

Some rejoice and exult that they have the gifts, which others have not. May God deliver His people from such gifts. What do these gifts do for them? Are they, through the exercise of these gifts, brought into the unity of the faith? And do they convince the unbeliever that God is with them of a truth? When these discordant ones, holding their different views, come together and there is considerable excitement and the unknown tongue, they let their light so shine that unbelievers would say, These people are not sane; they are carried away with a false excitement, and we know that they do not have the truth. Such stand directly in the way of sinners; their influence is effectual to keep others from accepting the Sabbath. Such will be rewarded according to their works. Would to God they would be reformed or give up the Sabbath! They would not then stand in the way of unbelievers.

A Sound Work

God has led out men who have toiled for years, who have been willing to make any sacrifice, who have suffered privation, and endured trials to bring the truth before the world, and by their consistent course remove the reproach that fanatics have brought upon the cause of God. They have met opposition in every form. They have toiled night and day in searching the evidences of our faith, that they might bring out the truth in its clearness, in a connected form, that it might withstand all opposition. Incessant labor and mental trials in connection with this great work have worn down more than one constitution, and prematurely sprinkled heads with gray hairs. They have not worn out in vain. God has marked their earnest, tearful, agonizing prayers that they might have light and truth, and that the truth might shine in its clearness to others. He has marked their self-sacrificing efforts, and He will reward them as their works have been.

On the other hand, those who have not toiled to bring out these precious truths, have come up and received some points, like the Sabbath truth, which are all prepared to their hand, and then all the gratitude they manifest for that which cost them nothing, but others so much, is to rise up like Korah, Dathan, and Abiram and reproach those upon whom God has laid the burden of His work. They would say, "Ye take too much upon you, seeing all the congregation are holy, every one of them, and the Lord is among them." They are strangers to gratitude. They possess a strong spirit, which will not yield to reason, and which will lead them on to their own destruction.

God has blessed His people who have moved forward, following His opening providence. He has brought out a people from every class upon the great platform of truth. Infidels have been convinced that God was with His people, and have humbled their hearts to obey the truth. The work of God moves steadily on.

Fruits of Inconsistency

Yet notwithstanding all the evidences that God has been leading the body, there are, and will continue to be, those who profess the Sabbath, who will move independent of the body, and believe and act as they choose. Their views are confused. Their scattered state is a standing testimony that God is not with them. By the world, the Sabbath and their errors are placed upon a level, and thrown away together.

Bibliography

God is angry with those who pursue a course to make the world hate them. If a Christian is hated because of his good works, and for following Christ, he will have a reward; but if he is hated because he does not take a course to be loved, hated because of his uncultivated manners and because he makes the truth a matter of quarrel with his neighbors, and takes a course to make the Sabbath as annoying as possible to them, he is a stumbling block to sinners, a reproach to the sacred truth, and unless he repents it were better for him that a millstone were hung about his neck, and he were cast into the sea.—Testimonies for the Church 1:417-420.

Bibliography

The Great Controversy, 388-390, 536-537	Babylon full of wine of false doctrine
Testimonies to Ministers and Gospel Workers, 20, 23, 32-62	S.D.A Church not Babylon

The Great Controversy, 388, 605-606; Early Writings, 273-274	Sins of Babylon
Testimonies for the Church 3:450-451; Testimonies for the Church 5:107-108; Gospel Workers, 444	Authority of church ordained of God
The Acts of the Apostles, 587-588; Testimonies to Ministers and Gospel Workers, 49; Testimonies for the Church 6:42; Testimonies for the Church 7:16	Church defective, yet loved by the Lord
The Acts of the Apostles, 162-164 (Gospel Workers, 443)	God acknowledges His organized church
Prophets and Kings, 590; Christ's Object Lessons, 298; Testimonies for the Church 9:228	God's love for the church
Early Writings, 270; Testimonies for the Church 1:181-183, 186-188; Testimonies for the Church 3:437-439	Laodicean message to cause a shaking, followed by loud cry
Life Sketches of Ellen G. White, 437-439	God with His ministering servants

Chapter 19—Apostasies

By Ellen G. White

I am in great travail of soul for our people. We are living in the perils of the last days. A superficial faith results in a superficial experience. There is a repentance that needs to be repented of. All genuine experience in religious doctrines will bear the impress of Jehovah. All should see the necessity of understanding the truth for themselves individually. We must understand the doctrines that have been studied out carefully and prayerfully. It has been revealed to me that there is among our people a great lack of knowledge in regard to the rise and progress of the third angel's message. There is great need to search the book of Daniel and the book of Revelation, and learn the texts thoroughly, that we may know what is written.

The light given me has been very forcible that many would go out from us, giving heed to seducing spirits and doctrines of devils. The Lord desires that every soul who claims to believe the truth shall have an intelligent knowledge of what is truth. False prophets will arise, and will deceive many. Everything is to be shaken that can be shaken. Then does it not become everyone to understand the reasons of our faith? In place of having so many sermons there should be a more close searching of the Word of God, opening the Scriptures, text by text, and searching for the strong evidences that sustain the fundamental doctrines that have brought us where we now are, upon the platform of eternal truth.

Charmed by Spurious Holiness

My soul is made very sad to see how quickly some who have had light and truth will accept the deceptions of Satan, and be charmed with a spurious holiness. When men turn away from the landmarks the Lord has established that we may understand our position as marked out in prophecy, they are going they know not whither.

I question whether genuine rebellion is ever curable. Study in *Patriarchs and Prophets* the rebellion of Korah, Dathan, and Abiram. This rebellion was extended, including more than two men. It was led by two hundred and fifty princes of the congregation, men of renown. Call rebellion by its right name and apostasy by its right name, and then consider that the experience of the ancient people of God with all its objectionable features was faithfully chronicled to pass into history. The Scripture declares, "These things ... are written for our admonition, upon whom the ends of the world are come." And if men and women who have the knowledge of the truth are so far separated from their Great Leader that they will take the great leader of apostasy and name him Christ our Righteousness, it is because they have not sunk deep into the mines of the truth. They are not able to distinguish the precious ore from the base material.

False Prophets

Read the cautions so abundantly given in the Word of God in regard to false prophets that will come in with their heresies, and if possible will deceive the very elect. With these warnings, why is it that the church does not distinguish the false from the genuine? Those who have in any way been thus misled need to humble themselves before God, and sincerely repent, because they have so easily been led astray. They have not distinguished the voice of the true Shepherd from that of a stranger. Let all such review this chapter of their experience.

For more than half a century God has been giving His people light through the testimonies of His Spirit. After all this time is it left for a few men and their wives to undeceive the whole church of believers, declaring Mrs. White a fraud and a deceiver? "By their fruits ye shall know them."

Those who can ignore all the evidences which God has given them, and change that blessing into a curse, should tremble for the safety of their own souls. Their candlestick will be removed out of its place unless they repent. The Lord has been insulted. The standard of truth, of the first, second, and third angels' messages has been left to trail in the dust. If the watchmen are left to mislead the people in this fashion, God will hold some souls responsible for a lack of keen discernment to discover what kind of provender was being given to His flock.

Apostasies have occurred and the Lord has permitted matters of this nature to develop in the past in order to show how easily His people will be misled when they depend upon the words of men instead of searching the Scriptures for themselves, as did the noble Bereans, to see if these things are so. And the Lord has permitted things of this kind to occur that warnings may be given that such things will take place.

Rebellion and Apostasy

Rebellion and apostasy are in the very air we breathe. We shall be affected by them unless we by faith hang our helpless souls upon Christ. If men are so easily misled now, how will they stand when Satan shall personate Christ, and work miracles? Who will be unmoved by his misrepresentations then—professing to be Christ when it is only Satan assuming the person of Christ, and apparently working the works of Christ? What will hold God's people from giving their allegiance to false christs? "Go not after them."

The doctrines must be plainly understood. The men accepted to preach the truth must be anchored; then their vessel will hold against storm and tempest, because the anchor holds them firmly. The deceptions will increase, and we are to call rebellion by its right name. We are to stand with the whole armor on. In this conflict we do not meet men only, but principalities and powers. We wrestle not against flesh and blood. Let Ephesians 6:10-18 be read carefully and impressively in our churches.

Voicing the Dragon's Words

Those who apostatize are voicing the words of the dragon. We have to meet the satanic agencies who went to make war with the saints. "The dragon was wroth with the woman, and went to make war with the remnant of her seed, which keep the commandments of God, and have the testimony of Jesus Christ." Those who apostatize leave the true and faithful people of God, and fraternize with those who represent Barabbas. "By their fruits ye shall know them."

I write this because many in the church are represented to me as seeing men like trees walking. They must have another and deeper experience before they discern the snares spread to take them in the net of the deceiver. There must be no halfway work done now. The Lord calls for stanch, decided, whole-souled men and women to stand in the gap, and make up the hedge. "And they that shall be of thee shall build the old waste places: thou shalt raise up the foundations of many generations; and thou shalt be called, The repairer of the breach, The restorer of paths to dwell in. If thou turn away thy foot from the Sabbath, from doing thy pleasure on My holy day; and call the Sabbath a delight, the holy of the Lord, honorable; and shalt honor Him, not doing thine own ways, nor finding thine own pleasure, nor speaking thine own words: then shalt thou delight thyself in the Lord; and I will cause thee to ride upon the high places of the earth, and feed thee with the heritage of Jacob thy father: for the mouth of the Lord hath spoken it."

There is a decided testimony to be borne by all our ministers in all our churches. God has permitted apostasies to take place in order to show how little dependence can be placed in man. We are always to look to God; His word is not Yea and Nay, but Yea and Amen.—Manuscript 185, 1897.

* * * * *

The Shadows of Satan

Bear in mind that the time will never come when the shadow of Satan will not be cast athwart our pathway to obstruct our faith and eclipse the light coming from the Sun of Righteousness. Our faith must not stagger, but cleave through that shadow. We have an experience that is not to be buried in the darkness of doubt. Our faith is not in feeling, but in truth. None of us need flatter ourselves that while the world is progressing in wickedness we shall have no difficulties.

Difficulties Lead to Prayer

It is these very difficulties that bring us to the audience chamber of the Most High, to seek counsel of the One who is infinite in wisdom. He loves to have us seek Him; He loves to have us trust Him and believe His Word. If we had no perplexities, no trials, we would become self-sufficient and lifted up in ourselves. The true saints will be purified, and made white, and tried.

Behold the Light

Let not depression and discouragement mar your representation of Christ. "Ye are a chosen generation, a royal priesthood, an holy nation, a peculiar people; that ye should show forth the praises of Him who hath called you out of darkness into His marvelous light." Let your light be seen. Educate your heart and lips to speak the praises of God for His matchless love for you. If you will educate your soul to be hopeful, and to see the light shining from the cross of Calvary, you will see His salvation brought near, and rejoice in the hope of a glorious immortality.

There is but one power that can bring us into conformity to the likeness of Christ, that can make us steadfast, and keep us constant. It is the grace of God that comes to us through obedience to the law of God which is the transcript of the divine character. It is a knowledge of Jesus Christ that we should cultivate to the uttermost of our power, in order that we may be doers of the Word.

Growth in Grace

Those who have Christ enthroned within, will manifest Christlike principles. They will make it evident that the Holy Spirit has imparted a new life to them, and that they are nourishing and cherishing that life. Its beginning is found in spiritual union with the Lord Jesus Christ, and as they go on increasing in the knowledge of God, they will manifest a growth in grace and will show Christlike love to others.

We are to be very humble in our work for God. We are to keep all His commandments that we may live. Let us seek to honor Christ in our daily lives, believing His Word, and following in His footsteps.—Letter 58, 1909.

[60]

An Active Conflict

Christ's manner of rule and government is to be established to counterwork the works of Satan, and to bring the world back to its loyalty to God. The Prince of heaven, He who was one with the Father, gave Himself that He might save the fallen race. Satan is actively at work to defeat His highest purposes. But Christ says, Where Satan has set his throne, there will I establish My cross. The prince of evil shall be cast out, and I will become the center of a world redeemed.

True conversion to the message of present truth embraces conversion to the principles of health reform. "I, if I be lifted up," said Christ, "will draw all men unto Me." Men who in their unconverted state are controlled by human ambitions and human passions, will, through faith in the sacrifice made in their behalf, embrace the terms of discipleship. Human ambitions will be sacrificed; evil passions will be converted; capabilities which through Satan's influence have been employed to counterwork all good, will be turned into channels for the upbuilding of that which once they destroyed.

Deceived Men Oppose God's Law

Satan is so deceiving men that many believe they are doing right in opposing the law of Jehovah. The enemy of God has led them to look upon His righteous law as an arbitrary requirement. All who unite on the side of righteousness in the conflict of good against evil will come into decided conflict with satanic forces; but this should not discourage the servant of God.

The Lord declares, "My Spirit shall strengthen every right principle in its opposition to evil. I will give power to every soul who will work on the side of righteousness and truth. I have a work for all to do who love Me, and who will hold aloft the banner of truth. And heavenly angels will be near to aid every human agency that is sanctified through the truth. All who preserve strict loyalty to God will do a righteous work in the earth in saving perishing souls."

Satan's Wiles

There are few among those who claim to be Christians who realize how deceptive are the wiles of Satan, and are prepared to oppose them firmly. Christ has promised His Spirit to go with those who will yield to His workings, and who will be loyal in opposing unrighteousness in every form. He has given to every human agent a work to do, that He may learn how to work in union with His Redeemer and in connection with heaven. It is the duty of every true Christian to unite the utmost powers of his being with the efforts of Him who made His life an example to mankind of what human agencies may accomplish in His name.—Letter 62, 1909.

* * * * *

Denying Christ

We may deny Christ in our life by indulging love of ease or love of self, by jesting and joking, and by seeking the honor of the world. We may deny Him in our outward appearance, by conformity to the world, by a proud look or costly apparel. Only by constant watchfulness and persevering and almost unceasing prayer, shall we be able to exhibit in our life the character of Christ or the sanctifying influence of the truth.—Testimonies for the Church 1:304.

Chapter 20—The Pillars of Our Faith*

By Ellen G. White

During the last fifty years of my life, I have had precious opportunities to obtain an experience. I have had an experience in the first, second, and third angels' messages. The angels are represented as flying in the midst of heaven, proclaiming to the world a message of warning, and having a direct bearing upon the people living in the last days of this earth's history. No one hears the voice of these angels, for they are a symbol to represent the people of God who are working in harmony with the universe of heaven. Men and women, enlightened by the Spirit of God and sanctified through the truth, proclaim the three messages in their order.

I have acted a part in this solemn work. Nearly all my Christian experience is interwoven with it. There are those now living who have an experience similar to my own. They have recognized the truth unfolding for this time; they have kept in step with the great Leader, the Captain of the Lord's host.

Prophecy Fulfilled

In the proclamation of the messages, every specification of prophecy has been fulfilled. Those who were privileged to act a part in proclaiming these messages have gained an experience which is of the highest value to them; and now when we are amid the perils of these last days, when voices will be heard on every side saying, "Here is Christ," "Here is truth"; while the burden of many is to unsettle the foundation of our faith which has led us from the churches and from the world to stand as a peculiar people in the world, like John our testimony will be borne:

"That which was from the beginning, which we have heard, which we have seen with our eyes, which we have looked upon,

---
*Written on the train en route to Lynn, Massachusetts, December, 1890.

and our hands have handled, of the Word of life;... that which we have seen and heard declare we unto you, that ye also may have fellowship with us."

I testify the things which I have seen, the things which I have heard, the things which my hands have handled of the Word of life. And this testimony I know to be of the Father and the Son. We have seen and do testify that the power of the Holy Ghost has accompanied the presentation of the truth, warning with pen and voice, and giving the messages in their order. To deny this work would be to deny the Holy Ghost, and would place us in that company who have departed from the faith, giving heed to seducing spirits.

Confidence Assailed

The enemy will set everything in operation to uproot the confidence of the believers in the pillars of our faith in the messages of the past, which have placed us upon the elevated platform of eternal truth, and which have established and given character to the work. The Lord God of Israel has led out His people, unfolding to them truth of heavenly origin. His voice has been heard, and is still heard, saying, Go forward from strength to strength, from grace to grace, from glory to glory. The work is strengthening and broadening, for the Lord God of Israel is the defense of His people.

Those who have a hold of the truth theoretically, with their fingertips as it were, who have not brought its principles into the inner sanctuary of the soul, but have kept the vital truth in the outer court, will see nothing sacred in the past history of this people which has made them what they are, and has established them as earnest, determined, missionary workers in the world.

[62]

The truth for this time is precious, but those whose hearts have not been broken by falling on the rock Christ Jesus, will not see and understand what is truth. They will accept that which pleases their ideas, and will begin to manufacture another foundation than that which is laid. They will flatter their own vanity and esteem, thinking that they are capable of removing the pillars of our faith, and replacing them with pillars they have devised.

This will continue to be as long as time shall last. Anyone who has been a close student of the Bible will see and understand the solemn position of those who are living in the closing scenes of this earth's history. They will feel their own inefficiency and weakness, and will make it their first business to have not merely a form of godliness, but a vital connection with God. They will not dare to rest until Christ is formed within, the hope of glory. Self will die; pride will be expelled from the soul, and they will have the meekness and gentleness of Christ.—Manuscript 28, 1890.

Instruction Given the Redeemed

Some among the redeemed will have laid hold of Christ in the last hours of life, and in heaven instruction will be given to those who, when they died, did not understand perfectly the plan of salvation. Christ will lead the redeemed ones beside the river of life, and will open to them that which while on this earth they could not understand.—Letter 203, 1905.

* * * * *

Christ's Abiding Presence

Christ's last words to His disciples were: "Lo, I am with you alway, even unto the end of the world." "Go ye therefore, and teach all nations." "Go to the farthest bounds of the habitable globe, and know that wherever you go, My presence will attend you." No more valuable legacy could He have left them than the promise of His abiding presence.

To us also the commission is given. We are bidden to go forth as Christ's messengers, to teach, instruct, and persuade men and women, to urge upon their attention the word of life. And to us also the assurance of Christ's abiding presence is given.—Manuscript 24, 1903.

* * * * *

Work of Minister and Doctor

We have a great work to do in our world. If ministers and doctors will work in God's lines, He will work with them. But they must change, decidedly change, in spirit and character. They must remember that they are not the only ones to whom the Lord will give wisdom. If His people will not follow in His way, the Lord will employ heathen princes to do His will....

Let ministers and physicians remember that their only safety is in being bound up together with Christ in God. They are to do their work by the Lord's appointment, and both occupy the same field.—Manuscript 14, 1901.

* * * * *

Chapter 21—Relation of Faith and Works

By Ellen G. White

Napier, New Zealand
April 9, 1893

Brother A. T. Jones:

I was attending a meeting, and a large congregation were present. In my dream you were presenting the subject of faith and the imputed righteousness of Christ by faith. You repeated several times that works amounted to nothing, that there were no conditions. The matter was presented in that light that I knew minds would be confused, and would not receive the correct impression in reference to faith and works, and I decided to write to you. You state this matter too strongly. There are conditions to our receiving justification and sanctification, and the righteousness of Christ. I know your meaning, but you leave a wrong impression upon many minds. While good works will not save even one soul, yet it is impossible for even one soul to be saved without good works. God saves us under a law, that we must ask if we would receive, seek if we would find, and knock if we would have the door opened unto us.

Christ offers Himself as willing to save unto the uttermost all who come unto Him. He invites all to come to Him. "Him that cometh to Me I will in no wise cast out." You look in reality upon these subjects as I do, yet you make these subjects, through your expressions, confusing to minds. And after you have expressed your mind radically in regard to works, when questions are asked you upon this very subject, it is not lying out in so very clear lines, in your own mind, and you cannot define the correct principles to other minds, and you are yourself unable to make your statements harmonize with your own principles and faith.

The young man came to Jesus with the question, "Good Master, what good thing shall I do, that I may have eternal life?" And Christ saith unto him, "Why callest thou Me good? there is none good but one, that is, God: but if thou wilt enter into life, keep the commandments." He saith unto Him, "Which?" Jesus quoted several, and the young man said unto Him, "All these things have I kept from my youth up: what lack I yet?" Jesus said unto him, "If thou wilt be perfect, go and sell that thou hast, and give to the poor, and thou shalt have treasure in heaven: and come and follow Me." Here are conditions, and the Bible is full of conditions. "But when the young man heard that saying, he went away sorrowful: for he had great possessions."

Then when you say there are no conditions, and some expressions are made quite broad, you burden the minds, and some cannot see consistency in your expressions. They cannot see how they can harmonize these expressions with the plain statements of the Word of God. Please guard these points. These strong assertions in regard to works, never make our position any stronger. The expressions weaken our position, for there are many who will consider you an extremist, and will lose the rich lessons you have for them, upon the very subjects they need to know My brother, it is hard for the mind to comprehend this point, and do not confuse any mind with ideas that will not harmonize with the Word. Please to consider that under the teaching of Christ many of the disciples were lamentably ignorant; but when the Holy Spirit that Jesus promised, came upon them and made the vacillating Peter the champion of faith, what a transformation in his character! But do not lay one pebble, for a soul that is weak in the faith to stumble over, in overwrought presentations or expressions. Be ever consistent, calm, deep, and solid. Do not go to any extreme in anything, but keep your feet on solid rock. O precious, precious Saviour. "He that hath My commandments, and keepeth them, he it is that loveth Me; and he that loveth Me shall be loved of My Father, and I will love him, and will manifest Myself to him." [64]

This is the true test—the doing of the words of Christ. And it is the evidence of the human agent's love to Jesus, and he that doeth His will giveth to the world the practical evidence of the fruit he manifests in obedience, in purity, and in holiness of character....

O my brother, walk carefully with God. But remember that there are some whose eyes are intently fixed upon you, expecting that you will overreach the mark, and stumble, and fall. But if you keep in humility close to Jesus, all is well....

There is no place in the school of Christ where we graduate. We are to work on the plan of addition, and the Lord will work on the plan of multiplication. It is through constant diligence that we will, through the grace of Christ, live on the plan of addition, making our calling and election sure.... "For if ye do these things ye shall never fall: for so an entrance shall be ministered unto you abundantly into the everlasting kingdom of our Lord and Saviour Jesus Christ."—Letter 44, 1893.

* * * * *

No Compromise With Sin

Let my brethren be very careful how they present the subject of faith and works before the people, lest minds become confused. The people need to be urged to diligence in good works. They should be shown how to be successful, how to be purified, and their offerings may be fragrant before God. It is by virtue of the blood of Christ. Messages of a decided character must be borne to the people. Men must go forth reproving, rebuking every manner of evil.

If there is given to the angel of any church a commission like unto that given to the angel of the church of Ephesus, let the message be heard through human agents rebuking carelessness, backsliding, and sin, that the people may be brought to repentance and confession of sin. Never seek to cover sin; for in the message of rebuke, Christ is to be proclaimed as the first and the last, He who is all in all to the soul.

His power awaits the demand of those who would overcome. The reprover is to animate his hearers so that they shall strive for the mastery. He is to encourage them to struggle for deliverance from every sinful practice, to be free from every corrupt habit, even if his denial of self is like taking the right eye, or separating the right arm from the body. No concession or compromise is to be made to evil habits or sinful practices.—Manuscript 26a, 1892.

* * * * *

No Short Route to Holiness

This is an age famous for surface work, for easy methods, for boasted holiness aside from the standard of character that God has erected. All short routes, all cut-off tracks, all teaching which fails to exalt the law of God as the standard of religious character, is spurious. Perfection of character is a lifelong work, unattainable by those who are not willing to strive for it in God's appointed way, by slow and toilsome steps. We cannot afford to make any mistake in this matter, but we want day by day to be growing up into Christ, our living head."—Testimonies for the Church 5:500.

* * * * *

Co-operation with God

Man is to co-operate with God, employing every power according to his God-given ability. He is not to be ignorant as to what are right practices in eating and drinking, and in all the habits of life. The Lord designs that His human agents shall act as rational, accountable beings in every respect....

We cannot afford to neglect one ray of light God has given. To be sluggish in our practice of those things which require diligence is to commit sin. The human agent is to co-operate with God, and keep under those passions which should be in subjection. To do this he must be unwearied in his prayers to God, ever obtaining grace to control his spirit, temper, and actions. Through the imparted grace of Christ, he may be enabled to overcome. To be an overcomer means more than many suppose it means.

Repentance the Gift of God

The Spirit of God will answer the cry of every penitent heart; for repentance is the gift of God, and an evidence that Christ is drawing the soul to Himself. We can no more repent of sin without Christ, than we can be pardoned without Christ, and yet it is a humiliation to man with his human passion and pride to go to Jesus straightway, believing and trusting Him for everything which he needs....

From First to Last, A Laborer Together With God

Let no man present the idea that man has little or nothing to do in the great work of overcoming; for God does nothing for man without his co-operation. Neither say that after you have done all you can on your part, Jesus will help you. Christ has said, "Without Me ye can do nothing." From first to last man is to be a laborer together with God. Unless the Holy Spirit works upon the human heart, at every step we shall stumble and fall.

Man's efforts alone are nothing but worthlessness; but co-operation with Christ means a victory. Of ourselves we have no power to repent of sin. Unless we accept divine aid we cannot take the first step toward the Saviour. He says, "I am Alpha and Omega, the beginning and the end," in the salvation of every soul.

But though Christ is everything, we are to inspire every man to unwearied diligence. We are to strive, wrestle, agonize, watch, pray, lest we shall be overcome by the wily foe. For the power and grace with which we can do this comes from God, and all the while we are to trust in Him, who is able to save to the uttermost all who come unto God by Him. Never leave the impression on the mind that there is little or nothing to do on the part of man; but rather teach man to co-operate with God, that he may be successful in overcoming.

Let no one say that your works have nothing to do with your rank and position before God. In the judgment the sentence pronounced is according to what has been done or to what has been left undone. (Matthew 25:34-40.)

Effort and Labor Required

Effort and labor are required on the part of the receiver of God's grace; for it is the fruit that makes manifest what is the character of the tree. Although the good works of man are of no more value without faith in Jesus than was the offering of Cain, yet covered with the merit of Christ, they testify [to] the worthiness of the doer to inherit eternal life. That which is considered morality in the world does not reach the divine standard and has no more merit before heaven than had the offering of Cain.—Manuscript 26a, 1892.

* * * * *

How Daniel Overcame

When Daniel was in Babylon, he was beset with temptations of which we have never dreamed, and he realized that he must keep his body under. He purposed in his heart that he would not drink of the king's wine or eat of his dainties. He knew that in order to come off a victor, he must have clear mental perceptions, that he might discern between right and wrong. While he was working on his part, God worked also, and gave him "knowledge and skill in all learning and wisdom: and Daniel had understanding in all visions and dreams." This is the way God worked for Daniel; and He does not propose to do any differently now. Man must co-operate with God in carrying out the plan of salvation.—The Review and Herald, April 2, 1889.

* * * * *

While Submitting to the Holy Spirit

Everyone who has a realizing sense of what it means to be a Christian, will purify himself from everything that weakens and defiles. All the habits of his life will be brought into harmony with the requirements of the word of truth, and he will not only believe, but will work out his own salvation with fear and trembling, while submitting to the molding of the Holy Spirit.—The Review and Herald, March 6, 1888.

* * * * *

He Becomes Our Righteousness

Christ looks at the spirit, and when He sees us carrying our burden with faith, His perfect holiness atones for our shortcomings. When we do our best, He becomes our righteousness. It takes every ray of light that God sends to us to make us the light of the world.—Letter 33, 1889.

Chapter 22—Doubting the Testimonies*

By Ellen G. White

When you find men questioning the Testimonies, finding fault with them, and seeking to draw away the people from their influence, be assured that God is not at work through them. It is another spirit. Doubt and unbelief are cherished by those who do not walk circumspectly. They have a painful consciousness that their life will not abide the test of the Spirit of God, whether speaking through His Word or through the Testimonies of His Spirit that would bring them to His Word. Instead of beginning with their own hearts, and coming into harmony with the pure principles of the gospel, they find fault, and condemn the very means that God has chosen to fit up a people to stand in the day of the Lord.

Let some skeptical one come along, who is not willing to square his life by the Bible rule, who is seeking to gain the favor of all, and how soon the class that are not in harmony with the work of God are called out. Those who are converted, and grounded in the truth, will find nothing pleasing or profitable in the influence or teaching of such a one. But those who are defective in character, whose hands are not pure, whose hearts are not holy, whose habits of life are loose, who are unkind at home, or untrustworthy in deal—all these will be sure to enjoy the new sentiments presented. All may see, if they will, the true measure of the man, the nature of his teaching, from the character of his followers.

Those who have most to say against the Testimonies are generally those who have not read them, just as those who boast of their disbelief of the Bible are those who have little knowledge of its teachings. They know that it condemns them, and their rejection of it gives them a feeling of security in their sinful course.

---

*Extract from a sermon at the General Conference of 1883.

Error's Bewitching Power

There is in error and unbelief that which bewilders and bewitches the mind. To question and doubt and cherish unbelief in order to excuse ourselves in stepping aside from the straight path is a far easier matter than to purify the soul through a belief of the truth, and obedience thereto. But when better influences lead one to desire to return, he finds himself entangled in such a network of Satan, like a fly in a spider's web, that it seems a hopeless task to him, and he seldom recovers himself from the snare laid for him by the wily foe.

When once men have admitted doubt and unbelief of the Testimonies of the Spirit of God, they are strongly tempted to adhere to the opinions which they have avowed before others. Their theories and notions fix themselves like a gloomy cloud over the mind, shutting out every ray of evidence in favor of the truth. The doubts indulged through ignorance, pride, or love of sinful practices, rivet upon the soul fetters that are seldom broken. Christ, and He alone, can give the needed power to break them.

Importance of Heeding Testimonies

The Testimonies of the Spirit of God are given to direct men to His Word, which has been neglected. Now if their messages are not heeded, the Holy Spirit is shut away from the soul. What further means has God in reserve to reach the erring ones, and show them their true condition?

The churches that have cherished influences which lessen faith in the Testimonies, are weak and tottering. Some ministers are working to attract the people to themselves. When an effort is made to correct any wrong in these ministers, they stand back in independence and say, "My church accepts my labors."

Jesus said, "Every one that doeth evil, hateth the light, neither cometh to the light, lest his deeds should be reproved." There are many today pursuing a similar course. In the Testimonies are specified the very sins of which they are guilty; hence they have no desire to read them. There are those who from their youth up have received warning and reproofs through the Testimonies; but have they walked in the light and reformed?—Not at all. They still indulge the same sins; they have the same defects of character. These evils mar the work of God, and make their impress upon the churches. The work the Lord would do to set the churches in order is not done, because the individual members—and especially the leaders of the flock—would not be corrected.

A Partial Acceptance

Many a man professes to accept the Testimonies, while they have no influence upon his life or character. His faults become stronger by indulgence until, having been often reproved and not heeding the reproof, he loses the power of self-control, and becomes hardened in a course of wrongdoing. If he is overworked, if weakness comes upon him, he has not moral power to rise above the infirmities of character which he did not overcome; they become his strongest points, and he is overborne by them. Then bring him to the test and ask, "Did not God reprove this phase in your character by the Testimonies years ago?" He will answer, "Yes, I received a written Testimony saying that I was wrong in these things." "Why, then, did you not correct these wrong habits?" "I thought the reprover must have made a mistake; that which I could see, I accepted; that which I could not see, I said was the mind of the one who gave the message. I did not accept the reproof."

The Cost of Rejection

In some cases the very faults of character which God would have His servants see and correct, but which they refuse to see, have cost these men their life. They might have lived to be channels of light. God wanted them to live, and sent them instruction in righteousness, that they might preserve their physical and mental powers to do acceptable service for Him; and had they received the counsel of God, and become altogether such as He would have them, they would have been able workmen for the advancement of the truth, men who would have stood high in the affections and confidence of our people. But they are sleeping in the grave, because they did not see that God knew them better than they knew themselves. His thoughts were not their thoughts, nor His ways, their ways. These one-sided men have molded the work wherever they have labored. The churches under their management have been greatly weakened.

What Are We Worth?

God reproves men because He loves them. He wants them to be strong in His strength, to have well-balanced minds and symmetrical characters; then they will be examples to the flock of God, leading them by precept and example nearer to heaven. Then they will build up a holy temple for God.—Manuscript 1, 1883.

Chapter 23—What Are We Worth?

[Portion of A sermon delivered in the st. Helena sanitarium chapel, January 23, 1904.]

By Ellen G. White

The Lord desires every one of us to be decidedly in earnest. We cannot afford to make a mistake in spiritual matters. The life-and-death question with us is, "What shall I do, that I may be saved, eternally saved?" "What shall I do, that I may inherit eternal life—a life that measures with the life of God?" This is a question that it becomes every one of us to consider carefully....

While living in this world, we are to be God's helping hand. Paul declared, "Ye are God's husbandry; ye are God's building." We are to co-operate with God in every measure that He desires to carry out. Are we fulfilling the purpose of the eternal God? Are we daily seeking to have the mind of Christ and to do His will in word and work?

What a condition the human family is in today! Have you ever seen before such a time of confusion—of violence, of murder, theft, and every other kind of crime? In this time, where are we individually standing?

A Hypocritical Fast

In the fifty-eighth of Isaiah we have read of those who "fast for strife and debate, and to smite with the fist of wickedness," and we have learned that God will not accept such a fast. "Ye shall not fast as ye do this day," He declares, "to make your voice to be heard on high.

"Is it such a fast that I have chosen? a day for a man to afflict his soul? is it to bow down his head as a bulrush, and to spread sackcloth and ashes under him? wilt thou call this a fast, and an acceptable day to the Lord?

The Acceptable Fast

"Is not this the fast that I have chosen? to loose the bands of wickedness, to undo the heavy burdens [instead of binding them on], and to let the oppressed go free, and that ye break every yoke? Is it not to deal thy bread to the hungry, and that thou bring the poor that are cast out to thy house? when thou seest the naked, that thou cover him; and that thou hide not thyself from thine own flesh?

The Reward

"Then [after they do these works of mercy and necessity] shall thy light break forth as the morning, and thine health shall spring forth speedily; and thy righteousness shall go before thee; the glory of the Lord shall be thy rereward."

We are to put into practice the precepts of the law, and thus have righteousness before us; the rereward will be God's glory. The light of the righteousness of Christ will be our front guard, and the glory of the Lord will be our rereward. Let us thank the Lord for this assurance. Let us constantly stand in a position where the Lord God of heaven can favor us. Let us consider that it is our high privilege to be in connection with God—to be His helping hand.

In God's great plan for the redemption of a lost race, He has placed Himself under the necessity of using human agencies as His helping hand. He must have a helping hand, in order to reach humanity. He must have the co-operation of those who will be active, quick to see opportunities, quick to discern what must be done for their fellow men.

Christ gave His life for sinful men and women. He desired to rescue the race from a life of transgression to a life of obedience and righteousness; and to those who accept Him as their Redeemer He offers the richest reward that Heaven can bestow—even the inheritance of life eternal....

What Are We Worth?

O that we might comprehend more fully the infinite price that has been paid for our redemption! Paul declares, "Ye are bought with a price;" and it is true; for the price paid is nothing less than the life of the only-begotten Son of God. Let us all consider this. We may refuse the invitations that Christ sends to us; we may neglect His offer of pardon and peace; but still it remains a fact that every one of us has been bought with a price, even with the precious blood of the Son of God. Therefore, "Consider Him."

You have cost much. "Glorify God in your body, and in your spirit, which are God's." That which you may regard as your own, is God's. Take care of His property. He has bought you with an infinite price. Your mind is His. What right has any person to abuse a body that belongs not to himself, but to the Lord Jesus Christ? What satisfaction can anyone take in gradually lessening the powers of body and mind by selfish indulgence of any form?

God has given to every human being a brain. He desires that it shall be used to His glory. By it, man is enabled to co-operate with God in efforts to save perishing fellow mortals. We have none too much brain power or reasoning faculties. We are to educate and train every power of mind and body—the human mechanism that Christ has bought—in order that we may put it to the best possible use. We are to do all we can to strengthen these powers; for God is pleased to have us become more and still more efficient colaborers with Him.

Of those who do their part faithfully, it is said, "We are laborers *together* with God." Apart from divine aid, man can do very little; but the heavenly Father and His Son are ready to work through every one who consecrates himself wholly on the altar of service. Every soul before me may co-operate with God, and labor for Him acceptably. The Lord desires us all to come into line. To every man He has given an appointed work, according to their several ability....

Personal Experience

At the age of seventeen, when all my friends thought I was an invalid for life on account of a severe accident I had sustained in my girlhood, a heavenly visitant came and spoke to me, saying, "I have a message for you to bear." "Why," I thought, "there certainly must be a great mistake somewhere." Again were spoken the words: "I have a message for you to bear. Write out for the people what I give you." Up to that time, my trembling hand had not been able to write a line. I replied, "I cannot do it; I cannot do it." "Write! write!" were the words spoken once again. I took the pen and paper, and I began to write; and how much I have written since, it is impossible to estimate. The strength, the power, was of God.

Since that time, the books that I have written have been published in many, many languages, and have gone to all parts of the earth. Just a short time ago I received word that a copy of one of my books had been graciously received by the queen of Germany, and that she had written a kind letter expressing her appreciation of the volume. To the Lord be all the praise.

Our Privilege

Of ourselves we can do nothing good. But it is our privilege to place ourselves in right relation to God, and to determine that by His help we will do our part in this work, to make it better. In the lives of those who humbly yet unfalteringly carry out this resolution, will be revealed the glory of God. I know this by experience. I have had no power of my own. I have realized that I must hang my helpless soul on Jesus Christ; and as the result of doing this, of praying, and of believing, the salvation of God has gone before me, and the glory of the Lord has followed.

I tell you that which I know, for your encouragement and comfort. Let us all place ourselves in right relation to God. What satisfaction is to be found in keeping pace with the fashions of this world? You have a better work to do. Fashion character. Use every ability, every nerve, every muscle, every thought, every action, to the glory of God. Then you will see, as you have never seen before, the salvation of God going before you.

In God Is Our Strength

O, I have nought to complain of. The Lord has never failed me. I laid my husband in the grave twenty-two years ago; and several years afterward, when the decision was made that more missionaries must go to Australia to unite with the few who had been sent, we went there ourselves to strengthen the hands of our brethren, and to establish the work on right lines in this new center. There we did much pioneer work.

Helping Establish A School

[71]

We saw the great need for a school in which promising young men and young women could be trained for the Master's service; and we went right into the woods in New South Wales, purchased fifteen hundred acres of land, and there established a training school away from the cities....

Three years ago we returned to America. Others were sent to Australia to take our places. The work has continued to grow; prosperity has attended every effort. I wish you could read the letters that come to us. Doubtless you have heard of the dreadful drought that has caused famine in so many places in Australia during the past two years. Hundreds of thousands of sheep and cattle and horses have perished. In all the colonies, and especially in Queensland, the suffering and the financial loss have been great.

But the spot that was chosen for our training school, has had sufficient rainfall for good pasture land and bountiful crops; in fact, in legislative assemblies and in the newspapers of the great cities it has been specified as "the only green spot in all New South Wales."

Is not this remarkable? Has not the Lord blessed? From one of the reports received, we learn that last year seven thousand pounds of honey of the best quality has been made on the school estate. Large quantities of vegetables have been raised, and the sale of the surplus has been a source of considerable revenue to the school. All this is very encouraging to us; for we took the wild land, and helped to bring it to its present fruitful state. To the Lord we ascribe all the praise.

Opportunities for Service

In every land and in every community there are many opportunities for helpful service. Even in these valleys in which we are now living, there are families that need help along spiritual lines. Look these ones up. Use your talent, your ability, by helping them. First give yourself to the Master; then He will work with you. To every man He gives his work.

Is Sister White Getting Rich?

Sometimes it has been reported that I am trying to get rich. Some have written to us, inquiring, "Is not Mrs. White worth millions of dollars? I am glad that I can say, "No." I do not own in this world any place that is free from debt. Why?—Because I see so much missionary work to be done. Under such circumstances, could I hoard money?—No, indeed. I receive royalties from the sale of my books; but nearly all is spent in missionary work.

The head of one of our publishing houses in a distant foreign land, upon hearing from others recently that I was in need of means, sent me a bill of exchange for five hundred dollars; and in the letter accompanying the money, he said that in return for the thousands upon thousands of dollars royalty that I had turned over to their mission field for the translation and distribution of new books and for the support of new missionary enterprises, they regarded the enclosed five hundred dollars as a very small token of their appreciation. They sent this because of their desire to help me in my time of special need; but heretofore I have given, for the support of the Lord's cause in foreign lands, all the royalties that come from the sale of my foreign books in Europe; and I intend to return this five hundred dollars as soon as I can free myself from debt.

A Gift to Our Schools

For the glory of God, I will tell you that about four years ago He enabled me to finish writing a book on the parables of Jesus, and then He put it into my heart to give this book for the advancement of our denominational educational work.

At that time some of our larger training schools and colleges were heavily in debt; but through the efforts of our people to sell this book and to devote the entire proceeds to the liquidation of these debts, over two hundred thousand dollars has already been raised and applied on the debts; and the good work is still going on. The success of this plan has been a source of great satisfaction to me. I am now completing another book, to be used in a similar way for other enterprises.

[72] But the financial gain is not the most encouraging feature to me. I love to dwell on the thought that the circulation of these books is bringing many souls into the truth. This thought makes my heart glad indeed. I have no time to sit down and mourn. I go right on with my work, and constantly keep writing, writing, writing. Early in the morning, when the rest of you are asleep, I am generally up, writing.

Perseverance Under Affliction

Even affliction has not caused me to cease writing. Not long after going to Australia, I was stricken with disease. Because of the dampness of the houses, I suffered an attack of inflammatory rheumatism, which prostrated me for eleven months. At times I was in intense agony. I could sleep in one position for only about two hours, then I had to be moved so that I could lie in another position. My rubber air mattress gave me very little relief, and I passed through periods of great suffering.

But in spite of this I did not cease my work. My right arm, from the elbow to the finger tips, was free from pain; the rest of the arm, the whole of the left arm, and both shoulders, could not be moved voluntarily. A framework was devised, and by the aid of this, I could write. During these eleven months, I wrote twenty-five hundred pages of letter paper, to send across the broad waters of the Pacific for publication in America.

A Pioneer

I feel so thankful to the Lord that He never disappoints me; that He gives me strength and grace. As I stood by the side of my dying husband, I placed my hand in his, and said, "Do you know me, husband?" He nodded. Said I: "All through the years I have allowed you to bear the business responsibilities, and to lead out in new enterprises. Now I promise you to be a pioneer myself." And I added, "If you realize what I say, grasp my hand a little more firmly." He did so; he could not speak.

After my husband had been laid away in the grave, his friends thought of putting up a broken shaft as a monument. "Never!" said I, "never! He has done, singlehanded, the work of three men. Never shall a broken monument be placed over his grave!" ...

God has helped me. Today I glorify His name in the presence of His people. I spent nearly ten years in Australia. A wonderful work has been done there; but more than twice as much could have been accomplished, if we had had the men and the means that we should have had. We thank God, nevertheless, for His sustaining presence, and for what we can now see in that field as the result of the efforts put forth.—Manuscript 8, 1904.

* * * * *

Earnest, Untiring Activity

Camp meetings should be held in our large cities. And if the speakers are careful in all they say, hearts will be reached as the truth is proclaimed in the power of the Spirit. The love of Christ received into the heart will banish the love of error. The love and benevolence manifested in the life of Christ is to be manifested in the lives of those who work for Him. The earnest, untiring activity that marked His life is to mark their lives. The character of the Christian is to be a reproduction of the character of Christ.

Let us never forget that we are not our own, that we have been bought with a price. Our powers are to be regarded as sacred trusts, to be used to the glory of God and the good of our fellow men. We are a part of the cross of Christ. With earnest, unwearying fidelity we are to seek to save the lost.—Manuscript 6, 1902.

* * * * *

Simple Agencies Will Be Used

Representations have been made to me, showing that the Lord will carry out His plans through a variety of ways and instruments. It is not alone the most talented, not alone those who hold high positions of trust, or are the most highly educated from a worldly point of view, whom the Lord uses to do His grand and holy work of soulsaving. He will use simple means; He will use many who have had few advantages to help in carrying forward His work. He will, by the use of simple means, bring those who possess property and lands to a belief of the truth, and these will be influenced to become the Lord's helping hand in the advancement of His work.—Letter 62, 1909.

Chapter 24—An Earnest Appeal

By Ellen G. White

**Battle Creek,
Oct. 15, 1880**
Elder D. M. Canright Dear Brother,

I was made sad to hear of your decision, but I have had reason to expect it. It is a time when God is testing and proving His people. Everything that can be shaken will be shaken. Only those will stand whose souls are riveted to the eternal Rock. Those who lean to their own understanding, those who are not constantly abiding in Christ, will be subject to just such changes as this. If your faith has been grounded in man, we may then expect just such results.

But if you have decided to cut all connection with us as a people, I have one request to make, for your own sake as well as for Christ's sake: keep away from our people, do not visit them and talk your doubts and darkness among them. Satan is full of exultant joy that you have stepped from beneath the banner of Jesus Christ, and stand under his banner. He sees in you one he can make a valuable agent to build up his kingdom. You are taking the very course I expected you would take if you yielded to temptation.

You have ever had a desire for power, for popularity, and this is one of the reasons for your present position. But I beg of you to keep your doubts, your questionings, your skepticism to yourself. The people have given you credit for more strength of purpose and stability of character than you possessed. They thought you were a strong man; and when you breathe out your dark thoughts and feelings, Satan stands ready to make these thoughts and feelings so intensely powerful in their deceptive character, that many souls will be deceived and lost through the influence of one soul who chose darkness rather than light, and presumptuously placed himself on Satan's side in the ranks of the enemy.

You have wanted to be too much, and make a show and noise in the world, and as the result your sun will surely set in obscurity. Every day you are meeting with an eternal loss. The schoolboy who plays truant thinks he is cheating his parent and his teacher; but who is meeting with the greatest loss? Is it not himself? Is he not cheating and deceiving himself, robbing himself of the knowledge he might have? God would have us become efficient in copying the example of Christ in good works; but you are playing truant, you are nursing a feeling which will sting and poison your soul to its own ruin, playing truant upon important eternal things, robbing your soul of the richness, the knowledge of the fullness of Christ. Your ambition has soared so high, it will accept of nothing short of elevation of self. You do not know yourself. What you have always needed was a humble, contrite heart.

Christ the Pattern Man

What a life was that of Christ? He was just as certainly fulfilling His mission as the Pattern Man when toiling as a carpenter, and hiding the great secret of His divine mission from the world, as when He trod the foaming white-capped billows on the Sea of Galilee, or when raising the dead to life, or when dying [as] man's sacrifice upon the cross, that He might lift up the whole race to a new and perfect life. Jesus dwelt long at Nazareth, unhonored and unknown, that the lesson in His example might teach men and women how closely they may walk with God in even the common course of daily life. How humiliating, how rude and homely, was this condescension of the Majesty of heaven, that He might be made one of us. He drew the sympathy of all hearts by showing Himself capable of sympathizing with all. The men of Nazareth in their questioning doubts asked, "Is not this the carpenter," the son of Joseph and Mary?

Heaven and earth are no wider apart today than when common men of common occupation met angels at noonday, or when on Bethlehem's plains shepherds heard the songs of the heavenly host as they watched their flocks by night. It is not the seeking to climb to eminence that will make you great in God's sight, but it is the humble life of goodness, of fidelity, that will make you the object of the heavenly angels' special guardianship. The Pattern Man, who thought it not robbery to be equal with God, took upon Himself our nature, and lived nearly thirty years in an obscure Galilean town, hidden away among the hills. All the angel host was at His command, yet He did not claim to be anything great or exalted. He did not attach "Professor" to His name to please Himself. He was a carpenter, working for wages, a servant to those for whom He labored, showing that heaven may be very near us in the common walks of life, and that angels from the heavenly courts will take charge of the steps of those who come and go at God's command.

O that the spirit of Christ might rest upon His professed followers. We must all be willing to work and toil, for this is the lesson Christ has given us in His life. If you had lived for God in common things, doing your work purely and faithfully when there was no one to say it was well done, you would not be in your present position. Your life you could make faithful by good words wisely spoken, by kind deeds thoughtfully done, by the daily manifestation of meekness, purity, and love. In view of all the light you have had, I fear you have made your final move. You have given Satan every advantage.

Hasty Decisions

Decisions may be made in a moment that fix one's condition forever. Satan has come to you as he came to Christ, with the presentation of worldly honor and glory, if you will only acknowledge his supremacy. This you are now doing. But before you take one more step, I beseech you to reflect.

What record are angels making in regard to you? How will you meet that record? What excuse will you render to God for the abrupt apostasy? There has ever been with you a desire to do a large work. Had you been content to do your small work with thoroughness and fidelity, this would meet the approval of the Master. But remember, it would take the work of a lifetime to recover what a moment of yielding to temptation and thoughtlessness throws away.

We are traveling, strangers and pilgrims, traveling to a better country; but it would be better for you and me to be beasts of burden to plow the field rather than to be in heaven without a heart to sympathize with its inhabitants. By a momentary act of will you may place yourself in the power of Satan, but it will require more than a momentary act of will to break his fetters and reach for a higher, holier life. The purpose may be formed, the work begun, but its accomplishment will require toil, time, and perseverance, patience and sacrifice. The man who deliberately wanders from God in the full blaze of light will find, when he wishes to set his face to return, that briars and thorns have grown up in his path, and he must not be surprised or discouraged if he is compelled to travel long with torn and bleeding feet. The most fearful and most to be dreaded evidence of man's fall from a better state is the fact that it costs so much to get back. The way of return can be gained only by hard fighting, inch by inch, every hour.

Heaven's path is too narrow for rank and riches to ride in state, too narrow for the play of ambition, too steep and rugged for carriages of ease to climb. Toil, patience, self-sacrifice, reproach, poverty, hard work, enduring the contradiction of sinners against Himself, was the portion of Christ, and it must be the portion of man if he ever enters the Paradise of God.

If your present faith is yielded so easily, it is because you never sent down the taproot in clinging faith. It has cost you too little. If it does not sustain you in trial and comfort you in affliction, it is because your faith has not been made strong by effort and pure by sacrifice. Those who are willing to suffer for Christ will experience more joy in suffering than in the fact that Christ has suffered for them, thus showing that He loved them. Those who win heaven will put forth their noblest efforts, and will labor with all long-suffering, that they may reap the fruit of toil.

There is a hand that will open wide the gates of Paradise to those that have stood the test of temptation and kept a good conscience by giving up the world, its honors, its applause, for the love of Christ, thus confessing Him before men, and waiting with all patience for Him to confess them before His Father and holy angels.

The Influence of Doubt

I do not ask an explanation of your course. Brother Stone wished to read your letter to me. I refused to hear it. The breath of doubt, of complaint and unbelief, is contagious; if I make my mind a channel for the filthy stream, the turbid, defiling water proceeding from

Satan's fountain, some suggestion may linger in any mind, polluting it. If his suggestions have had such power on you as to lead you to sell your birthright for a mess of pottage—the friendship of the Lord's enemies—I want not to hear anything of your doubts, and I hope you will be guarded, lest you contaminate other minds; for the very atmosphere surrounding a man who dares to make the statements you have made is as a poisonous miasma.

I beg of you to go entirely away from those who believe the truth; for if you have chosen the world and the friends of the world, go with those of your own choice. Do not poison the minds of others and make yourself Satan's special agent to work the ruin of souls. If you have not fully taken your stand, make haste to resist the devil before it shall be forever too late. Do not take another step into darkness, but take your position as a man of God.

If you would secure the grand aim and purpose of life without mistake in your choice or fear of failure, you must make God first and last and best in every plan and work and thought. If you want a path that leads straight into darkness, you have only to cast the light of God behind you, live without God. When God points out your path and says, "This is your way of safety and peace," you have only to set your face in an opposite direction from the way of the Lord and your feet will take hold on perdition. The voice of the Lamb of God is heard speaking to us, "Follow Me, and ye shall not walk in darkness."

A Commission from the King of Kings

God has chosen you for a great and solemn work. He has been seeking to discipline, to test, to prove you, to refine and ennoble you, that this sacred work may be done with a single eye to His glory which belongs wholly to God. What a thought that God chooses a man and brings him into close connection with Himself, and gives him a mission to undertake, a work to do, for Him. A weak man is made strong, a timid man is made brave, the irresolute becomes a man of firm and quick decision. What! is it possible that man is of so much consequence as to receive a commission from the King of kings!! Shall worldly ambition allure from the sacred trust, the holy commission?

The Majesty of heaven came to our world to give to man an example of a pure and spotless life, and to sacrifice Himself to the joy of saving the perishing. Whoever follows Christ is a colaborer with Him, sharing with Him the divine work of saving souls. If you have a thought of being released from it because you see some prospect of forming an alliance with the world which shall bring yourself to greater notice, it is because you forget how great and noble it is to do anything for God, how exalted a position it is to be a colaborer with Jesus Christ, a light bearer to the world, shedding light and love upon the pathway of others.

Reward of Fidelity

You will have a great conflict with the power of evil in your own heart. You have felt that there was a higher work for you, but, oh, if you would only take up the work lying directly in your path, and do it with fidelity, not seeking in any way to exalt self, the peace and joy would come to your soul, purer, richer, and more satisfying than the conquerors in earthly warfare. To live and work for God and make the best use we can of all our time and faculties, is to grow in grace and knowledge. This we can do, because it is *our* work. You must needs put away your questioning doubts, and have full faith in the reality of your divine mission, to be indeed successful in labor.

The joy, the success, the glory of your ministry, is to be ever ready with listening ear to answer the call of the Master, "Here am I; send me." Here, Lord, with my heart's best and holiest affections; here, take my mind with its purest and noblest thoughts, take me, and qualify me for Thy service.

I now appeal to you to make back tracks as fast as possible; take up your God-given mission, and seek for purity and holiness to sanctify that mission. Make no delay; halt not between two opinions. If the Lord be God, serve Him; but if Baal, serve him. You have the old lesson of trust in God to learn anew in the hard school of suffering. Let D. M. Canright be swallowed up in Jesus. What is your life? The answer was given by a voice from heaven long ago. It is like a vapor of the morning, that appeareth for a little time, and then vanisheth way.

Our names may be called in a little while, and there will be none to answer. Let that life be hid in God, and that name be registered in heaven, and it is immortalized. Follow on whether Christ leads the way, and let the footprints which you leave behind you on the sands of time be such that others may safely follow in the path of holiness.

The Two Paths

All along the path that leads to death there are pains and penalties, there are sorrows and disappointments, there are warnings from God's messengers not to go on, and God will make it hard for the heedless and the headstrong to destroy themselves. All the way up the steep path leading to eternal life are wellsprings of joy to refresh the weary. The true, strong joy of the soul begins when Christ is formed within, the hope of glory. If you now choose the path where God leads, and go forward where the voice of duty calls, the difficulties which Satan has magnified before you will disappear.

No path is safe, save that which grows clearer and firmer the farther it is pursued. The foot may sometimes slip upon the safest path. In order to walk without fear, you must know that your hand is firmly held by the hand of Christ. You must not for a moment think there is no danger for you. The wisest make mistakes. The strongest sometimes falter. The foolish, self-confident, heady and high-minded who press heedlessly on upon forbidden paths, flattering themselves that they can change their course when they please are walking upon a path of pitfalls. They may recover a fall, a mistake they make, but how many make one misstep which will prove their eternal ruin. If you play the policy of non-committal in order to gain objects you would otherwise fail to obtain, if you secure by art and cunning what should be won by perseverance, toil, and conflict, you will be entangled in a net of your own weaving, and will be ruined, not only for this world, but for the future life.

God forbid that you should make shipwreck of faith here. Look at Paul; listen to his words sounding along the line to our time: "I have fought a good fight, I have finished my course, I have kept the faith: henceforth there is laid up for me a crown of righteousness, which the Lord, the righteous judge, shall give me at that day: and not to me only, but unto all them also that love His appearing." Here is the battle shout of victory from Paul. What will be yours?

Now, Elder Canright, for your soul's sake grasp firmly again the hand of God, I beseech you. I am too weary to write more. God deliver you from Satan's snare is my prayer.—Letter 1, 1880.

* * * * *

Exalting Christ

Every soul who truly accepts Christ by faith will walk in humility of heart. There will be no exalting of self; but Christ will be exalted as the One on whom the hope of eternal life depends. "By grace are ye saved through faith," the apostle Paul declared. And it is the grace of Christ in us that makes us His witnesses. We can be overcomers only by the blood of the Lamb, and by the word of our testimony. By a well-ordered life and a godly conversation, we become lights in the church and in the world. Spiritual things must be spiritually discerned. Those who drink most deeply of the waters of salvation will reveal most fully the meekness and lowliness of Christ.

I am bidden to say to those who have been called to teach the Word of God to others: Never encourage men to look to you for wisdom. When men come to you for counsel, point them to the One who reads the motives of every heart. A different spirit must come into our ministerial work. No persons must act as confessors; no man must be exalted as supreme. Our work is to humble self and to exalt Christ before the people. After His resurrection, the Saviour promised that His power would be with all who would go forth in His name. Let this power and this name be exalted. We need to keep continually before our minds the prayer of Christ when He prayed that self might be sanctified by truth and righteousness.

The power of the eternal Father and the sacrifice of the Son should be studied more than it is. The perfect work of Christ was consummated in His death upon the cross. In His sacrifice and His intercession at the right hand of the Father, is our only hope of salvation. It should be our joy to exalt the character of God before men, and make His name a praise in the earth.—Manuscript 137, 1907.

Education

Chapter 25—The Church School Question*

By Ellen G. White

I promised that I would speak this morning in regard to the necessity of withdrawing our children from the public schools, and of providing suitable places where they can be educated aright. I have felt surprised at the apparently indifferent attitude of some, notwithstanding the oft-repeated warnings given that parents must provide for their families not merely with reference to their present interests, but especially with reference to their future, eternal interests. The characters that we form in this life are to decide our destiny. If we choose, we may live a life that measures with the life of God.

The Home A School

Every Christian family is a church in itself. The members of the family are to be Christlike in every action. The father is to sustain so close a relation to God that he realizes his duty to make provision for the members of his family to receive an education and training that will fit them for the future, immortal life. His children are to be taught the principles of heaven. He is the priest of the household, accountable to God for the influence that he exerts over every member of his family. He is to place his family under the most favorable circumstances possible, so that they shall not be tempted to conform to the habits and customs, the evil practices and lax principles, that they would find in the world.

Influence of the Home

Setting a right example in the home, parents are able to exert a good influence in the church.... Into the home there must be brought the heavenly rule. This will fit us for church relationship as laborers together with God, and will make us examples to the world.

---
*An address given in the St. Helena Sanitarium (California) chapel, July 14, 1902.

The Lord desires us to understand that we must place our children in right relation to the world, the church, and the family. Their relation to the family is the first point to be considered. Let us teach them to be polite to one another, and polite to God. "What do you mean," you may inquire, "by saying that we should teach them to be polite to God?" I mean that they are to be taught to reverence our heavenly Father, and to appreciate the great and infinite sacrifice that Christ has made in our behalf.

Christ placed Himself at the head of humanity in order that He might exemplify what humanity could be in connection with divinity. Teach them that together, as children and parents, it is your privilege to be members of the church of God—living stones in His beautiful temple.

Companionship of Angels

Parents and children are to sustain so close a relation to God that the heavenly angels can communicate with them. These messengers are shut out from many a home where iniquity and impoliteness to God abound. Let us catch from His Word the spirit of heaven, and bring it into our life here below.

Miracle-Working Powers

Some may say, "If we believe the Bible, why does not the Lord work miracles for us?" He will, if we will let Him. When a human mind is allowed to come under the control of God, that mind will reveal the miracle-working power of God; the power of that mind in action is like the miracle-working power of God.

In our prayers we are to hold on by faith to the children in our home; and we are to do faithfully the duties that belong to us. From the light that God has given me, I know that the husband and the wife are to be, in the home, minister, physician, nurse, and teacher, binding their children to themselves and to God, training them to avoid every habit that will in any way militate against God's work in the body, and teaching them to care for every part of the living organism. Parents are under a most solemn responsibility to keep themselves in physical soundness and in spiritual health, that the light of heaven may shine into the chambers of the mind and illuminate the soul temple. Such parents are able to give their children instruction from babyhood as to what God wants them to do. Taking His Word as their counselor, they bring them up in the nurture and admonition of the Lord.

Not Allowed to Drift

Many parents allow their children to drift, as it were, hither and thither. But this is not right. Parents are held accountable to God for the salvation of their children. They are also held accountable for their physical health. In every way possible they should help them to grow up with a sound constitution. They should teach them not to indulge appetite or to imperil their physical and mental capabilities by wrong habits; for God desires to use all their powers. Every word spoken by fathers and mothers has its influence over the children, for good or for evil. If the parents speak passionately, if they show the spirit shown by the children of this world, God counts them as the children of this world, not as His sons and daughters.

Politeness and Courtesy

Parents, from the moment that we are born again into the kingdom of heaven, we are in God's service. Our lives are to be such that He can approve. The principles of heaven are to be brought into the government of the home. Every child is to be taught to be polite, compassionate, loving, pitiful, courteous, tenderhearted. Peter speaks of these characteristics of a Christian, and also instructs us how to rid ourselves of all evil by living on the plan of addition. "Giving all diligence," he says, "add to your faith virtue; and to virtue knowledge; and to knowledge temperance; and to temperance patience; and to patience godliness; and to godliness brotherly kindness; and to brotherly kindness charity [love]."

We want the knowledge of our Saviour. Is it not best for every one of us to begin to teach our children to be polite in the home and polite to God? Is not this the work that as "laborers together with God" it is our bounden duty to do?

From the light that God has given me for years, I know that the households of His people are in great need of purification. The end is nearer than when we first believed. As fathers and mothers, we are to purify ourselves, even as Christ is pure; that is, we are to be perfect in our sphere, even as God is perfect in His sphere. Instead of backsliding, we should now be conformed to the will of heaven, the heavenliness of heaven. Let us put away the spirit of murmuring and complaining, remembering that by cherishing such a spirit we are disrespectful to God. We are living in His dwelling place; we are members of His family—His by creation and by redemption.

Everyone is to cherish feelings of respect and tenderness for those with whom he associates. In our relations with one another we should be careful never to mar and scar the life and the spirit of others. When in life and character we show the miracle-working power of God, the world will take knowledge of us that we have been with Jesus and learned of Him....

We are not to feel that we have reached perfection. We need to be melted over, that we may be purified from all dross. We are in need of the rich blessings that Heaven is so ready to bestow, the blessings promised to every believer.

Faith to Be Exercised

The Lord withholds from us no good thing. He declares, "Ask what ye will, and it shall be done unto you." He does not tell us to restrict our asking to certain things, but assures us that He will bless us according to the riches of His grace. He is more willing to give the Holy Spirit to those who ask Him than parents are to give good gifts to their children. To show his willingness, He refers to the tender relationship that a father sustains to his son. "What man is there of you," He says, "whom if his son ask bread, will he give him a stone? or if he ask a fish, will he give him a serpent? If ye then, being evil, know how to give good gifts unto your children, how much more shall your Father which is in heaven give good things to them that ask Him?"

Parents can learn this lesson in all its significance. Children who ask for something that is not for their best good are not to be rebuffed, but kindly told, "That would not be for your good. You cannot have it, because it would injure you. But although we cannot give it to you, we will try in every way possible to make you happy."

Lessons in Fellowship

The father should always feel kindly disposed toward his children. How sad it is that the father's disposition is not always that which it should be! The father of the boys is to come into close connection with his sons, giving them the benefit of his larger experience, and talking with them in such simplicity and tenderness that he binds them to his heart. He is to let them see that he has their best interest, their happiness, in view all the time.

[79]

Parents, let us constantly keep before our children the relation that we sustain to our heavenly Father. Let us tell them that we are His children, and that we desire to treat them as He treats us. He does not indulge us in injurious things. He gives us only the things that are for our best good. He says, "Ask, and it shall be given you; seek and ye shall find; knock, and it shall be opened unto you; for every one that asketh receiveth; and he that seeketh findeth; and to him that knocketh it shall be opened."

We are all amenable to God. When we take into consideration our accountability to Him for every action, when we remember that we are "a spectacle unto the world, and to angels, and to men," we will desire to be purged from our fretfulness and harshness, our lack of sympathy and tenderness for one another. These evils are as tares amid the wheat, and must be destroyed.

Children to be Shielded From Contaminating Influences

Upon fathers and mothers devolves the responsibility of giving a Christian education to the children entrusted to them. They are never to neglect their children. In no case are they to let any line of business so absorb mind and time and talents that their children, who should be led into harmony with God, are allowed to drift until they are separated far from Him. They are not to allow their children to slip out of their grasp into the hands of unbelievers. They are to do all in their power to keep them from imbibing the spirit of the world. They are to train them to become helpers together with God.

They are God's human hand, fitting themselves and their children for an endless life in the heavenly home....

Some fathers and mothers are so indifferent, so careless, that they think it makes no difference whether their children attend a church school or a public school. "We are in the world," they say, "and we cannot get out of it." But, parents, we can get a good way out of the world, if we choose to do so. We can avoid seeing many of the evils that are multiplying so fast in these last days. We can avoid hearing about much of the wickedness and crime that exist.

Evils of Newspapers

Everything that can be done should be done to place ourselves and our children where we shall not see the iniquity that is practiced in the world. We should carefully guard the sight of our eyes and the hearing of our ears, so that these awful things shall not enter our minds. When the daily newspaper comes into the house, I feel as if I wanted to hide it, that the ridiculous, sensational things in it may not be seen. It seems as if the enemy is at the foundation of the publishing of many things that appear in newspapers. Every sinful thing that can be found is uncovered and laid bare before the world.

An Unmistakable Distinction

The line of demarcation between those who serve God and those who serve Him not, is ever to remain distinct. The difference between believers and unbelievers should be as great as the difference between light and darkness. When God's people take the position that they are the temple of the Holy Ghost, Christ Himself abiding within, they will so clearly reveal Him in spirit, words, and actions, that there will be an unmistakable distinction between them and Satan's followers....

A Lesson from Israel

While the judgments of God were falling upon the land of Egypt, the Lord directed the Israelites not only to keep their children within their houses, but to bring in even their cattle from the fields....

As the Israelites kept their children within their houses during the time when the judgments of God were in the land of Egypt, so in this time of peril we are to keep our children separate and distinct from the world. We are to teach them that the commandments of God mean much more than we realize. Those who keep them will not imitate the practices of the transgressors of God's law.

Bible Principles Diligently Taught

Parents must regard God's Word with respect, obeying its teachings. To the parents in this day, as well as to the Israelites, God declares: "These words ... shall be in thine heart: and thou shalt teach them diligently unto thy children, and shalt talk of them when thou sittest in thine house, and when thou walkest by the way, and when thou liest down, and when thou risest up. And thou shalt bind them for a sign upon thine hand, and they shall be as frontlets between thine eyes. And thou shalt write them upon the posts of thy house, and on thy gates." ...

Christian parents, you must make provision for your children to be educated in Bible principles. And do not rest satisfied merely with having them study the Word in the church school. Teach the Scriptures to your children yourselves when you sit down, when you go out, when you come in, and when you walk by the way. Walk with your children much oftener than you do. Talk with them. Set their minds running in a right channel. As you do this, you will find that the light and the glory of God will come into your homes. But how can you expect His blessing when you do not teach your children aright? ...

A Reformation Necessary

Seventh-day Adventists must move in a way altogether different from the way in which they have been moving, if they expect the approval of God to rest upon them in their homes.

Every faithful parent will hear from the lips of the Master the words, "Well done, good and faithful servant; ... enter thou into the joy of thy Lord." May the Lord help us to be good and faithful servants in our dealings with one another. He tells us to "consider one another to provoke unto love and to good works," helping and strengthening one another.—Manuscript 100, 1902.

* * * * *

Regarding Children

Christ is waiting in gracious mercy, waiting to make you vessels unto honor. The Holy Ghost inspired Paul to lift up his voice in earnest, solemn words, saying, "None of us liveth to himself." We should take these words to heart. Money has been worse than thrown away for needless adornment of yourselves and your children. You should turn this current of means into the channel that reaches the treasury of the Lord.

God requires that you should educate and discipline your children for His work; and the very first lesson that you should teach them is that of self-denial and self-sacrifice. You should set before them the great Pattern, Christ Jesus, and imitate Him yourselves, and teach your children to walk in His footsteps.

We may manufacture many wants, we may place snares before our children by allowing them to gratify their every desire. We may curtail their usefulness by granting them the free use of means that they may make a display.

Children are a gift of God to increase the experience and happiness of parents. Parents through discipline may become more useful in teaching their children to be Christ's children and so increase their influence for good.

Instead of denying self, how many will give a trifle to the cause of God, and then indulge their children in the gratification of selfish desires, thus educating them to place their influence on Satan's side. It would be better had such parents never been born, for if the grace of Christ's has never controlled your souls, how can you expect it to control the souls of your children?

Self-indulgence is the curse of our families, and as a consequence, the curse of our churches.

The world lives for pleasure, for selfishness, and how can we hope to draw the world to Christ, when we also live for the gratification of self? Christ has said, "Go ye into all the world, and preach the gospel to every creature."—Manuscript 53, 1895.

* * * * *

In this connection see also:
F. E., pp. 64-70, "The Home and the School."
F. E., pp. 149-161, "Home Education."
Education, 186-189, "Family Study."
C. T., pp. 173-177, "The Work of the Church School."
C. T., pp. 150-157, "Co-operation Between the Home and the School."
Testimonies for the Church 6:193-205, "Church Schools."
Testimonies for the Church 6:119, "Teaching Home Religion."

Chapter 26—Appeal to Young Men*

By Ellen G. White

My mind is exercised in regard to the young men who have crossed the broad waters to America, in order to obtain an education that they thought they could not obtain in their own country.

I am much pleased with New Zealand. I think it a very fine country, and would have no objection to making my home here if this were the will of God. But my mission and work require me to be a pilgrim and a stranger, waiting, watching, and working, till the time shall fully come, when with the saints in light, I shall enter the city which hath foundations, whose Maker and Builder is God.

For many years I have seen by faith the inheritance of the saints afar off, and I have been persuaded of the promises, and have embraced them. I have perfect confidence in the God who is behind the promises. I am pleased to confess that I am a pilgrim and a stranger in the earth. My earnest determination is to declare plainly by my life and character to all with whom I am brought in contact, that I seek a better country, even a heavenly, as did those men of old who loved and feared God. "Wherefore God is not ashamed to be called their God; for He hath prepared for them a city."

The Expectation of Friends

I feel very anxious that our New Zealand boys who have gone to America to obtain an education shall be a credit in every respect to those who have assisted them. I would say to these students, Those who have interested themselves in your behalf have flattering hopes of you, as I well know. They have taken upon themselves much responsibility for you; and they earnestly desire that you shall reach a high standard, and be signalized as useful men, men of moral worth and unswerving integrity.

---
*Written from Gisborne, New Zealand, October 28, 1893.

Remember that you will never reach a higher standard than you yourselves set. Set your mark high, and then step by step, even though it be by painful effort, by self-denial and self-sacrifice, ascend the whole length of the ladder of progress. Let nothing hinder you. Christ will be to you a present help in every time of trouble. Stand like Daniel, the faithful statesman, a man whom no temptation could corrupt. Do not disappoint your parents and friends. And there is another to be considered. Do not disappoint Him who so loved you that He gave His own life to cancel your sins. He says: "Without Me ye can do nothing." Remember this, If you have made mistakes, you certainly gain a victory if you see these mistakes, and regard them as beacons of warning. I need not tell you that thus you turn defeat into victory, disappointing the enemy and honoring your Redeemer.

Sympathy with Teachers

We feel sorry indeed that any weakness of character should mar the record of the past, because we know that if you had watched unto prayer, this need not have been. We feel sorry for your teachers; for your wrong conduct places upon them burdens they ought not to be asked to bear. They may have moved unwisely; for each one has the weakness of his own natural character to contend against. They may have thought they were doing right when they were making mistakes. But how much better it would be if every student would place himself upon his honor, and cherish pure, high, noble motives, feeling it his duty to help his teachers in every possible way, thinking how he would like to be treated were he in a position of trust and responsibility.

If teachers are disciples of Christ, and engaged in a work that is approved by God, Satan will surely assault them with every possible temptation. And if he can stir up in the student elements of character that will aid him in bringing perplexities and discouragements to the educators, he has gained a great advantage. If the tempted one reveals weakness in any respect, his influence is weakened; and the one who has by a wrong course of action proved to be an agent under the controlling power of the adversary of souls, must render an account to God for the part he has acted in laying a stumbling block in the way of his fellow man. Will our students study carefully this phase of the subject? Why should they link themselves with the great apostate? Why should they become his agents in temptation, in their turn to tempt others? Why do they not realize that every human being has his own trials, peculiar to himself, and that no one is free from temptation? Students, study to help sustain and encourage your teachers in their position in the school. Thus doing, you are not sowing tares, but wheat; and God's Word declares, "Whatsoever a man soweth, that shall he also reap."

Fun and Lawlessness

Students will be tempted to do lawless things, to please themselves. They may think this only fun. But if they would put themselves upon their honor, and realize that in doing these things they bless no one, but involve others as well as themselves in difficulty, they would be more careful of their actions. How much more manly and honorable it would be to act like gentlemen, who do not ask that all sympathy be shown them, but who realize that they must put their will on Christ's side, and work in His lines by helping their teachers to carry burdens and perplexities that Satan would make discouragingly heavy. By helping to bear these burdens, instead of making them more taxing, what a blessing students would receive. They would create an atmosphere in the school that would be helpful and exhilarating, not depressing and enfeebling. Every student would enjoy the consciousness that he had acted his part on Christ's side, and had not given one jot of his ability or influence to the great adversary of all that is good or ennobling. How much more satisfactory it would be for the students to think that they had not given their sanction to any plans showing disrespect for order, diligence, and obedience, even against the clamoring of inclination for indulgence.

Will not students remember that it is in their power to help and not to hinder? They are at school for the purpose of gaining a knowledge of books, and especially a knowledge of the Scriptures. "The fear of the Lord is the beginning of wisdom." Lay the foundation, and you will be happy men and women.

Agents of Righteousness

Students are in no case to cheapen and decrease their value in Christian endeavor lines. They are to prepare to go forth as missionaries to warn the world. They should have their seasons of prayer. From them earnest, fervent prayers should ascend to heaven for the president of the school, that God may bless him with health, and give him moral power, clearness of mind, and spiritual discernment. They should pray that the teachers may be blessed and qualified by the grace of Christ to do their work with fidelity, with an active, fervent love that is in harmony with the mind of the Saviour. They are to be His agents through whom He works that good may prevail over evil. May God give the students who attend our institutions of learning, grace and courage to act up to the principles revealed in the laws of God.

By dying for man, Jesus exalted humanity in the scale of moral value with God. The Son of the infinite God clothed His divinity with humanity, that He might become a steppingstone for every human being to heaven, that by His power humanity might be a partaker of the divine nature, having escaped the corruption that is in the world through lust. He is working to uplift and ennoble man, and He requires every soul that He has redeemed from hopeless misery to co-operate with Him in the great work of saving souls. Oh, if all could see this matter as it is presented before me, how soon would they cease to aid the enemy in his work! How they would despise his efforts to bring sin into the world! With what a perfect hatred they would hate sin, as they thought of how it cost the life of the Commander of heaven!

Choosing a Leader

Christ died that man might not be bound hopelessly to Satan's chariot as the trophies of his victory. Who then will link with Satan? Who will choose to wear his badge? Who will choose him as their leader, refusing to stand under a banner stained with the blood of the Captain of their salvation? Christ died for every son and daughter of Adam. It was for us He manifested this amazing love. How can the subjects of His love be indifferent, standing in sin and disobedience, refusing to confess Christ? How can they love to do evil? How can they prostitute their reasoning faculties, and place their influence on Satan's side? By doing this they weaken their moral power and efficiency, instead of strengthening every faculty to do the will of Him who so loved the world that He gave His only-begotten Son, that whosoever believeth on Him should not perish, but have everlasting life. [83]

The Lord has greatly honored men by giving Christ as their ransom, that they might be recovered from the enemy's service. But are they willing to be recovered? Will they accept the precious gift Christ Jesus, or will they refuse to do Him service? Christ declared, "He that gathereth not with Me scattereth abroad." Those who try to do well in their finite strength will fail. But those who accept Jesus are upheld by a higher than human power. They confess Christ. They become His soldiers in their school associations. They will realize that they are enlisted to make the school the most orderly, elevated, and praiseworthy institution in the world. They will place every jot and tittle of their influence on the side of Christ and heavenly intelligences.

Help-One-Another Societies

They will feel it their duty to form Christian endeavor societies, to help every student to see the consistency of a course of action that God will approve. They will draw with Christ, doing their utmost to perfect a Christian character. They will take upon themselves the work of leading the lame and the weak into the safe, upward paths that Christ has cast up for His chosen ones. They will plan to do all they can to make the institution in which they are all that God designed it to be when He signified that it should be brought into existence.

Be Helpers

Students, never be found disparaging the schools which God has established. If you have failed at any time, if you have fallen under temptation, it was because you did not make God your strength, because you did not have that faith that works by love and purifies the soul. If you had felt that as human agents for whom Christ has given His precious life, it was your privilege to do all you possibly could to aid the work God has recognized as His work, if you had called into existence every ability in an effort to co-operate with Christ in blessing and saving the youth, you would have made great advance upward and onward. When each student in our institutions of learning acts his part with fidelity, as Daniel acted his part in wicked Babylon, these institutions will resemble the schools of the prophets. No wrong influence will then go from the students. As consecrated instrumentalities, they will help to do the work they see necessary to be done. They will help to carry the burdens borne by the president and the teachers, and instead of disparaging the school, they will speak of the excellence and personal merit of the teachers.

Let all who have any connection with the schools already established be firm and determined, in the strength of Him who has paid the ransom for their souls to be faithful servants in the cause of Christ, to help their fellow students to be faithful, pure, and holy in life and character. Let everyone who loves God seek to win those who have not confessed Christ to do this without delay. A silent, prayerful interest may be manifest every day. The very best experience in missionary lines may be gained by thus co-operating with Jesus, the missionary in chief to our world. Let every soul grow in excellence of character, in devotion, in purity, in holiness, exercising aright every God-given ability, that the enemies of our faith shall not triumph, that those in open rebellion against God shall not mold and fashion the characters of His children. Let the influence of the sons and daughters of God, united by the bonds of holy faith, be wholly on the Lord's side. Give evidence that you have a living connection with God, and that you are ambitious, for the Master's glory, to cultivate every grace of character. May the love of Christ constrain all to help their associates, by their love and sympathy, to walk in the heavenly way, the path cast up for the ransomed of the Lord to walk in.

A Right Choice

When the students in our schools learn to choose God's will, they will find it comparatively easy to do His will. Let every student remember that he is a member of God's firm, and that he is to make the school what God would have it. If you see defects in students or in church members, be thankful to God you have discerned these defects. Do not grieve your Redeemer by imitating them. Avoid them. You will see those who are weak in spiritual understanding, who are not learning in the school of Christ His meekness and lowliness, who manifest a vain, frivolous, worldly character, which loves display. The only remedy for these is to talk of Jesus and behold Jesus. If they can be led to look at Him, and study His character, they will learn to despise everything that is vain and frivolous; for Christ was intensely earnest, full of goodness, mercy, forbearance, patience, and unexampled love. By continuing to behold Jesus, they will rise above the littleness of the things that so molded them that they were unlovely and unholy in character. They will feel contempt for themselves. They will say, "I will not sit with vain persons, neither will I go in with dissemblers." "He that walketh with wise men shall be wise: but a companion of fools shall be destroyed." ...

Even some who are striving for the mastery over the enemy develop a predisposition to do wrong. Evil prevails over good, because they do not trust wholly in Christ. They do not abide in Him, and because of their lack of dependence on God, they show inconsistency of character. But no one is compelled to choose this class as familiar associates. The temptations of life are met everywhere, and those who complain of the church members, being cold, proud, haughty, un-Christlike, need not associate with this class. There are many who are warmhearted, self-denying, self-sacrificing, who would if necessary lay down their lives to save souls. Let none, then, become accusers of the brethren, but let the tares grow together with the wheat; for thus Christ has said it should be. But we are not under the necessity of being tares ourselves, because the harvest is not all wheat.

He who rejects the life and character of Jesus, refusing to be like Him, declares himself to be in controversy with God. "He that is not with Me is against Me," Christ declares, "and he that gathereth not with Me scattereth abroad." Those who love God will not choose His enemies as their friends. The question is asked, "Shouldest thou help the ungodly, and love them who hate the Lord?" True Christians will not choose the society of non-Christians. If the Lord gives them a special position in the world, as He gave Joseph and Daniel, He will keep them from being contaminated. We need to discern good from evil. We need all the help and instruction that comes from a true faith. We need to listen to the inculcation of Scripture doctrines, which are free from the sophistry and deception of the great deceiver. We need to live in as pure a religious atmosphere as possible, that we may bring solid timbers into our character building.

Evil Associations to be Shunned

By association with those who have no faith in God, wrong ideas are imperceptibly insinuated into mind and heart by the masterwork of deception. These prove the ruin of many. Will you choose the association of the irreligious and the disloyal, who are openly transgressing God's law? Will you separate yourselves by your own choice from those who love God? Will you place yourselves as far from the light as possible? This is a way of delusion. You will never be where you will find too much light, but woe to those who choose darkness rather than light.—Manuscript 74, 1893.

* * * * *

In this connection see also:
F. E., pp. 541-545, "The True Ideal for Our Youth."
F. E., pp. 191-195, "Christian Character Exemplified."
F. E., pp. 245-252, "Students Deciding Their Eternal Destiny."
F. E., pp. 291-296, "Students Required to Be Workers With God."
Testimonies for the Church 3:221-227, "Dangers and Duties of Youth."

Chapter 27—Parents and Children*

By Ellen G. White

I felt that if I should come before you again I should say the same things that I was saying last night in my dreams. I seemed to be speaking to a company of people, who listened earnestly to my words. I was pleading with them to devote their energies to training their children for the future life. There were many in the congregation who were condemned by the truths spoken; for they had been giving misguided instruction, with scoldings and denials. They had not brought up their children in the nurture and admonition of the Lord.

There are many among us who, though they stand in the position of guardians of the young, are not awake to the danger of letting the children and youth drift with the world. They do not seem to realize the possibilities and probabilities of the early years of training. The first years of that life which is to measure with the life of God begin here. None who stand in positions of accountability can afford to turn the youth away to go whither they will, taking no account of the influences to which they are exposed.

There are those here who, if truly converted, could do a far-reaching work for God in the training of the youth. But those who would win souls to Christ, must first have Christ themselves. Only in His wisdom can they teach how the heart may be safeguarded against the assaults of temptation, and be able to reveal to others the transforming power of grace.

As a people we need the truth of God. We need to understand its power to convert the soul and transform the life. We need to appreciate the great sacrifice that has made possible a home for us in the heavenly courts.

Our children need this truth. We do not do half enough in instructing them in its principles. If we could realize the responsibilities

---
*Remarks at the ministerial institute held in Los Angeles, Monday, March 18, 1912.

that rest upon us as their teachers and guardians, we would be much more careful and persevering in their education in religious things.

Not one parent in a hundred fully understands the work committed to him in the training of the youth. It is important that ministers and teachers act their part in this special line of service for God. It is for them to see that these little ones understand what the Bible approves and disapproves. The Lord is coming soon; there is not much time in which to redeem the past.

Converted Parents

Day and night I am burdened with the thought of our great need of converted parents. How many there are who need to humble their hearts before God and come into right relation to heaven if they would exert a saving influence over their families. They should know what they must do to inherit eternal life, if they would train their children for the inheritance of the redeemed. Every day they should be receiving the light of heaven into their souls; every day be receiving the impressions of the Holy Spirit upon heart and mind. Every day they should be receiving the word of truth and letting it control the life.

Terrible will be the revelations of the day of judgment regarding the neglect of parents to bring up their children in the nurture and admonition of the Lord. What does this mean—in the nurture and admonition of the Lord? It means to teach them to order the life by the requirements and the lessons of the Word; to help them to a clear understanding of the terms of entrance into the city of God. The gates of that city will not be opened to all who would enter, but to those only who have studied God's will, and have yielded their lives to His control.

One great reason why there is so much evil in the world today is that parents occupy their minds with other things than that which is all-important—how to adapt themselves to the work of patiently and kindly teaching their children the way of the Lord. If the curtain could be drawn aside, we should see that many, many children who have gone astray have been lost to good influence through this neglect. Parents, can you afford to have it so in your experience? You should have no work so important that it will prevent you from giving to your children all the time that is necessary to make them understand what it means to obey and trust the Lord fully.

A Training for Eternity

These children are to be trained for eternity. Do not then occupy your time by endeavoring to follow all the foolish fashions in dress. Dress neatly and becomingly, but do not make yourself the subject of remarks either by being overdressed or by dressing in a lax, untidy manner. Act as though you know that the eye of heaven is upon you, and that you are living under the approbation or disapprobation of God.

Before visitors, before every other consideration, your children should come first. This will teach them that they are worth being cared for. They will see that you value them above everything else.

And what will you reap as a reward of your effort?—You will find your children right by your side, willing to take hold and cooperate with you in the lines that you suggest. You will find your work made easy. But if you give yourself up to visitors and to things that are unessential, while you let your children drift for want of proper instruction, when they go astray, remember that you must give account to God for their wrongdoing.

The less attention we give to spiritual things, the more satisfied we are with our own righteousness. There are many who claim to be righteous, and who think that they are righteous. These souls need to study Christ's life of self-renunciation.

When the Spirit of God dwells in our hearts and controls our actions, we shall not fail of giving our children and youth the training that will fit them for a place in the heavenly courts. But when parents are careless in regard to these things, what hope is there that the children will be converted? They are forming character of another kind—character that Christ cannot accept. Can we afford to have it so?

Co-Operation

We want the children to honor us. Then we must honor God, acting our part in the fashioning of their characters. We must not do haphazard work here. Every Christian parent is responsible to God for the training of his children. And this should be a united work on the part of fathers and mothers. And the Holy Spirit waits to co-operate with them, to impress the heart and mind, to take the life under His control.

Parents should be careful not to allow the spirit of dissension to creep into the home; for this is one of Satan's agents to make his impression on the character. If parents will strive for unity in the home by inculcating the principles that governed the life of Christ, dissension will be driven out and unity and love will abide there. Parents and children will partake of the gift of the Holy Spirit.

Kindness and Patience

I shall not speak very long this morning, but I want you to carry away with you the few thoughts that I shall suggest. Let it be deeply impressed on your hearts that when you speak angry words to your children, you are helping the cause of the enemy of all righteousness. Let every child have a fair chance from babyhood up. The work of teaching should begin in childhood, not accompanied by harshness and fretting, but in kindness and patience; and this instruction should be continued through all their years to manhood and womanhood. It is the blessed privilege of every Christian parent to reveal the Lord to the child as merciful and good and full of kindness. He will put His Holy Spirit on the children, even though they sometimes make mistakes and do wrong. These children may hear the "Well done" as verily as the older members of the Lord's family.

It is not bringing up the children in the nurture and admonition of the Lord to meet their mistakes with anger and chiding, to send them off feeling that you do not care what they do. To manifest passion toward an erring child is to increase the evil. It arouses the worst passion of the child, and leads him to feel that you do not care for him. He reasons with himself that you could not treat him so if you cared.

And think you that God takes no cognizance of the way in which these children are corrected? He knows, and He knows also what might be the blessed results if the work of correction were done in a way to win rather than to repel.

A Blessed Work

My brethren and sisters, it takes time to give nurture and admonition. Tell them of the Father who loved them so that He gave His only Son for their salvation. Tell them the story of Christ's earthly life and His sacrifice in their behalf. This will touch their hearts. By such instruction they will see that you want them to be conformed to His likeness.

It is a great work, and a simple work—a work that, as we carry it forward, will soften the spirit and tender the heart. It will strengthen our hold on heaven. It will teach us to control the temper, and yield the life to the influence of truth.

Jesus loves us. The seventeenth chapter of John shows how full and how broad is the mercy and love that He waits to bestow upon all who will walk in obedience and humility before Him.

Arouse, Arouse, Arouse!

My brethren and sisters, have you improved your opportunities to bring up your children in the nurture and admonition of the Lord? God wants you to co-operate with Him in this work. Will you do it? May God help every father and every mother to arouse to the responsibilities that rest upon them. You must not let mischief come to your children; you must not see it coming, and say no word of warning to them. I am now grown old, and my children are men; but I could not today see one of them going into wrong ways and say nothing to him about it. I would be responsible if I did not counsel them in regard to the way of the Lord.

We are too independent in our ideas and ways. Many want to lead, and thus they get out of the path of meekness and obedience. We take our own way altogether too much. We act too often like stubborn children. This is not pleasing to the Lord.

I ask you to consider these words. Do not, I beg of you, correct your children in anger. That is the time of all times when you should act with humility and patience and prayer. Then is the time to kneel down with the children and ask the Lord for pardon. Seek to win them to Christ by the manifestation of kindness and love, and you

[88]

will see that a higher power than that of earth is co-operating with your efforts....

When the time of final award shall come, you will want to hear from the lips of the Saviour the words, "Well done, good and faithful servant." May God help you to be converted daily. Fathers and mothers, sisters and brothers, old and young, work in harmony with Christ, so that the Spirit of God and holy angels can dwell with you and mold your lives. And if these influences are fashioning the lives of parents, the characters of the children will be renewed after the likeness of Christ. If parents do their work faithfully, the children will not be left to go to ruin.

"The eyes of the Lord are upon the righteous, and His ears are open to their cry. The face of the Lord is against them that do evil." "Sanctify the Lord God in your hearts; and be ready always to give an answer to every man that asketh you a reason of the hope that is in you with meekness and fear."...

I want you to get your minds on the possibilities of a thorough conversion; for when this experience comes to you, you will strike a note that will be recognized as having its origin in God. Let us seek for such a conversion.... Let us seek for a deeper consecration. God will accept us as we come to Him in our weakness, and will impart to us that which we so greatly need—the spirit of perfect submission to the will of God.—Manuscript 53, 1912.

Chapter 28—A Work of Co-operation

By Ellen G. White

"Work out your own salvation with fear and trembling. For it is God which worketh in you both to will and to do of His good pleasure." The work of salvation is a work of co-partnership, a joint operation. No man can work out his own salvation without the aid of the Holy Spirit. The co-operation of divine and human forces is necessary for the formation of right principles in the character.

Man is to make the most strenuous efforts to overcome the tempter, to subdue natural passions; but he is wholly dependent upon God for success in the work of overcoming the propensities that are not in harmony with correct principles. Success depends wholly upon willing obedience to the will and way of God.

Character develops in accordance with conformity to the divine plan. But man must work in Christ's lines. He must be a laborer together with God. He must submit to God's training, that he may be complete in Christ.

God has originated and proclaimed the principles on which divine and human agencies are to combine in temporal matters as well as all spiritual achievements. They are to be linked together in all human pursuits, in mechanical and agricultural labor, in mercantile and scientific enterprises. In all lines of work it is necessary that there be co-operation between God and man.

God has provided facilities with which to enrich and beautify the earth. But the strength and ingenuity of human agencies are required to make the very best use of the material. God has filled the earth with treasure, but the gold and silver are hidden in the earth, and the exercise of man's powers is required to secure this treasure which God has provided. Man's energy and tact are to be used in connection with the power of God in bringing the gold and silver from the mines, and trees from the forest. But unless by His miracle-working power God co-operated with man, enabling him to use his physical and mental capabilities, the treasures in our world would be useless.

We cannot keep ourselves for one moment. We are kept by the power of God through faith unto salvation. We are utterly dependent upon God every moment of our lives.

God desires every human being in our world to be a worker together with Him. This is the lesson we are to learn from all useful employment, making homes in the forest, felling trees to build houses, clearing land for cultivation. God has provided the wood and the land, and to man He has given the work of putting them in such shape that they will be a blessing. In this work man is wholly dependent upon God.

The fitting of the ships that cross the broad ocean is not alone due to the talent and ingenuity of the human agent. God is the great Architect. Without His co-operation, without the aid of the higher intelligences, how worthless would be the plans of men! God must aid, else every device is worthless.

The human organism is the handiwork of God. The organs employed in all the different functions of the body were made by Him. The Lord gives us food and drink, that the wants of the body may be supplied. He has given the earth different properties adapted to the growth of food for His children. He gives the sunshine and the showers, the early and the latter rain. He forms the clouds and sends the dew. All are His gifts. He has bestowed His blessings upon us liberally. But all these blessings will not restore in us His moral image unless we co-operate with Him, making painstaking effort to know ourselves, to understand how to care for the delicate human machinery. Man must diligently help to keep himself in harmony with nature's laws. He who co-operates with God in the work of keeping this wonderful machinery in order, who consecrates all his powers to God, seeking intelligently to obey the laws of nature, stands in his God-given manhood, and is recorded in the books of heaven as a man.

God has given man land to be cultivated. But in order that the harvest may be reaped, there must be harmonious action between divine and human agencies. The plow and other implements of labor must be used at the right time. The seed must be sown in its season. Man is not to fail of doing his part. If he is careless and negligent, his unfaithfulness testifies against him. The harvest is proportionate to the energy he has expended.

A Divine Relationship

So it is in spiritual things. We are to be laborers together with God. Man is to work out his own salvation with fear and trembling, for it is God that worketh in him, both to will and to do of His good pleasure. There is to be co-partnership, a divine relation, between the Son of God and the repentant sinner. We are made sons and daughters of God. "As many as received Him, to them gave He power to become the sons of God." Christ provides the mercy and grace so abundantly given to all who believe in Him. He fulfills the terms upon which salvation rests. But we must act our part by accepting the blessing in faith. God works and man works. Resistance of temptation must come from man, who must draw his power from God. Thus he becomes a co-partner with Christ.

The infinitely wise and all-powerful God proposes co-operation with His frail, erring creatures, whom He has placed on vantage ground. On the one side there is infinite wisdom, goodness, compassion, power; on the other, weakness, sinfulness, absolute helplessness, poverty, dependence. We are dependent upon God, not only for life and all its blessings, but for our entrusted talents, and for all the resources required in the work we must do if we accept the invitation to work with God. Man's intellect, his understanding, his every valuable thought, the opportunities and privileges that are placed within his reach, all come from Him who is the Way, the Truth, and the Life. We have nothing of ourselves. Our success in the Christian life depends upon our co-operation with Christ, and our submission to His will. It is not a sign of pure, consecrated service for a worker to follow his own way. Every worker is to willingly obey his Leader, to receive and practice every word of God.

Perfection of Character

We are to be individual toilers. Character cannot be bought or sold. It is formed by patient, continuous effort. Much patience is required in the striving for that life which is to come. We may all strive for perfection of character, but all who come into possession of it will earn it step by step, by the cultivation of the virtues which God commends. The Holy Spirit presents before man the agencies provided for his transformation. If he heeds the words, "He that will come after Me, let him deny himself, and take up his cross and follow Me," he will receive help from a power that is infinite.

[91] Man is given the privilege of working with God in the saving of his own soul. He is to receive Christ as his personal Saviour and believe in Him. Receiving and believing is his part of the contract. This means abiding in Christ, showing in Him at all times and under all circumstances a faith that works by love and purifies the soul from all defilement. Christ is the author of this faith, and He demands that it be constantly exercised. Thus we receive a constant supply of grace.—*Article 21, 1899.*

* * * * *

Words to Parents

Is it at all necessary that there should be so large a number of feeble, helpless women in our world? No; I answer, decidedly; no. The opinion prevails in this generation that women do not need active, vigorous muscles and strong, sturdy frames; but does not reason tell us differently? It is argued that by nature their muscles are softer and feebler, and their strength and power of endurance less. We admit that this is the case, but why? Because for many generations back false ideas, degenerating in their influence, have been brought in through their efforts to meet the standard of fashion. The great master worker, Satan, has not been idle. He has brought in a variety of fashions, and has led men and women to encourage delicate idleness.

If food were prepared with more simplicity and in less variety, if mothers dressed their children in neat, modest apparel, without striving to meet the demands of fashion, there would be far more well-balanced minds, calm nerves, and sweet tempers. Mothers wear out their nerves by doing needless things, in order to keep pace with fashion. One third of the time now devoted to this work should be spent with their children in the open air, weeding the garden, picking berries, teaching the children to help. Enough time is wasted on fashionable dress and in the preparation of articles of food that irritate the digestive organs, to purchase a spot of ground which the children could have as their own, and from which mothers and fathers could derive precious lessons, to be given to their children. Teach your children that the garden in which they place the tiny seed represents the garden of the heart, and that God has enjoined upon you, their parents, to cultivate the soil of their hearts, as they cultivate the garden.

Cultivate the Soil of the Heart

The Lord has entrusted to parents a solemn, sacred work. They are to cultivate carefully the soil of the heart. Thus they may be laborers together with God. He expects them to guard and tend carefully the garden of their children's hearts. They are to sow the good seed, weeding out every unsightly weed. Every defect in character, every fault in disposition, needs to be cut away; for if allowed to remain, these will mar the beauty of the character.

Patiently, lovingly, as faithful stewards of the manifold grace of God, parents are to do their appointed work. It is expected of them that they will be found faithful. Everything is to be done in faith. Constantly they must pray that God will impart His grace to their children. Never must they become weary, impatient, or fretful in their work. They must cling closely to their children and to God.

If parents work in patience and love, earnestly endeavoring to help their children to reach the highest standard of purity and modesty, they will succeed. In this work parents need to manifest patience and faith, that they may present their children to God, polished after the similitude of a palace.—Manuscript 138, 1898.

Why God Chose Abraham

[92]

God judges a man by what he is in his family. Abraham is called the father of the faithful. "I know him," said the Searcher of hearts, "that he will command his children and his household after him, and they shall keep the way of the Lord, to do justice and judgment." The Lord chose Abraham as a representative man, because He knew that he would cultivate home religion, that he would cause the fear of the Lord to circulate through his tent. There would be no betrayal of sacred trust on Abraham's part. He would acknowledge and keep God's law. Blind affection and indulgence, which is the veriest cruelty, would not be shown by him. By the combined influence of authority and affection he would rule his house. Mercy and justice were blended in his rule.

The Harvest

"Whatsoever a man soweth, that shall he also reap." Parents, your work is to win the confidence of your children, and in love patiently sow the precious seed. Do your work with contentment, never complaining of the hardship, care, and toil. If by patient, kindly, Christlike efforts, you may present one soul perfect in Christ Jesus, your life will not have been in vain. Keep your own soul hopeful and patient. Let no discouragement be traced in your features or attitude. You have in your hands the making of a character, through the help of God, that may work in the Master's vineyard, and win many souls to Jesus. Ever encourage your children to reach a high standard in all their habits and tendencies. Be patient with their imperfections, as God is patient with you in your imperfections, bearing with you, watching over you, that you may bring forth fruit unto His glory. Encourage your children to strive to add to their attainments the virtues they lack. Let no cheap, frivolous conversation be indulged. Take your Bible, and read to your children the words of the inspired apostle. (Read Titus 2:6-8 and 1 Peter 1:13-16.)

There is need of guarding the conversation, that the words shall be pure, chaste, elevated. If parents would strictly guard their words, they would by precept and example teach their children to be select in their words.

The home may be a school where the children are indeed fashioned in character after the similitude of a palace. No coarseness or roughness is to be indulged; for it is entirely contrary to heaven's custom.—Manuscript 136, 1898.

Chapter 29—Home Training

By Ellen G. White

Watch, pray, work. Watching, working, and waiting for the Lord: this is our proper position. We are to act as servants who strive faithfully to do the Master's will. I am particularly burdened in reference to home training. The father is the house-band of the family. This is his position, and if he is a Christian, he will maintain right government in every respect. His authority is to be recognized, but in many families parental authority is never fully acknowledged. Various excuses are framed for the disobedience of children, and the life is a scene of endless variance between parents and children. Often the mother works to counteract the influence of the father, who, she thinks, is too severe, too exacting.

If the father is a Christian, he represents the divine authority of God, whose vicegerent he is, and whose work it is to carry out the gracious designs of an infinite God in the establishment of upright principles and the foundation of pure, virtuous, well-balanced characters. But if the father and mother are at variance with each other, the condition of things in the home is demoralizing. Neither the father nor mother receives the respect and confidence essential to correct management. The mother leaves on the minds of the children the impression that she thinks the father too severe; for children are quick to see anything that casts the slightest reflection on rules or regulations, especially if they restrict them in carrying out their inclinations.

Working in Unity

I would that parents had sanctified intelligence, that they might see the necessity of working in unity. The husband, wife, and children are a firm. They should look upon themselves as God's agents who are to work together intelligently, regarding the family as a divine institution. The parents are to instruct their children wisely, and patiently, teaching them line upon line, precept upon precept, here a little and there a little. With faith and perseverance they are to educate, train, and discipline, requiring their children to be obedient, allowing no disrespect. Thus the seeds of reverence and respect for the heavenly Father are sown. The home should be a preparatory school, where children and youth may be fitted to do service for the Master, preparatory to joining the higher school in the kingdom of God.

Parents need to remember that they occupy the place of God to their children. Just as you deal with your children, parents, so will God deal with you. Their lack of experience is to be supplied by wise precepts and godly practice. This work is to begin in their early years, when the heart is tender and impressible, and is to be carried forward step by step. Every word, every action, of the parents is to be an object lesson of the right kind. They should not act impulsively, but as though realizing that God sees them, that the heavenly universe witnesses every act when dealing with each other and with their children.

Children are the Lord's heritage, purchased by the blood of the only-begotten Son of God. With intense interest heavenly intelligences watch to see how children are dealt with by their parents, guardians, and teachers. And what strange management they witness at times, when father and mother disagree, and express their variance by words and actions.

[94]

Sometimes the father casts reflections on the mother. He sternly disciplines the children, as if to disparage the mother's tenderness and love. Because of this the mother thinks she must bestow on them increased affection, and gratify and indulge their inclinations. Thus she seeks to counteract the father's impatience and severity; but oh, how God is dishonored. The family is demoralized, and the children are confused in regard to true discipline and correct education.

Govern with Wisdom

There is danger of too severely criticizing small things. Criticism that is too severe, rules that are too rigid, lead to the disregard of all regulations; and by and by children thus educated will show the same disrespect for the laws of Christ.

Parents must be converted before they can guide their children aright. They must become submissive to the requirements of God before they can expect their children to submit to them. Then their words and even their thoughts will be brought into captivity to Jesus Christ. Day by day they must learn from Jesus, catching His Spirit, that they may reveal the Christlikeness in their lives. In childhood and youth the powers of imitation are strong, and children should have the most perfect pattern set before them, that they may have unquestionable confidence in the wisdom of their parents.

Religion in the home—what will it not accomplish? It will do the very work that God designed should be done in every family. Children will be brought up in the nurture and admonition of the Lord. They will be educated and trained, not to be society devotees, but members of the Lord's family. They will not be sacrificed to Moloch. Parents will become willing subjects of Christ. Both father and mother will consecrate themselves to the work of properly training the children given them. They will firmly decide to work in the love of God with the utmost tenderness and compassion to save the souls under their guidance. They will not allow themselves to be absorbed with the customs of the world. They will not give themselves up to parties, concerts, dances, to give feasts and attend feasts, because after this manner do the Gentiles.

Vigilance

Eternal vigilance must be manifested with regard to our children. With his manifold devices Satan begins to work with their tempers and their wills as soon as they are born. Their safety depends upon the wisdom, and the vigilant care of the parents. They must strive in the love and fear of God to preoccupy the garden of the heart, sowing the good seeds of a right spirit, correct habits, and the love and fear of God.

Obedience to parental authority must be inculcated in babyhood, childhood, and youth. The will of the parents must be under the discipline of Christ. Molded and controlled by God's pure, Holy Spirit, they may establish unquestioned dominion over the children.

Effects of Misrule

But if the parents are severe and exacting in their discipline, they do a work which they themselves can never undo. By their arbitrary course of action they stir up a sense of injustice. Many parents have to meet in their children their own temper and disposition. But instead of ruling with wisdom and kindness, they are harsh and exacting. They do not make the religious life attractive, and the children say, "If this is religion, we want none of it." Enmity against the rules of God is created. The rebellious spirit which refused to render obedience to parental authority is the last to yield to divine authority. Thus, by misrule, parents fix the eternal destiny of their children. By mismanagement they drive them to the enemy's ranks, to serve the prince of darkness rather than the Prince of light.

Such parents will have a fearful account to settle with God. In the great day of judgment He will ask them, "What have you done with My heritage? Where are the children I entrusted to your care?" Then with terrible distinctness the parents will see that their neglect has not only proved the ruin of their children, but of themselves, and that the wrong traits of character they cherished have been transmitted from parent to child to the third and fourth generation. The seeds which have been sown have produced a harvest they will not care to garner. The course of action which confirmed the children in irreligious practices has reacted upon themselves, making their influence a curse instead of a blessing.

Educate for the Master

The family should be a school where the father and mother, under the control of Christ, seek to educate their children for the Master. They should not try to evade the responsibilities of this work. They should not give their time to visiting, to the entertainment of visitors, neglecting their children to do this. If parents neglect to teach their children to be useful and helpful, Satan takes them and instructs them in his school, and those who learn in this school show who has been their instructor.

Parents lose much when they are only half converted. Of Abraham Christ said, "I know him, that he will command his children and his household after him, and they shall keep the way of the Lord."

By the combined influence of love and authority, Abraham was to rule his home. He was to walk before his household without hypocrisy or deception. He would do nothing to betray the truth. The rule for master and servant, parent and child, is obedience to the great standard of righteousness. But how few bring religion into the home life! Parents, what course are you pursuing? Are you acting on the theory that in things concerning the religious life your children shall be left free from restraint, that all you have to do is to counsel with them, and then leave them to do as they please? If so, you are neglecting your duty, neglecting the souls for whom God holds you responsible.—Manuscript 7, 1899.

* * * * *

So great is the value of the human soul that Christ paid an infinite price for the redemption of the race. God gave His Son up to shame and reproach and to an ignominious death that man might have eternal life. In view of this, why are we not working more earnestly to save sinners? Why are we so indifferent, so careless? Where is our faith, where our works?—Manuscript 24, 1903.

* * * * *

A Sacred Circle

I have been shown that around every family there is a sacred circle, which should be kept unbroken. Within this circle no other person has a right to come.

The husband and the wife should have confidence in each other. The wife should keep no secret from her husband and the husband should keep no secret from his wife. Neither should relate family secrets to others. The heart of the wife should be the grave for her husband's faults and the heart of the husband should be the grave for his wife's faults.

Never should either husband or wife indulge in a joke at the expense of the other's feelings. Never should either one in sport or

[96] in any other way complain to others concerning their companion; for frequently indulgence in foolish and what may apparently be harmless joking will eventually become habit, and may end in trial and possibly in estrangement.—Manuscript 21, 1902.

* * * * *

Husband the Time

The closing scenes of this earth's history are near at hand. The unfulfilled predictions of the book of Revelation are soon to be fulfilled. This prophecy is now to be studied with diligence by the people of God, and should be clearly understood. It does not conceal the truth; it clearly forewarns, telling us what will be in the future.

Our work now is to husband the time, the influence, and the means that God has given us, and to cooperate with the Lord at every step. We are to be true, courageous, and faithful. Unless we stand firmly and intelligently for the truth, there will be serious misconceptions, and the work that the Lord would have done will be left undone.

Let us not be in any way deceived. Let us realize the weakness of humanity, and see where man fails in his self-sufficiency. We shall then be filled with a desire to be just what God desires us to be—pure, noble, sanctified. We shall hunger and thirst after the righteousness of Christ. To be like God will be the one desire of the soul.

This is the desire that filled Enoch's heart. And we read that he walked with God. He studied the character of God to a purpose. He did not mark out his own course, or set up his own will, as if he thought himself fully qualified to manage matters. He strove to conform himself to the divine likeness.

The Lord calls upon our young people to enter our schools, and quickly fit themselves for service. In various places, outside of the cities, schools are to be established, where our youth can receive an education that will prepare them to go forth to do evangelical work and medical missionary work.—Letter 210, 1903.

* * * * *

Why Men are Condemned

The wrath of God is not declared against men merely because of the sins which they have committed, but for choosing to continue in a state of resistance, and, although they have light and knowledge, repeating their sins of the past. If they would submit, they would be pardoned; but they are determined not to yield. They defy God by their obstinacy. These souls have given themselves to Satan, and he controls them according to his will.—Testimonies to Ministers and Gospel Workers, 74, 75.

Chapter 30—Useful Occupation Better Than Games[*]

By Ellen G. White

Educate men and women to bring up their children free from false, fashionable practices, to teach them to be useful. The daughters should be educated under the mothers to do useful labor, not merely indoor labor but out-of-door labor as well. Mothers could also train the sons, to a certain age, to do useful things indoors and out-of-doors.

There are plenty of necessary, useful things to do in our world that would make the pleasure amusement exercise almost wholly unnecessary. Brain, bone, and muscle will acquire solidity and strength in using them to a purpose, doing good hard thinking, and devising plans which shall train them to develop powers of intellect, and strength of the physical organs, which will be putting into practical use their God-given talents with which they may glorify God.

This was plainly laid out before our health institution and our college as the forcible reason why they should be established among us; but as it was in the days of Noah and Lot, so it is in our time. Men have sought out many inventions and have widely departed from God's purposes and His ways.

The Danger in Sports

I do not condemn the simple exercise of playing ball; but this, even in its simplicity, may be overdone. I shrink always from the almost sure result which follows in the wake of these amusements. It leads to an outlay of means that should be expended in bringing the light of truth to souls that are perishing out of Christ. The

---

[*]Portion of a letter addressed to a college student, written from Napier, New Zealand, October 2, 1893.

amusements and expenditures of means for self-pleasing, which lead on step by step to self-glorifying, and the educating in these games for pleasure, produce a love and passion for such things that is not favorable to the perfection of Christian character.

The way that they have been conducted at the college does not bear the impress of heaven. It does not strengthen the intellect. It does not refine and purify the character. There are threads leading out through the habits and customs and worldly practices, and the actors become so engrossed and infatuated that they are pronounced in heaven, lovers of pleasure more than lovers of God. In the place of the intellect becoming strengthened to do better work as students, to be better qualified as Christians to perform the Christian duties, the exercise in these games is filling their brains with thoughts that distract the mind from their studies.

The More Excellent Way

Now the same power of exercise of mind and muscle might invent ways and means of altogether a higher class of exercise, in doing missionary work which would make them laborers together with God, and would be educating for higher usefulness in the present life, in doing useful work, which is a most essential branch in education.

There are many ways in which the youth can be putting to usury the talents entrusted to them of God, to build up the work and cause of God, not to please themselves but to glorify God. The Majesty of heaven, the King of glory, made the infinite sacrifice in coming to our world in order that He might elevate and ennoble humanity. He was a persevering, diligent worker. We read, He "went about doing good."

Is not this the work that every youth should be seeking to do, working in Christ's lines? You have Christ's help. The ideas of the students will broaden. They will be far-reaching, and the powers of usefulness, even in your student's life, will be continually growing. The arms, the hands, which God has given, are to be used in doing good which shall bear the signet of heaven, that you can at last hear the "Well done, thou good and faithful servant."

I do not think, from the way the matter has been presented to me, that your ball games are so conducted that the record of the students will be of that character, in the estimation of Him who weighs actions, that will bring a reward to the actors.

Missionary Work for Students

Let there be a company formed somewhat after the plan of the Christian Endeavor order, and see what can be done by each accountable human agent, in watching and improving opportunities to do work for the Master. He has a vineyard in which everyone can perform good work. Suffering humanity needs help everywhere. The students may win their way to hearts, by speaking words in season, by doing favors for those who need even physical labor. This will not degrade any one of you, and it will bring a consciousness of the approval of God. It will be putting the talents, entrusted to you for wise improvement, to the exchangers. It will increase them by trading upon them.

Beneficial Methods of Exercise

There are healthful methods of exercise that may be planned which will be beneficial to both soul and body. There is a great work to be done and it is essential that every responsible agent shall educate himself to do this work acceptably to God. There is much for all to learn, and there cannot be invented a better use for brain, bone, and muscle than to accept the wisdom of God in doing good, and adopting some human device for remedying the existing evils of this profligate, extravagant age.

It is our duty ever to seek to do good in the use of the muscles and brain God has given to youth, that they may be useful to others, making their labors lighter, soothing the sorrowing, lifting up the discouraged, speaking words of comfort to the hopeless, turning the minds of the students from fun and frolic which often carries them beyond the dignity of manhood and womanhood to shame and disgrace. The Lord would have the mind elevated, seeking higher, nobler channels of usefulness.

The Dangers to Spirituality

Is the eye single to the glory of God in these games? I know that this is not so. There is a losing sight of God's way and His purposes. The employment of intelligent beings, in probationary time, is superseding God's revealed will, and substituting for it the speculations and inventions of the human agent, with Satan by his side to imbue with his spirit. Keep the Word of God close by your side. Guided by it you will be wise, you will be steadfast, immovable, always abounding in the work of the Lord. We must in these last days watch unto prayer. The Lord God of heaven protests against the burning passion cultivated for supremacy in the games that are so engrossing.

In no time in your life have you been more critically placed than you are while prosecuting your medical studies in Ann Arbor. Satan is watching every avenue whereby he can take advantage to enter with his specious temptations to spoil the soul. You will meet with infidel sentiments in very intelligent men who call themselves Christians. Cling to the wisdom which is revealed to you in the Word of God, for it will bind you, if you obey its teachings, to the throne of God.

I am fearful now, more than at any other period of time, that Christians, as individuals, may separate from God because they lose sight of the Pattern Jesus Christ, and think it is safe to walk in the sparks of their own kindling, deceiving the soul with thinking it is the way of the Lord.—Letter 17a, 1893.

* * * * *

Need of Self-Sacrificing Effort

Will young men and young women accept the holy trust from the Master's hands? Will they offer themselves for service, and put all the fervor of the soul into the work of reforming themselves, that they may labor acceptably for the youth who are wholly given to pleasure and self-gratification?

Because of our artificial civilization people are sick; they need a physician who can cure them. Each human being is entrusted with talents. These talents are to be appreciated; they are to be used, not abused. The love of Christ alone can enable us to properly appreciate our talents. In every school established, the most simple theory of theology should be taught. In this theory the atonement of Christ should be the great substance, the central truth. The wonderful theme of redemption should be presented to the students....

Those who claim to believe the truth do not possess that power that God would bestow upon them if they really believed, and were striving for conformity to His image. The church is in the Laodicean state. The presence of God is not in her midst. If Christ were formed within, the hope of glory, conformity to His image would be seen, and the church trials which separate the members from Christ would disappear....

Mission work must not cease because of limited means. Let every church member practice self-denial. The Word of God gives the commission, "Go ye into all the world, and preach the gospel to every creature." There is no restriction, no limit, to the work. And the promise is "Lo, I am with you alway, even unto the end of the world." Abridge the work, limit your labors, and you remove your Helper. The sickly, unhealthy state of the church reveals a church afraid to work, fearing that self-denial will be required. The presence of the Lord is ever seen where every energy of the church is aroused to meet the spiritual responsibilities. But many of the churches who have had the light of present truth are dwarfed and crippled by the evils existing in their midst, by the selfishness cherished, by spending on self that which should be given to the Lord. Because of self-indulgence, they have nothing to give toward the work of saving souls.

Angels of God are sent to measure the temple and the worshipers therein. The Lord looks with sadness upon those who are serving their idols, with no care for the souls perishing in darkness and error. He cannot bless the church who feel it no part of their duty to be laborers together with God. What a terrible thing it is to exclude Christ from His own temple! What a loss to the church!

A Gracious Invitation

Our Redeemer sends His messengers to bear a testimony to His people. He says, "Behold, I stand at the door, and knock. If any man hear My voice, and open the door, I will come in to him, and will sup with him, and he with Me." But many refuse to receive Him, because they fear that He will be an expensive guest. The Holy Spirit waits to soften and subdue hearts, but they are not willing to open the door and let the Saviour in; for they fear that He will require something from them. And so Jesus of Nazareth passes by. He longs to bestow on them His rich blessings and gifts of grace, but they refuse to accept them.

The Lord requests His church to have a higher grade of piety, a more just sense of duty; a clear realization of their obligation to their Creator. All who will read the third chapter of Malachi will see that God calls for systematic contributions from His people. The funds so given will be abundantly blessed. If all whose names are on the church books would give to the Lord a tenth of their increase, as He has prospered them, abundant resources would swell the revenues of the church. God desires even the poorest to give their gifts, small though they may be. By giving as we have been prospered, we acknowledge God's mercy and liberality in supplying our necessities.—Manuscript 156, 1898.

* * * * *

Example of Faithfulness

There are two great principles, one of loyalty and the other of disloyalty. Christian strength is obtained by serving the Lord faithfully. We all need greater Christian courage, that we may uplift the standard on which is inscribed, The commandments of God and the faith of Jesus. We are to make no compromise with the leaders of rebellion. The line of demarcation between the obedient and the disobedient must be plain and distinct. We must have a firm determination to do the Lord's will at all times and in all places.

Young men and young women should learn the lesson that to be one with Christ is the highest honor to which they can attain. By the strictest fidelity they should strive for a moral independence, and this independence they should maintain against every influence that tries to turn the soul from righteous principles. Stronger minds may, yes, they will, make assertions which have no foundation in truth. Let the heavenly eyesalve be applied to the eyes of your understanding, that you may distinguish between truth and error. Search the Word, and when you find a "Thus saith the Lord," take your stand.

The wrong customs, practices, and theories of the world are to find no recognition in the life of the one who has chosen to be on the Lord's side. Consecrate all that there is of you, soul, body, and spirit, to the Saviour. Yield every power that you have to the control of the Holy Spirit.—Manuscript 121, 1898.

Methods

Chapter 31—Admonition Will Be Heard

By Ellen G. White

Dangers of the Last Days

We are living in the last days of this earth's history, and we may be surprised at nothing in the line of apostasies and denials of the truth. Unbelief has now come to be a fine art which men work at to the destruction of their souls. There is constant danger of there being shams in pulpit preachers, whose lives contradict the words they speak; but the voice of warning and of admonition will be heard as long as time shall last; and those who are guilty of transactions that should never be entered into, when reproved or counseled through the Lord's appointed agencies, will resist the message and refuse to be corrected. They will go on as did Pharaoh and Nebuchadnezzar, until the Lord takes away their reason, and their hearts become unimpressible. The Lord's word will come to them; but if they choose not to hear it, the Lord will make them responsible for their own ruin.

An Unflinching Testimony

In John the Baptist the Lord raised up for Himself a messenger to prepare the way of the Lord. He was to bear to the world an unflinching testimony in reproving and denouncing sin. Luke, in announcing his mission and work, says, And he shall go before Him in the spirit and power of Elias, to turn the hearts of the fathers to the children, and the disobedient to the wisdom of the just; to make ready a people, prepared for the Lord."

Many of the Pharisees and Sadducees came to the baptism of John, and addressing these, he said, "O generation of vipers, who hath warned you to flee from the wrath to come? Bring forth therefore fruits meet for repentance: and think not to say within yourselves, We have Abraham to our father: for I say unto you, that God is able of these stones to raise up children unto Abraham. And now also the ax is laid unto the root of the trees: therefore every tree which bringeth not forth good fruit is hewn down, and cast into the fire. I indeed baptize you with water unto repentance: but He that cometh after me is mightier than I, whose shoes I am not worthy to bear: He shall baptize you with the Holy Ghost, and with fire; whose fan is in His hand, and He will thoroughly purge His floor, and gather His wheat into the garner; but He will burn up the chaff with unquenchable fire."

The voice of John was lifted up like a trumpet. His commission was, "Show My people their transgression, and the house of Jacob their sins." He had obtained no human scholarship. God and nature had been his teachers. But one was needed to prepare the way before Christ who was bold enough to make his voice heard like the prophets of old, summoning the degenerate nation to repentance.

Heard by All Classes

And all went forth into the wilderness to hear him. Unlearned fishermen and peasants came from the surrounding countries and from regions nigh and afar off. The Roman soldiers from the barracks of Herod came to hear. Chieftains came with their swords girded by their sides, to put down anything that savored of riot or rebellion. The avaricious taxgatherers came from the regions round about; and from the Sanhedrim came forth the phylacteried priests. All listened as if spellbound; and all came away, even the Pharisee, the Sadducee, and the cold, unimpressionable scoffer of the age, with the sneer gone, and cut to the heart with a sense of their sin. There were no long arguments, no finely cut theories, elaborately delivered in their "firstly," "secondly," and "thirdly." But pure native eloquence was revealed in the short sentences, every word carrying with it the certainty and truth of the weighty warnings given.

[102]

Nineveh an Example

The warning message of John was in the same lines as the warning to Nineveh, "Yet forty days, and Nineveh shall be overthrown." Nineveh repented, and called upon God, and God accepted their acknowledgement of Him. Forty years of probation was granted them in which to reveal the genuineness of their repentance and to turn from sin. But Nineveh turned again to the worship of images; her iniquity became deeper and more desperate than before, because the light had come and had not been heeded.

False Hopes Exposed

John called every class to repentance. To the Pharisees and Sadducees he said, Flee from the wrath to come. Your claims to Abraham as your father are not of the least value to you. They will not impart to you pure principles and holiness of character. Ceremonial sacrifices possess no value unless you discern their object, the Lamb of God, that taketh away the sin of the world. You turn from God's requirements and follow your own perverted ideas; and you lose those characteristics which constitute you children of Abraham. And pointing to the rocks in wild confusion around through which the stream was winding its course, he said, "God is able of these stones to raise up children unto Abraham."

John the Baptist met sin with open rebuke in men of humble occupation and in men of high degree. He declared the truth to kings and nobles, whether they would hear or reject it. He spoke personally and pointedly. He reproved the Pharisees of the Sanhedrim because their religion consisted in forms and not in righteousness of pure, willing obedience.... He spoke to Herod in regard to his marriage with Herodias, saying, It is not lawful for thee to have her. He spoke to him of a future retribution, when God would judge every man according to his works....

What Shall We Do?

"Then came also publicans to be baptized, and said unto him, Master, what shall we do?" Did he say, Leave your toll and custom houses? No, he said to them, "Exact no more than that which is appointed you." If they were taxgatherers still, they could hold just weights and balances of truth in their hands. They could reform in those things that savored of dishonesty and oppression.

"And the soldiers likewise demanded of him, saying, And what shall we do? And he said unto them, Do violence to no man, neither accuse any falsely; and be content with your wages."...

The Sword of Truth at Work

Christ also spoke pointedly to every class of men. He reproved those who dominated over their fellow men, those whose passions and prejudices caused many to err and compelled many to blaspheme God. The sword of truth was blunted by apologies and suppositions; but Christ called things by their right names. The ax was laid to the root of the tree. He showed that all the religious forms of worship could not save the Jewish nation, because they did not behold and receive by faith the Lamb of God as their Saviour.

Just such a work and message as that of John will be carried on in these last days. The Lord has been giving messages to His people, through the instruments He has chosen, and He would have all take heed to the admonitions and warnings He sends.

Repent! Repent!

The message preceding the public ministry of the Son of God was, Repent, publicans, repent, Pharisees and Sadducees, "for the kingdom of heaven is at hand." Our message is not to be one of "peace and safety." As a people who believe in Christ's soon appearing, we have a work to do, a message to bear—"Prepare to meet thy God." We are to lift up the standard, and bear the third angel's message—the commandments of God, and the faith of Jesus.

The Message for Today

The message we bear must be as direct as was the message of John. He rebuked kings for their iniquity. He rebuked the adultery of Herod. Notwithstanding his life was in peril, the truth did not languish upon his lips. And our work in this age must be as faithfully done. The inhabitants of the world at this time are represented by the dwellers upon the earth at the time of the flood. The wickedness of the inhabitants of the old world is plainly stated: "And God saw that the wickedness of man was great in the earth, and that every imagination of the thoughts of his heart was only evil continually." God became weary of these people whose only thoughts were of pleasure and indulgence. They sought not the counsel of the God who had created them, nor cared to do His will. The rebuke of God was upon them because they followed the imagination of their own hearts continually; and there was violence in the land. "And it repented the Lord that He had made man on the earth, and it grieved Him at His heart. And God looked upon the earth, and, behold, it was corrupt; for all flesh had corrupted his way upon the earth. And God said unto Noah, The end of all flesh is come before Me; for the earth is filled with violence through them; and behold, I will destroy them with the earth."...

Stern Rebuke Called For

There are special duties to be done, special reproofs to be given in this period of the earth's history. The Lord will not leave His church without reproofs and warnings. Sins have become fashionable; but they are none the less aggravating in the sight of God. They are glossed over, palliated, and excused; the right hand of fellowship is given to the very men who are bringing in false theories and false sentiments, confusing the mind of the people of God, deadening their sensibilities as to what constitutes right principles. Conscience has thus become insensible to the counsels and the reproofs which have been given. The light given, calling to repentance, has been extinguished in the clouds of unbelief and opposition brought in by human plans and human inventions.

It is living earnestness that God requires. Ministers may have little learning from books; but if they do the best they can with their talents; if they work as they have opportunity; if they clothe their utterances in the plainest and most simple language; if they are humble men who walk in carefulness and humility, seeking for heavenly wisdom, working for God from the heart, and actuated by one predominating motive—love for Christ and the souls for whom He has died—they will be listened to by men of even superior ability and talents. There will be a charm in the simplicity of the truths they present. Christ is the greatest teacher that the world has ever known.

John had not learned in the schools of the rabbis. Yet kings and nobles, Pharisees and Sadducees, Roman soldiers and officers, trained in all court etiquette, wily, calculating taxgatherers, and world-renowned men, listened to his words. They had confidence in his plain statements, and were convicted of sin. They asked of him, "What shall we do?" ...

Earnestness is Necessary

In this age, just prior to the second coming of Christ in the clouds of heaven, the Lord calls for men who will be earnest and prepare a people to stand in the great day of the Lord. The men who have spent long terms in the study of books are not revealing in their lives that earnest ministry which is essential for this last time. They do not bear a simple, straightforward testimony. Among ministers and students there is need of the infusion of the Spirit of God. The prayerful, earnest appeals that come from the heart of a whole-souled messenger will create convictions. It will not need the learned men to do this; for they depend more on their learning from books than upon their knowledge of God and Jesus Christ whom He has sent. All who know the only true and living God will know Jesus Christ, the only-begotten Son of God, and will preach Jesus Christ and Him crucified....

Does anyone suppose that the messages of warning will not come to those whom God reproves? The ones reproved may rise up in indignation and seek to bring the law to bear upon God's messenger, but in doing this, they are not bringing the law upon the messenger, but upon Christ, who gave the reproof and the warning. When men endanger the work and cause of God by their own wrong course of action, shall they hear no voice of reproof? If the wrongdoer only were concerned, and the work reached no farther than him, he alone should have the words of warning; but when his course of action is doing positive harm to the cause of truth, and souls are imperiled, God requires that the warning be as broad as the injury done. The testimonies will not be hindered. The words of rebuke and warning, the plain, "Thus saith the Lord," will come from God's appointed agencies; for the words do not originate with the human instrument; they are from God, who appointed them their work. If a suit is instituted in earthly tribunals, and God suffers it to come to trial, it is that His own name may be glorified. But a woe will be upon the man who gives himself to do this work. God reads the motives, whatever they may be. I pray that the Lord will teach our brethren to be straightforward, and make no compromise in the matter. The cause of God has been bruised and wounded by any such men connecting with it, and the sooner they are separated from it, the better....

God calls for men of decided fidelity. He has no use in an emergency for two-sided men. He wants men who will lay their hand upon a wrong work and say, "This is not according to the will of God."—Letter 19a, 1897.

Chapter 32—How to Present Truth

By Ellen G. White

Our success will depend on carrying forward the work in the simplicity in which Christ carried it forward, without any theatrical display....

All our preparations for presenting and illustrating the truth must correspond with the solemnity of the message we bear. The Lord never designed the advancement of His work to depend on outward display. Thus the means would quickly be spent, and little would be left with which to open new fields....

Creating A False Appetite

Every part of the work is to be carried forward solidly. When large, expensive preparations are made in connection with the public effort made in cities, these preparations may at first attract a large number of people. But they cannot be maintained for any length of time. It is found, however when an effort is made to dispense with them, that they have created an appetite for such things, and that they cannot be dispensed with without a falling off in interest and in the number of hearers.

Works of Healing

The way in which Christ worked was to preach the Word, and to relieve suffering by miraculous works of healing. But I am instructed that we cannot now work in this way; for Satan will exercise his power by working miracles. God's servants today could not work by means of miracles; because spurious works of healing, claiming to be divine, will be wrought.

For this reason the Lord has marked out a way in which His people are to carry forward a work of physical healing, combined with the teaching of the Word. Sanitariums are to be established, and with these institutions are to be connected workers who will carry forward genuine medical missionary work. Thus a guarding influence is thrown around those who come to the sanitariums for treatment.

This is the provision the Lord has made whereby gospel medical missionary work is to be done for many souls. These institutions are to be established out of the cities, and in them educational work is to be intelligently carried forward....

Christ's Work Our Example

In our work we are not to go onto a hilltop to shine. We are not told that we must make a special, wonderful display. The truth must be proclaimed in the highways and the byways, and thus work is to be done by sensible, rational methods. The life of every worker, if he is under the training of the Lord Jesus Christ, will reveal the excellence of His life. The work that Christ did in our world is to be our example, as far as display is concerned. We are to keep as far from the theatrical and the extraordinary as Christ kept in His work. Sensation is not religion, although religion will exert its own pure, sacred, uplifting, sanctifying influence, bringing spiritual life and salvation....

Best Methods for Large Cities

How shall we carry on evangelistic work in large cities?—As you are carrying it on in Washington, without the parade that some who are deceiving their own souls are inclined to think necessary. The truth that we have to proclaim is the most solemn truth ever entrusted to mortals, and it is to be proclaimed in a way that corresponds to its solemnity and importance. There is to be attached to it no fantastic display. Such display meets the minds of some, but how few are really convicted and converted by a fanciful blending of display with the proclamation of the solemn gospel message for this time. The display counterworks the impression made by the gospel message.

Were all to connect with the preaching of the Word the display that some deem so essential, how soon there would be a dearth of means. Extravagance would be seen on every side, and all through our ranks an appetite for display would be created and developed.

God expects us to follow the example of the Majesty of heaven, who clothed His divinity with humanity that divinity might touch humanity and humanity might partake of the divine nature. It is only as we are clothed with humility that God can accept us as Christ's followers.

Avoid Peculiar Ideas

We are not to try to gather together strange, peculiar ideas, which are not revealed in the Word of God. If the shepherds of the flock of God are partakers of the divine nature, they will be clothed with genuine humility. They will fill contentedly the place God gives them, shining brightly amidst the moral darkness. Realizing the sacredness of the truth, they will refuse to be drawn out of their place by the attractions of the world or the praise of men. They will stand firmly at their post of duty as brave soldiers.

How to Shine

Christ does not say to us, "Strive to shine." He says, "Let your light shine." He in whose heart Christ abides cannot help shining. "*Let* your light shine." Do not allow your light to be dimmed by selfishness or unrighteous actions. Never gather clouds about you; for this means concealment of your light. Do not dim it by speaking words of harshness or anger. Let the light shine forth brightly to those within and without the home. Gather rays of light from Him who is the Light of the world, and shine more and more brightly. Let your lamp be always trimmed and burning.

Bring the Lord Jesus very near you in your home life; then when you speak the Word of God, this Word will be as a sharp, two-edged sword, cutting through the sinful practices of the sinner. The Lord will make the application of the word spoken.

Keep your lamp trimmed and burning, that the light may shine forth to all who are in the house. "Let your light so shine before men that they may see your good works, and glorify your Father which is in heaven."—Letter 53, 1904.

Chapter 33—Deeper Consecration

By Ellen G. White

I long to be able to rest, but the burden continues to weigh heavily upon my soul, as night after night I am calling upon our medical missionary workers to seek the Lord while He may be found, and call upon Him while He is near. I am instructed to say that the teachers of our people need to have a work done for themselves. Their spirit needs to be brought under the control of God. Those who have a knowledge of the truth should live the truth. Our ministers and physicians need real conversion of soul, that they may be imbued with power from on high. They need to rend their hearts before God. A thorough work needs to be done in the hearts of the workers in every line of the cause of God. I call upon them to awake, while they still have opportunity to repent, and prepare to meet their God.

A Real Conversion Needed

Over and over again I am instructed that our ministers and physicians need to have a decided work done for them. I beg of them not to flatter themselves that they know how to carry forward the work of the Lord. They need a reformation, a real conversion. When they get a glimpse of their need of God, there will come to them a humiliation of heart that will be a savor of life unto life.

God calls upon the men in charge of His work to arouse themselves. They are not now awake. Their hearts need to be changed. Their human desires and inclinations need to be brought under the control of the Holy Spirit.

I heard the voice of a mighty general crying in trumpet tones, "Prepare to meet thy God. Prepare for the great conflict before you. Quit yourselves as brave soldiers of the Lord's army. Put on the whole armor of God, that ye may be able to stand against the wiles of the enemy. We wrestle not against flesh and blood, but against principalities, against powers, against the rulers of the darkness of this world, against spiritual wickedness in high places. Wherefore take unto you the whole armor of God, that ye may be able to withstand in the evil day, and having done all, to stand. Stand therefore, having your loins girt about with truth, and having on the breastplate of righteousness; and your feet shod with the preparation of the gospel of peace; above all, taking the shield of faith, wherewith ye shall be able to quench all the fiery darts of the wicked. And take the helmet of salvation, and the sword of the Spirit, which is the Word of God."

An Inspiring Message

I seemed to see a company bowed in prayer. Confessions of sin were made that till then had been withheld. Then One of authority arose, and with deep feeling read the following scripture:

"If there be therefore any consolation in Christ, if any comfort of love, if any fellowship of the Spirit, if any bowels and mercies, fulfill ye my joy, that ye be like-minded, having the same love, being of one accord, of one mind. Let nothing be done through strife or vainglory; but in lowliness of mind let each esteem others better than themselves. Look not every man on his own things, but every man also on the things of others. Let this mind be in you, which was also in Christ Jesus: who, being in the form of God, thought it not robbery to be equal with God: but made Himself of no reputation, and took upon Him the form of a servant, and was made in the likeness of men; and being found in fashion as a man, He humbled himself, and became obedient unto death, even the death of the cross."

"The Father loveth the Son, and hath given all things into His hands." "It pleased the Father that in Him should all fullness dwell." "God also hath highly exalted Him, and given Him a name which is above every name: that at the name of Jesus every knee should bow, of things in heaven, and things in earth; and things under the earth; and that every tongue should confess that Jesus Christ is Lord, to the glory of God the Father." "For by Him were all things created, that are in heaven, and that are in earth, visible and invisible, whether they be thrones, or dominions, or principalities, or powers: all things were created by Him, and for Him: and He is before all things, and by Him all things consist."

"Christ both died, and rose, and revived, that He might be Lord both of the dead and living." "In Him dwelleth all the fullness of the Godhead bodily. And ye are complete in Him."

A Timely Warning

I am instructed to warn our physicians and ministers not to become exalted, but to walk as children, wholly consecrated to God's service, wholly dependent on Him. My brethren, my prayer for you is "that the God of our Lord Jesus Christ, the Father of glory, may give unto you the spirit of wisdom and revelation in the knowledge of Him: the eyes of your understanding being enlightened; that ye may know what is the hope of His calling, and what the riches of the glory of His inheritance in the saints, and what is the exceeding greatness of His power to usward who believe, according to the working of His mighty power, which He wrought in Christ, when He raised Him from the dead, and set Him at His own right hand in the heavenly places, far above all principality, and power, and might, and dominion, and every name that is named, not only in this world, but also in that which is to come."

Working Together

You are God's husbandry, God's building. You are to be laborers together with Him. Will you not remember that word "together"? Keeping it ever in mind sanctifies the soul. You come far short of appreciating the advantages that are for those who are called and chosen. Will you not walk worthy of the high honor that God will place upon you if you are faithful? You must walk humbly before Him. Put away all abruptness of speech and action....

Work in unity. Press together. Let each one stand in his place. Speak the truth plainly, but in love. Keep the standard of truth uplifted.

May God help you to heed these words.—Letter 266, 1903.

Chapter 34—The Teaching of Extreme Views

By Ellen G. White

St. Helena, Calif.

May 19, 1890
Dear Brother,

I expected ere this to see you and talk with you, or write to you; but I have not been able to do either, neither am I now able; but I feel a deep interest in you and am desirous that you shall not be separated from the work. I have not strength to do justice in conversation with you; your mind is so quick and your tongue so fluent, that I fear I should become very much wearied, and that which I might say would not remain distinct in your mind.

I see your danger; you can readily put your thoughts into words. You put things in a strong light; and your language is not guarded. Your views on some points are so expressed that you make your brethren afraid of you. This need not be. You should not try to get as far from your brethren as you can, making it appear that you do not see alike.

I have been shown that your influence for good is greatly lessened because you feel it your duty to express your ideas on certain points which you do not fully comprehend yourself, and which, with all your efforts, you cannot make others comprehend. I have been shown that it was not necessary for you to feel that you must dwell upon these points. Some of your ideas are correct, others incorrect and erroneous.

Dwell on Essential Themes

If you would dwell on such subjects as Christ's willingness to forgive sins, to receive the sinner, to save that which is lost, subjects that inspire hope and courage, you would be a blessing. But while you strive to be original and take such extreme views, and use such strong language in presenting them, there is danger of doing much harm. Some may grasp your thought and seem to be benefited, but when tempted and overcome, they lose courage to fight the good fight of faith.

If you will dwell less on these ideas, which seem to you so important, and will restrain your extravagant expressions, you yourself will have more faith. I saw that your mind was at times unbalanced from trying very hard to study into and explain the mystery of godliness, which is just as great a mystery after your study and explanations as it was before.

Differing Experiences in Conversion

Lead the people to look to Jesus as their only hope and helper; leave the Lord room to work upon the mind, to speak to the soul, and to impress the understanding. It is not essential for you to know and tell others all the whys and wherefores as to what constitutes the new heart, or as to the position they can and must reach so as never to sin. You have no such work to do.

All are not constituted alike. Conversions are not all alike. Jesus impresses the heart, and the sinner is born again to new life. Often souls have been drawn to Christ when there was no violent conviction, no soul rending, no remorseful terrors. They looked upon an uplifted Saviour, they lived. They saw the soul's need, they saw the Saviour's sufficiency, and His claims, they heard His voice saying, "Follow Me," and they rose up and followed Him. This conversion was genuine, and the religious life was just as decided as was that of others who suffered all the agony of a violent process.

Our ministers must cease to dwell upon their peculiar ideas with the feeling, "You must see this point as I do, or you cannot be saved." Away with this egotism. The great work to be done in every case is to win souls to Christ. Men must see Jesus on the cross, they must look and live. It is not your ideas they must feed upon, but it is the flesh and blood of the Son of God. He says, "My flesh is meat indeed." "The words that I speak unto you, they are spirit, and they are life."

Leave Christ Room to Work

The soul that accepts Jesus places himself under the care of the Great Physician, and let men be careful how they come between the patient and the physician who discerns all the needs of the soul. Christ, the Physician of the soul, understands its defects and its maladies, and knows how to heal with the purchase of His own blood. What the soul lacks, He can best supply. But men are so officious, they want to do so much, that they overdo the matter, leaving Christ no room to work.

[110]

Whatever molding and fashioning needs to be wrought in the soul, Christ can best do. The conviction may not be deep, but if the sinner comes to Christ, viewing Him upon the cross, the just dying for the unjust, the sight will break every barrier down. Christ has undertaken the work of saving all who trust in Him for salvation. He sees the wrongs that need to be righted, the evils that need to be repressed. He came to seek and save that which was lost. "Him that cometh to Me," He says, "I will in no wise cast out."

Through the goodness and mercy of Christ the sinner is to be restored to the divine favor. God in Christ is daily beseeching men to be reconciled to God. With outstretched arms He is ready to receive and welcome not only the sinner but the prodigal. His dying love, manifested on Calvary, is the sinner's assurance of acceptance, peace, and love. Teach these things in the simplest form, that the sin-darkened soul may see the light shining from the cross of Calvary.

Idolizing Fine-Drawn Theories

Satan is working in many ways, that the very men who ought to preach the message may be occupied with fine-drawn theories which he will cause to appear of such magnitude and importance as to fill the whole mind; and while they think they are making wonderful strides in experience, they are idolizing a few ideas, and their influence is injured, and tells but little on the Lord's side.

Let every minister make earnest efforts to ascertain what is the mind of Christ. Unless your mind becomes better balanced in regard to some things, your course will separate you from the work, and you will not know at what you stumble. You will advance ideas which you might better never have originated.

Detached Sentences

There are those who pick out from the Word of God, and also from the Testimonies, detached paragraphs or sentences that may be interpreted to suit their ideas, and they dwell upon these, and build themselves up in their own positions, when God is not leading them. Here is your danger.

You will take passages in the Testimonies that speak of the close of probation, of the shaking among God's people, and you will talk of a coming out from this people of a purer, holier people that will arise. Now all this pleases the enemy. We should not needlessly take a course that will make differences or create dissension. We should not give the impression that if our particular ideas are not followed, it is because the ministers are lacking in comprehension and in faith, and are walking in darkness.

Truth Mingled with Supposition

Your mind has been on an unnatural strain for a long time. You have much truth, precious truth, but mingled with suppositions. Your extreme ideas and strong language often destroy the effect of your best efforts. Should many accept the views you advance, and talk and act upon them, we would see one of the greatest fanatical excitements that has ever been witnessed among Seventh-day Adventists. This is what Satan wants.

Now there are in the lessons of Christ, subjects in abundance that you can speak upon. And mysteries which neither you nor your hearers can understand or explain might better be left alone. Give the Lord Jesus Christ room Himself to teach; let Him by the influence of His Spirit open to the understanding the wonderful plan of salvation.

There is a time of trouble coming to the people of God, but we are not to keep that constantly before the people, and rein them up to have a time of trouble beforehand. There is to be a shaking among God's people, but this is not the present truth to carry to the churches....

The ministers should not feel that they have some wonderful advanced ideas, and unless all receive these, they will be shaken out and a people will arise to go forward and upward to the victory. Some of those who are resisting the very principles of the message God has sent for this time, present just such cases as yourself. They point to your extreme views and teaching as an excuse for their neglect of receiving the Lord's messages.

Satan's object is accomplished just as surely when men run ahead of Christ and do the work He has never entrusted to their hand, as when they remain in the Laodicean state, Lukewarm, feeling rich and increased with goods, and in need of nothing. The two classes are equally stumbling blocks.

Straining for Originality [111]

Some zealous ones who are aiming and straining every energy for originality have made a grave mistake in trying to get something startling, wonderful, entrancing before the people, something that they think others do not comprehend; but they do not themselves know what they are talking about. They speculate upon God's Word, advancing ideas that are not a whit of help to themselves or to the churches. For the time being they may excite the imagination, but there is a reaction, and these very ideas become a hindrance. Faith is confounded with fancy, and their views may bias the mind in a wrong direction.

Let the plain, simple statements of the Word of God be food for the mind; this speculating upon ideas that are not clearly presented there is dangerous business.

You are naturally combative. You do not care much whether you harmonize with your brethren or not. You would like to enter into controversy, would like to fight for your particular ideas; but you should lay this aside, for this is not developing the Christian graces. Work with all your power to answer the prayer of Christ, that His disciples may be one, as He is one with the Father.

Not a soul of us is safe unless we learn of Jesus daily, His meekness, His lowliness of heart. When you go to any place to labor, do not be dictatorial, do not be severe, do not be antagonistic. Preach the love of Christ, and this will melt and subdue hearts. Seek to be of one mind and of one judgment, coming close in harmony with your brethren, and to speak the same things.

Talk Not of Divisions

This talking about divisions because all do not have the same ideas as present themselves to your mind, is not the work of God, but of the enemy. Talk the simple truths wherein you can agree. Talk of unity; do not become narrow and conceited; let your mind broaden.

Christ does not weigh character in scales of human judgment. He says, "I, if I be lifted up from the earth, will draw all men unto Me." Every soul who responds to this drawing will turn from iniquity. Christ is able to save to the uttermost all who come unto Him. He who comes to Jesus is setting his feet upon a ladder that reaches from earth to heaven. Teach it by pen, by voice, that God is above the ladder; the bright rays of His glory are shining upon every round of the ladder. He is looking graciously upon all who are climbing painfully upward, that He may send them help, divine help, when the hand seems to be relaxing and the foot trembling. Yes, tell it, tell it in words that will melt the heart, that not one who shall perseveringly climb the ladder will fail of an entrance into the everlasting kingdom of our Lord and Saviour Jesus Christ; those who believe in Christ shall never perish, neither shall any pluck them out of His hand.

Tell the people in clear, hopeful language how they may escape the heritage of shame which is our deserved portion. But for Christ's sake do not present before them ideas that will discourage them, that will make the way to heaven seem very difficult. Keep all these overstrained ideas to yourself.

While we must often impress the mind with the fact that the Christian life is a life of warfare, that we must watch and pray and toil, that there is peril to the soul in relaxing the spiritual vigilance for one moment, the completeness of the salvation proffered us from Jesus who loves us and gave Himself that we should not perish, but have everlasting life, is to be the theme.

Walk Day by Day with God

Day by day we may walk with God, day by day following on to know the Lord, entering into the holiest by the blood of Jesus, laying hold on the hope set before us. If we reach heaven it must be by binding the soul to the Mediator, becoming partakers of the divine nature. Leaning on Christ, your life being hid with Christ in God and led by His Spirit, you have the genuine faith.

Believing fully in the efficacy of His atoning sacrifice, we shall be laborers together with God. Trusting in His merits, we are to work out our own salvation with fear and trembling; for it is God that worketh in us both to will and to do of His good pleasure. Always keeping hold of Christ, we are coming nearer and nearer to God. Jesus desires us to keep this always prominent. Do not arouse your combative spirit; the wisdom that is from above is first pure, then peaceable, easy to be entreated, full of mercy and good fruits....

Harmonize with Your Brethren

Do not think that you must make prominent every idea your imagination receives. Jesus said to His disciples, "I have yet many things to say unto you, but ye cannot bear them now." How much more should we, who are constantly liable to err, beware of urging upon others that which they are not prepared to receive. Constantly looking unto Jesus, restrain your strong extravagant expressions. But while you should be cautious as to your words and ideas, it is not necessary that your labors should entirely cease. Seek to be in harmony with your brethren, and there will be plenty for you to do in the vineyard of the Lord. But exalt Christ, not your ideas and views. Put on the armor, and keep step with God's workers, shoulder to shoulder; press the battle against the enemy. Hide in Jesus. Dwell on the simple lessons of Christ, feed the flock of God, and you will become settled, strengthened, established; you will work to build up others in the most holy faith.

Avoid Foolish Contentions

If you differ with your brethren as to your understanding of the grace of Christ and the operations of His Spirit, you should not make these differences prominent. You view the matter from one point; another, just as devoted to God, views the same question from another point, and speaks of the things that make the deepest impression on his mind; another viewing it from a still different point, presents another phase; and how foolish it is to get into contention over these things, when there is really nothing to contend about. Let God work on the mind and impress the heart.

The Lord is constantly at work to open the understanding, to quicken the perceptions, that man may have a right sense of sin and of the far-reaching claims of God's law. The unconverted man thinks of God as unloving, as severe, and even revengeful; His presence is thought to be a constant restraint, His character an expression of "Thou shalt not." His service is regarded as full of gloom and hard requirements. But when Jesus is seen upon the cross, as the gift of God because He loved man, the eyes are opened to see things in a new light. God as revealed in Christ is not a severe judge, an avenging tyrant, but a merciful and loving Father.

As we see Jesus dying upon the cross to save lost man, the heart echoes the words of John, "Behold what manner of love the Father hath bestowed upon us, that we should be called the sons of God: therefore the world knoweth us not, because it knew Him not." There is nothing that more decidedly distinguishes the Christian from the worldly man than the estimate he has of God. (Hebrews 2:16-18; 12:12-15.)

Some workers in the cause of God have been too ready too hurl denunciations against the sinner; the grace and love of the Father in giving His Son to die for the sinful race have been put in the background. The teacher needs the grace of Christ upon his own soul, in order to make known to the sinner what God really is—a Father waiting with yearning love to receive the returning prodigal, not hurling at him accusations in wrath, but preparing a festival of joy to welcome his return. (Zephaniah 3:14-17.)

God's Way of Winning Souls

O that we might all learn the way of the Lord in winning souls to Christ! We should learn and teach the precious lessons in the light that shineth from the sacrifice upon the cross of Calvary. There is but one way that leads from ruin, and continuously ascends, faith all the time reaching beyond the darkness into the light, until it rests upon the throne of God. All who have learned this lesson have accepted the light which has come to their understanding. To them this upward way is not a dark, uncertain passage; it is not the way of finite minds, not a path cut out by human device, a path in which toll is exacted from every traveler.

You cannot gain an entrance by penance nor by any works that you can do. No, God Himself has the honor of providing a way, and it is so complete, so perfect, that man cannot, by any works he may do, add to its perfection. It is broad enough to receive the greatest sinner if he repents, and it is so narrow, so holy, lifted up so high, that sin cannot be admitted there.

When God is seen as He is, the blessed truth shines with a new and clearer light. That which kept the mind in perplexity is cleared away by the bright beams of the Sun of Righteousness. And yet there are many things we shall not comprehend; but we have the blessed assurance that what we know not now, we shall know hereafter.—Letter 15a, 1890.

Chapter 35—Appeal to a Popular Evangelist

By Ellen G. White

God will richly bless those who are humble and sincere, those who are kind and benevolent, who relieve the wants of the widow and the fatherless.

This is an age of extravagance and display. Men think that it is necessary to make a display in order to gain success. But this is not so. Take up your work in the name of Jesus Christ of Nazareth, and show the fallacy of expending means needlessly for effect. Preach and practice economy. Labor with simplicity, humility, and graceful dignity, and your work will make a lasting impression. Trustful dependence on God, earnest prayer to Him for help, obedience to His Word—these are as gold and silver and precious stones brought to the foundation.

Make it stand out with the greatest clearness that all created things are dependent on and under the control of Jehovah, and that as He sees best, He uses them as His instruments for the salvation of those who believe, and as instruments for the destruction of those who harden their-hearts in impenitence.

To Reach Thousands

There are thousands to be reached by the truth. There are thousands who are to receive Christ as a personal Saviour. Greater New York must be worked on an altogether more economical plan than the plan on which you have been working. Christ says, "Whosoever will come after Me, let him deny himself, and take up his cross, and follow Me." Talk the truth, live the truth, walk before God in all humility of mind and in all simplicity of action. Let the angels see that you love God, and that you practice the humility of Christ. This all must do who enter the courts of the Lord. In this life they must walk in the new and precious way that Christ has provided for His followers.

My brother, I write you this at this time because I want you to be prepared to engage in camp meeting work, prepared to speak to thousands, making plain by word and illustration the truths that must be presented. Suffer me to say the things that must be said to you. Hasty decisions, formed under the influence of strong feeling, without time for deliberation or for asking counsel from God, are generally wrong and are often exceedingly unjust.

Cultivate Gentleness

I have the word of the Lord for you. You need to cultivate the gentleness of Christ. Communion with God will give you increased influence for good. Bring humility into your business life and into your religious life. Watch, watch, watch! For the sake of your children, watch!

Unite with your brethren in counsel. Do not, I beg of you, stand apart as a separate whole. Unify! unify! Exercise care to avoid discord and strife. Do not speak words such as I heard you speak when in the night season I was in a council meeting at which you were present. Speak the words that Christ would speak were He in your place.

The Lord is your only safeguard. Fear Him, and tremble at His word. He will manifest Himself to His people as He does not to the world.

Those who claim to believe the truth are to guard carefully the powers of body and mind, so that God and His cause will not be in any way dishonored by their words or actions. The habits and practices are to be brought into subjection to the will of God. We are to give careful attention to our diet.

The Use of Flesh Meats

It has been clearly presented to me that God's people are to take a firm stand against meat eating. Would God for thirty years give His people the message that if they desire to have pure blood and clear minds, they must give up the use of flesh meat, if He did not want them to heed this message?

By the use of flesh meat the animal nature is strengthened and the spiritual nature weakened. Such men as you, who are engaged in the most solemn and important work ever entrusted to human beings, need to give special heed to what they eat.

Remember that when you eat flesh meat, you are but eating grains and vegetables secondhand; for the animal receives from these things the nutrition that makes it grow and prepares it for market. The life that was in the grains and vegetables passes into the animal, and becomes part of its life, and then human beings eat the animal. Why are they so willing to eat their food secondhand?

In the beginning, fruit was pronounced by God as "good for food." The permission to eat flesh meat was a consequence of the fall. Not till after the flood was man given permission to eat the flesh of animals. Why then need we eat flesh meat? Few who eat this know how full it is of disease. Flesh meat never was the best food, and now it is cursed by disease.

The thought of killing animals to be eaten is in itself revolting. If man's natural sense had not been perverted by the indulgence of appetite, human beings would not think of eating the flesh of animals.

Our Relation to Health Reform

We have been given the work of advancing health reform. The Lord desires His people to be in harmony with one another. As you must know, we shall not leave the position in which, for the last thirty-five years, the Lord has been bidding us stand. Beware how you place yourself in opposition to the work of health reform. It will go forward; for it is the Lord's means of lessening the suffering in our world, and of purifying His people.

Be careful what attitude you assume, lest you be found causing division. My brother, even while you fail to bring into your life and into your family the blessing that comes from following the principles of health reform, do not harm others by opposing the light God has given on this subject.

While we do not make the use of flesh meat a test, while we do not want to force anyone to give up its use, yet it is our duty to request that no minister of the conference shall make light of or oppose the message of reform on this point. If, in the face of the light God has given concerning the effect of meat eating on the system, you will still continue to eat meat, you must bear the consequences. But do not take a position before the people that will permit them to think that it is not necessary to call for a reform in regard to meat eating, because the Lord is calling for reform. The Lord has given us the work of proclaiming the message of health reform, and if you cannot step forward in the ranks of those who are giving this message, you are not to make this prominent. In counterworking the efforts of your fellow laborers, who are teaching health reform, you are out of order, working on the wrong side.

Be Like Minded

Christ is our Example. He was next to God in the heavenly courts. But He came to this earth to live among men. "If there be therefore any consolation in Christ, if any comfort of love, if any fellowship of the Spirit, if any bowels and mercies, fulfill ye my joy, that ye be like minded, having the same love, being of one accord, of one mind. Let nothing be done through strife or vainglory; but in lowliness of mind let each esteem other better than themselves. Look not every man on his own things, but every man also on the things of others. Let this mind be in you, which was also in Christ Jesus: who, being in the form of God, thought it not robbery to be equal with God: but made Himself of no reputation, and took upon Him the form of a servant, and was made in the likeness of men: and being found in fashion as a man, He humbled Himself, and became obedient unto death, even the death of the cross. Wherefore God also hath highly exalted Him, and given Him a name which is above every name: that at the name of Jesus every knee should bow, of things in heaven, and things in earth, and things under the earth; and that every tongue should confess that Jesus Christ is Lord, to the glory of God the Father."—Letter 48, 1902.

* * * * *

Divine and Human Agencies in the Work of Saving Souls

Our fidelity to Christian principles calls us to active service for God. Those who do not use their talents in the cause and work of God, will have no part with Jesus in His glory. Light is to shine forth from every soul that is a recipient of the grace of God. There are many souls in darkness, but what rest, and ease, and quietude many feel in this matter!

Thousands enjoy great light and precious opportunities, but do nothing with their influence or their money to enlighten others. They do not even take the responsibility of keeping their own souls in the love of God, that they may not become a burden to the church. Such ones would be a burden and a clog in heaven. For Christ's sake, for the truth's sake, for their own sakes, such should arouse and make diligent work for eternity. Heavenly mansions are preparing for all who will comply with the conditions laid down in the Word of God.

In behalf of the souls for whom Christ has died, who are in the darkness of error, it is enjoined upon all true followers of Christ to be a light to the world. God has done His part in the great work, and is waiting for the co-operation of His followers. The plan of salvation is fully developed.

The blood of Jesus Christ is offered for the sins of the world, the Word of God is speaking to man in counsels, in reproofs, in warnings, in promises, and in encouragement, and the efficacy of the Holy Spirit is extended to help him in all his efforts. But with all this light the world is still perishing in darkness, buried in error and sin.

Messengers of Mercy

Who will be laborers together with God, to win these souls to the truth? Who will bear to them the good tidings of salvation? The people whom God has blessed with light and truth are to be the messengers of mercy. Their means is to flow into the divine channel. Their earnest efforts are to be put forth. They are to become laborers together with God, self-denying, self-sacrificing, like Jesus, who for our sakes became poor, that we through His poverty might be made rich....

Has God enlightened you with a knowledge of Himself? Have the treasures of His Word been opened to your understanding, so that you have become intelligent in regard to the truths therein? Then go to work with your ability. If you are only humble, pure in heart, single in purpose, you will see the needs and wants of God's cause. You will see that there are foreign countries to be visited, that missionaries must go forth with the spirit of self-sacrifice and devotion, to labor, to deny self, to suffer for Christ's sake.

[116]

And even in our own country there are thousands of all nations, and tongues, and peoples who are ignorant and superstitious, having no knowledge of the Bible or its sacred teachings. God's hand was in their coming to America, that they might be brought under the enlightening influence of the truth revealed in His Word, and become partakers of His saving faith. How many have felt any interest for these strangers? How many have been stirred with the spirit of the Master to act as missionaries to those brought, as it were, to our very doors? What will arouse our churches to their true condition of sleepiness and inactivity while souls are perishing within their reach?

Where there is one laborer there ought to be hundreds receiving every word that proceeds out of the mouth of God, and giving it to the people as they can bear it. A hundredfold more might have been done than has been done.

A worldly spirit has prevailed among the professed servants of God, and the souls of men have not been counted of half as much value as their cattle, their farms, and their business. God will hold them accountable for this terrible neglect in the past; but what are they going to do in the future? Will they come into co-operation with our great Benefactor? Will they as men who have had the light of truth, let that light shine forth to those in darkness?

God has honored them with the privilege of being colaborers with Christ in the great harvest field. Will they thankfully, heartily receive all the advantages God has provided, and diligently improve them by exercise, using every ability and every sacred trust in the service of the Master? Their success in advancement in the divine life depends upon the improvement of the talents lent them. Their future reward will be proportioned to the integrity and earnestness with which they serve the Master.—The Review and Herald, March 1, 1887.

Chapter 36—Christ's Lifework and Ours

By Ellen G. White

We read of One who walked this earth in meekness and lowliness, who went about "doing good," who spent His life in loving service, comforting the sorrowing, ministering to the needy, lifting up the bowed down. He had no home in this world, only as the kindness of His friends provided it for Him as a wayfarer. Yet it was heaven to be in His presence. Day by day He met trials and temptations, yet He did not fail or become discouraged. He was surrounded by transgression, yet He kept His Father's commandments. He was always patient and cheerful, and the afflicted hailed Him as a messenger of life and peace and health. He saw the needs of men and women, and to all He gives the invitation, "Come unto Me, all ye that labor and are heavy laden, and I will give you rest. Take my yoke upon you, and learn of Me; for I am meek and lowly in heart: and ye shall find rest unto your souls. For My yoke is easy, and My burden is light."

What an example Christ has left us in His lifework! Who of His children are living as He did, for the glory of God? He is the light of the world, and he who works successfully for the Master must kindle his taper from His divine life.

To His disciples Christ said, "Ye are the salt of the earth: but if the salt have lost his savor, ... it is thenceforth good for nothing, but to be cast out, and to be trodden under foot of men." How careful then we should be to follow the example of Christ in our lifework. Unless we do this, we are worthless to the world—salt which has lost its savor....

God uses a diversity of talents in His cause. He carries on His work for the church by a variety of instruments. No man who desires to make of himself the only teacher in the church is working for God. No one who says, I want my influence only to tell in the church over which I preside, is letting his light shine for God. Those who are uncourteous to their fellow workers must reckon with God. By their influence they keep out of the church the light which God desires His people to have. They manifest a spirit which God does not endorse.

Christ the Pattern

Christ was sent to the world to look after His Father's interests. He is our pattern in all things. The variety of His teaching is a lesson we need to study.

All workers are not alike in their understanding and experience or in their administration of the Word. Some are constantly partaking of Christ's flesh and blood. They eat the leaves of the tree of life. They are constant learners in the school of Christ. They make daily progress in goodness, and gain an experience which fits them to labor for the Master. Their influence is a savor of life unto life. So spiritually minded are they that they readily discern spiritual things. The Bible is their study. Magazines, newspapers, and books which treat of nothing heavenly or divine have no attraction for them. But the Word of God grows constantly more precious to them. God draws near and speaks to them in language which cannot be misunderstood.

[118] There are others who have not learned how to fix their minds so intently upon the Scriptures that they draw from them each day a fresh supply of grace.

Some men have a special message from heaven. They are to be sent forth to waken the people, not to hover over the churches to their own detriment and the hindrance of the work of God. It does a church no good to have two or three ministers waiting upon it. Were these ministers to go forth to labor for those in darkness, their work would show some results. Let the experienced men take the young men who are preparing for the ministry and go forth into new territory to proclaim the message of warning.

Those who believe the truth will be greatly blessed as they impart the blessings God has given them, letting their light shine forth in good works. As they let their light shine by personal piety, by revealing sound principles in all business transactions, they will magnify the principles of God's law. God calls upon His workers to annex new territory for Him. With intense earnestness we are to work for those who are without hope and without God in the world. There are rich fields of toil waiting for the faithful worker.

The laborers in God's cause should bow before Him in humble, earnest prayer, and then go forth, Bible in hand, to arouse the benumbed senses of those represented in the Word as dead in trespasses and sins. Those who do this work will be greatly blessed. Those who know the truth are to strengthen one another, saying to the ministers, "Go forth into the harvest field in the name of the Lord, and our prayers shall go with you as sharp sickles." Thus our churches should bear decided witness for God, and they should also bring Him their gifts and offerings, that those who go forth into the field may have wherewith to labor for souls.

Who is working faithfully for the Master in this age of the world, when the corruption of the earth is even as the corruption of Sodom and Gomorrah? Who is helping those around him to win eternal life? Are we cleansed and sanctified, fit to be used by the Lord as vessels unto honor? Will every church member now remember that deformity is not from God? The Divine Being is to be worshiped in the beauty of holiness; for He is excellent in majesty and power....

God desires His people to show by their lives the advantage of Christianity over worldliness. We are to live so that God can use us in His work of converting men and women and leading them to wash their garments of character and make them white in the blood of the Lamb. We are His workmanship, "created in Christ Jesus unto good works." Through us God desires to reveal His manifold wisdom. Therefore He bids us let our light shine forth in good works.—Manuscript 73a, 1900.

* * * * *

When divine power is combined with human effort, the work will spread like fire in the stubble. God will employ agencies whose origin man will be unable to discern; angels will do a work which men might have had the blessing of accomplishing, had they not neglected to answer the claims of God.—The Review and Herald, December 15, 1885.

Chapter 37—The Attitude in Prayer

By Ellen G. White

I have received letters questioning me in regard to the proper attitude to be taken by a person offering prayer to the Sovereign of the universe. Where have our brethren obtained the idea that they should stand upon their feet when praying to God? One who has been educated for about five years in Battle Creek was asked to lead in prayer before Sister White should speak to the people. But as I beheld him standing upright upon his feet while his lips were about to open in prayer to God, my soul was stirred within me to give him an open rebuke. Calling him by name, I said, "Get down upon your knees." This is the proper position always.

"And He was withdrawn from them about a stone's cast, and kneeled down, and prayed." Luke 22:41.

"Peter put them all forth, and kneeled down, and prayed; and turning him to the body said, Tabitha, arise. And she opened her eyes: and when she saw Peter, she sat up." Acts 9:40.

"They stoned Stephen, calling upon God, and saying, Lord Jesus, receive my spirit. And he kneeled down, and cried with a loud voice, Lord, lay not this sin to their charge. And when he had said this, he fell asleep." Acts 7:59, 60.

"When he had thus spoken, he kneeled down, and prayed with them all." Acts 20:36.

"When we had accomplished those days, we departed and went our way; and they all brought us on our way, with wives and children, till we were out of the city: and we kneeled down on the shore, and prayed." Acts 21:5.

"At the evening sacrifice I arose up from my heaviness; and having rent my garment and my mantle, I fell upon my knees, and spread out my hands unto the Lord my God, and said, O my God, I am ashamed and blush to lift up my face to Thee, my God: for our iniquities are increased over our head, and our trespass is grown up unto the heavens." Ezra 9:5, 6.

"O come, let us worship and bow down: let us kneel before the Lord our maker." Psalm 95:6.

"For this cause I bow my knees unto the Father of our Lord Jesus Christ." Ephesians 3:14. And this whole chapter will, if the heart is receptive, be as precious a lesson as we can learn.

To Bow Down

To bow down when in prayer to God is the proper attitude to occupy. This act of worship was required of the three Hebrew captives in Babylon.... But such an act was homage to be rendered to God alone—the Sovereign of the world, the Ruler of the universe; and these three Hebrews refused to give such honor to any idol, even though composed of pure gold. In doing so, they would, to all intents and purposes, be bowing to the king of Babylon. Refusing to do as the king had commanded, they suffered the penalty, and were cast into the burning fiery furnace. But Christ came in person and walked with them through the fire, and they received no harm.

Both in public and private worship it is our duty to bow down upon our knees before God when we offer our petitions to Him. This act shows our dependence upon God.

At the dedication of the temple, Solomon stood facing the altar. [120] In the court of the temple was a brazen scaffold or platform and after ascending this, he stood and lifted up his hands to heaven, and blessed the immense congregation of Israel, and all the congregation of Israel stood....

"Then said Solomon, The Lord hath said that He would dwell in the thick darkness. But I have built an house of habitation for Thee, and a place for Thy dwelling forever. And the king turned his face and blessed the whole congregation of Israel: and all the congregation of Israel stood. And he said, Blessed be the Lord God of Israel, who hath with His hands fulfilled that which He spake with His mouth to my father David, saying, Since the day that I brought forth My people out of the land of Egypt I chose no city among all the tribes of Israel to build an house in, that My name might be there; neither chose I any man to be a ruler over My people Israel:

but I have chosen Jerusalem, that My name might be there; and have chosen David to be over My people Israel. Now it was in the heart of David my father to build an house for the name of the Lord God of Israel. But the Lord said to David my father, Forasmuch as it was in thine heart to build an house for My name, thou didst well in that it was in thine heart: notwithstanding thou shalt not build the house; but thy son which shall come forth out of thy loins, he shall build the house for My name. The Lord therefore hath performed His word that He hath spoken: for I am risen up in the room of David my father, and am set on the throne of Israel as the Lord promised, and have built the house for the name of the Lord God of Israel. And in it have I put the ark, wherein is the covenant of the Lord, that He made with the children of Israel....

"For Solomon had made a brazen scaffold, of five cubits long, and five cubits broad, and three cubits high, and had set it in the midst of the court: and upon it he stood, and kneeled down upon his knees before all the congregation of Israel, and spread forth his hands toward heaven." 2 Chronicles 6:1-13.

The lengthy prayer which he then offered was appropriate for the occasion. It was inspired of God, breathing the sentiments of the loftiest piety blended with the deepest humility.

A Growing Laxness

I present these proof texts with the inquiry, "Where did Brother -----obtain his education?"—At Battle Creek. Is it possible that with all the light that God has given to His people on the subject of reverence, that ministers, principals, and teachers in our schools, by precept and example teach young men to stand erect in devotion as did the Pharisees? Shall we look upon this as significant of their self-sufficiency and self-importance? Are these traits to become conspicuous?

"And He spake this parable unto certain which trusted in themselves that they were righteous, and despised others: Two men went up into the temple to pray; the one a Pharisee, and the other a publican. The Pharisee stood and prayed thus with himself, God, I thank Thee, that I am not as other men are, extortioners, unjust, adulterers, or even as this publican. I fast twice in the week, I give tithes of all that I possess." Mark you it was the self-righteous Pharisee who was not in a position of humility and reverence before God; but standing in his haughty self-sufficiency, he told the Lord all his good deeds. "The Pharisee stood and prayed thus with himself"; and his prayer reached no higher than himself.

"And the publican, standing afar off, would not lift up so much as his eyes unto heaven, but smote upon his breast, saying, God be merciful to me a sinner. I tell you, this man went down to his house justified rather than the other: for every one that exalteth himself shall be abased; and he that humbleth himself shall be exalted."

We hope that our brethren will not manifest less reverence and awe as they approach the only true and living God than the heathen manifest for their idol deities, or these people will be our judges in the day of final decision. I would speak to all who occupy the place of teachers in our schools. Men and women, do not dishonor God by your irreverence and pomposity. Do not stand up in your Phariseeism and offer your prayers to God. Mistrust your own strength. Depend not in it; but often bow down on your knees before God, and worship Him.

A Token of Complete Subjection

And when you assemble to worship God, be sure and bow your knees before Him. Let this act testify that the whole soul, body, and spirit are in subjection to the Spirit of truth. Who have searched the Word closely for examples and direction in this respect? Whom can we trust as teachers in our schools in America and foreign countries? After years of study shall students return to their own country with perverted ideas of the respect and honor and reverence that should be given to God, and who feel under no obligation to honor the men of gray hairs, the men of experience, the chosen servants of God who have been connected with the work of God through almost all the years of their life? I advise all who attend the schools in America or in any other place, do not catch the spirit of irreverence. Be sure you understand for yourself what kind of education you need that you may educate others to obtain a fitness of character, that will stand the test that is soon to be brought upon all who live upon the earth. Keep company with the soundest Christians. Choose not the pretentious instructors or pupils, but those who show the deepest piety, those who have a spirit of intelligence in the things of God.

"And this is life eternal, that they might know Thee, the only true God, and Jesus Christ whom Thou hast sent." This is the only safe knowledge that students can obtain. The light reading of the Scriptures makes my heart ache. Whilst I am writing I groan in spirit as I see how superficial is the understanding of the Scriptures. There is an abundance of profession of Christianity, but very little practice. Jesus says, I am the Way, the Truth, and the Life. Who will prove themselves wise virgins? Who the foolish virgins who have no oil in their vessels with their lamps? Shall it be as represented—half wise, and half foolish?

On Bended Knee

We are living in perilous times. Seventh-day Adventists are professedly the commandment-keeping people of God; but they are losing their devotional spirit. This spirit of reverence for God teaches men how to approach their Maker—with sacredness and awe through faith, not in themselves, but in a Mediator. Thus man is kept fast, under whatever circumstances he is placed. Man must come on bended knee, as a subject of grace, a suppliant at the footstool of mercy. And as he receives daily mercies at the hand of God, he is ever to cherish gratitude in his heart, and give expression to it in the words of thanksgiving and praise for these unmerited favors. Angels have been guarding his pathway through all his life, and many of the snares he has been delivered from he has not seen. And for this guardianship and watchcare by eyes that never slumber and never sleep, he is to recognize in every prayer the service of God for him.

All should lean upon God in their helplessness and daily necessity. They should keep humble, watchful, and prayerful. Praise and thanksgiving should flow forth in gratitude and sincere love for God.

Witnesses for God

In the assembly of the upright and in the congregation should they praise the Most High God. All who have a sense of their vital connection with God should stand before the Lord as witnesses for

Him, giving expression of the love, the mercies, and the goodness of God. Let the words be sincere, simple, earnest, intelligent, the heart burning with the love of God, the lips sanctified to His glory to make known the mercies of God not only in the assembly of the saints, but to be His witnesses in every place. The inhabitants of the earth are to know that He is God, the only true and living God.

There should be an intelligent knowledge of how to come to God in reverence and godly fear with devotional love. There is a growing lack of reverence for our Maker, a growing disregard of His greatness and His majesty. But God is speaking to us in these last days. We hear His voice in the storm in the rolling thunder. We hear of the calamities He permits in the earthquakes, the breaking forth of waters, and the destructive elements sweeping all before them. We hear of ships going down in the tempestuous ocean. God speaks to families who have refused to recognize Him, sometimes in the whirlwind and storm, sometimes face to face as He talked with Moses. Again He whispers His love to the little trusting child and to the gray-haired sire in his dotage. And earthly wisdom has a wisdom as it beholds the unseen.

When the still small voice which succeeds the whirlwind and the tempest that moves the rocks out of position, is heard, let all cover their face, for God is very near. Let them hide themselves in Jesus Christ; for He is their hiding place. The cleft in the rock is hidden with His own pierced hand while the humble seeker waits in bowed attitude to hear what saith the Lord unto His servant.—Manuscript 84b, 1897.

* * * * *

Prayer Never Inappropriate

There is no time or place in which it is inappropriate to offer up a petition to God.... In the crowds of the street, in the midst of a business engagement, we may send up a petition to God, and plead for divine guidance, as did Nehemiah when he made his request before King Artaxerxes.—Steps to Christ, 103.

* * * * *

We may speak with Jesus as we walk by the way, and He says, I am at thy right hand. We may commune with God in our hearts; we may walk in companionship with Christ. When engaged in our daily labor, we may breathe out our heart's desire, inaudible to any human ear; but that word cannot die away into silence, nor can it be lost. Nothing can drown the soul's desire. It rises above the din of the street, above the noise of machinery. It is God to whom we are speaking, and our prayer is heard.—Gospel Workers, 258.

* * * * *

It is not always necessary to bow upon your knees in order to pray. Cultivate the habit of talking with the Saviour when you are alone, when you are walking, and when you are busy with your daily labor.—The Ministry of Healing, 510, 511.

Chapter 38—Be Earnest and Steadfast

By Ellen G. White

Never was there a time when it is more plainly the duty of the people of God to understand that actions are determined by motives. Those in positions of responsibility are very apt to judge others by themselves. Doing many things that are not in harmony with their profession, they judge others according to their own deviation from righteousness. But as they pronounce judgment upon others, they condemn themselves.

We need now to repent before God. Those who show a repentance that means reconversion will not be left to beat about in the fog of uncertainty and discouragement. He who knocks at the door of mercy and asks forgiveness will receive that for which he asks. The Lord understands the voice of petition. Ask, then; in everything by prayer and supplication let your requests be made known unto God.

"Every one that asketh receiveth; and he that seeketh findeth; and to him that knocketh it shall be opened." Continue to present your requests to God; continue to ask for the blessings which you must receive from His never-failing goodness. Knock at the door of mercy and grace with a sincerity and earnestness which shows that you will continue to knock and seek until your efforts are rewarded by the bestowal of the gifts that are needed by all who perfect a Christian character. Read John 16:32, 33; 15:16, 18-21.

The Conflict of Two Leaders

Here are two opposing elements, with two different leaders. One party is under the control of Satan. He is their captain. Jesus Christ, the only-begotten Son of God, is the leader of the other party. He laid off His royal robe and kingly crown, and clothed Himself with the garment of humanity, that He might stand at the head of the human race, bearing the trials that we must bear, and meeting the temptations that we must meet. The power of the temptations brought against Him was as much greater as He is higher and purer than we are, and yet not for an instant during His sojourn in this earth did He swerve from His loyalty to God. He lived a life pure and undefiled, unmarred by spot or stain of sin. It was in His right to place one hand upon the throne of God in heaven, while with the other He laid hold of fallen human beings, and has raised them from their degradation. To all who receive Him He gives power to become the sons of God.

"Go ye therefore, and teach all nations, baptizing them in the name of the Father, and of the Son, and of the Holy Ghost: teaching them to observe all things whatsoever I have commanded you: and, lo, I am with you alway, even unto the end of the world."

Fanciful Theories Regarding God

Be careful what you teach. Those who are learners of Christ will teach the same things that He taught.

The religious bodies all over Christendom will become more and more closely united in sentiment. They will make of God a peculiar something in order to escape from loyalty to Him who is pure, holy, and undefiled, and who denounces all sin as a production of the apostate. Christ came to counterwork the theories of the great deceiver. In His life, no sin appeared. He could say to His enemies, Which of you convinceth Me of sin? He was in a world of sinful human beings, yet He "did no sin, neither was guile found in His mouth."

No requirement is laid upon man that Christ has not obeyed. We can overcome as He overcame, if we will avail ourselves of the help of the three great powers of heaven, who are waiting to answer the demand made upon them by God's people for power to defeat satanic agencies.

"Sanctify them through Thy truth; Thy Word is truth." Christ's teachings are truth. Those who surrender their wills to the divine guidance will be protected from Satan's snares. Draw nigh to God in your helplessness, and He will draw nigh to you. He will lift up for you a standard against the enemy.

"As Thou hast sent Me into the world, even so have I also sent them into the world. And for their sakes I sanctify Myself, that they also might be sanctified through the truth."

Let not the theory be presented that God would dwell in the soul-temple of a wicked man. No greater falsehood could be presented.

"Neither pray I for these alone, but for them also which shall believe on Me through their word; that they all may be one; as Thou, Father, art in Me, and I in Thee, that they also may be one in us."

Distinct Personalities

These words present God and Christ as two distinct personalities.

Christ prays that a pure, holy love may bind His followers to Himself, and to the Father, that this close fellowship may be a sign that God loves as His own Son those who believe in Him.

Still the Son of God urges His petition to His Father, Read John 17:24-26.

Let no man claim that the subjects of the enemy are the temples of God. Read 1 Corinthians 6:9-20.

The Lord is speaking through His apostle to those who claim to be Christians. He is not speaking to those who have made no profession of righteousness. We are to make no concessions to the enemy. We are not to change one principle of the truth that we have received from God. We cannot hold converse with those who are in league with evil angels. Christ never purchased peace by compromise.—Manuscript 181, 1905.

* * * * *

New Glories of the Word of God

In the Scriptures thousands of gems of truth lie hidden from the surface-seeker. The mine of truth is never exhausted. The more you search the Scriptures with humble hearts, the greater will be your interest, and the more you will feel like exclaiming with Paul: "O the depth of the riches both of the wisdom and knowledge of God! how unsearchable are His judgments, and His ways past finding out!"

Every day you should learn something new from the Scriptures. Search them as for hid treasures, for they contain the words of eternal life. Pray for wisdom and understanding to comprehend these holy writings. If you would do this, you would find new glories in the Word of God; you would feel that you had received new and precious light on subjects connected with the truth, and the Scriptures would be constantly receiving a new value in your estimation.—Testimonies for the Church 5:266.

Chapter 39—Brace Your Souls for Action

By Ellen G. White

I ask the believers in Los Angeles to seek for a deeper, higher experience in the things of God. The Father seeketh such to worship Him. Arise, and brace your souls for action. Take an extensive survey of the work that is to be done. Read your Bibles with an increasing determination to have a larger experience in the things of God. Stand in the light of the Sun of Righteousness.

What could induce the pure, sinless Son of God to tabernacle with men in a world filled with crime and strife and wickedness. He did this that He might better reach the lost and perishing. He suffered, being tempted. Proportionate to the perfection of His holiness was the strength of the temptation. Because of the depravity so revolting to His purity, His residence in the world was a perpetual sorrow. On every hand He saw men and women destroying themselves by yielding to perverted appetite and passion.

Christ gave His life for the life of the world. He came to this earth in the likeness of man, to present before human beings an example of the character that all must form in order to be saved. He came to bring them power to overcome all the temptations of the enemy.

O that every soul might be awakened, and led to become a subject of the heavenly kingdom, surrendering all to Christ. The Word of God gives us no encouragement that a sinner is pardoned in order that he may continue in sin. He is pardoned on condition that he receives Christ, confessing and repenting of his sin, and becoming renewed. Many who pass under the name of Christian are not converted. Conversion means renovation. The sinner must enter into the renovating process for himself. He must come to Jesus. He must give up the wrong habits in which he has indulged. He must bring his unsubdued, un-Christlike tendencies under the control of Christ, else he cannot be made a laborer together with God. Christ works, and the sinner works. The life of Christ becomes the life of the human agent. It is through the renewing power of the divine Spirit that man is fashioned into a perfect man in Christ.

By the character that he is forming, every man is deciding his future destiny. In the books of heaven is made the record. There the character is photographed. There is seen a picture of the unclothed soul.

The promise is given, "As many as received Him, to them gave He power to become the sons of God, even to them that believe on His name." It is the striving souls who receive the assistance of heaven, and partake of its elements. It is by test and trial that the followers of Christ are fitted to dwell with Him in the heavenly courts.—Letter 161, 1905.

*****

Work in the Cities

The importance of making our way in the great cities is still kept before me. For many years the Lord has been urging upon us this duty, and yet we see but comparatively little accomplished in our great centers of population. If we do not take up this work in a determined manner, Satan will multiply difficulties which will not be easy to surmount. We are far behind in doing the work that should have been done in these long-neglected cities.

Barriers Broken Down

The work will now be more difficult than it would have been a few years ago. But if we take up the work in the name of the Lord, barriers will be broken down, and decided victories will be ours.

In this work physicians and gospel ministries are needed. We must press our petitions to the Lord, and do our best, pressing forward with all the energy possible to make an opening in the large cities. Had we in the past worked after the Lord's plans, many lights would be shining brightly that are going out.

Work for Laymen in Cities

In connection with the presentation of spiritual truth, we should also present what the Word of God says upon the questions of health and temperance. In every way possible, we must seek to bring souls under the convincing and converting power of God. The believers in our churches need to be aroused to act their part. Let seasons of prayer be appointed, and let us earnestly seek the Lord for an increase of faith and courage. Let ministers and other church members labor for souls as never before. We are not to spend our time merely in repeating over and over again the same things to the churches where the truth is well known. Let the church members labor unitedly in their several lines to create an interest. The disciples of Christ are to unite in labor for perishing souls. Let the laborers invite others to unite with them in their efforts, that many may be fired with zeal to work for the Master.

I entreat of the church members in every city that they lay hold upon the Lord with determined effort for the baptism of the Holy Spirit. Be assured that Satan is not asleep. Every obstacle possible he will place in the way of those who would advance in this work. Too often these obstacles are regarded as insurmountable. Let everyone now be soundly and truly converted, and then lay hold of the work intelligently and with faith.—Letter 148, 1909.

* * * * *

Growing in Grace

No Christian reaches the highest point of attainment that overloads himself with worries about this world or in carrying his pet sins along with him. We can and should breathe a purer atmosphere and taste more heavenly joys. We need Jesus every day and with His strength we may gain strength, yes, grow in grace for heavier conflicts and obtain inspiring views of heavenly things. The pierced hand of our divine Master holds the signal for us to come up higher. "This one thing I do, forgetting those things which are behind, and reaching forth unto those things which are before, I press toward the mark for the prize of the high calling of God in Christ Jesus." O that we might arise and shine, for our light has come and the glory of the Lord hath arisen upon us. The more closely we copy the Pattern the more wisdom and intelligence we will have of His matchless loveliness.—Manuscript 10, 1889.

Chapter 40—A Variety of Gifts

By Ellen G. White

Last night I seemed to be in an assembly of men who had been entrusted with large and important responsibilities. There were ministers present, and all seemed to be filled with apprehension for the future. After prayer had been offered, the cases of canvassers who had been appropriating means from the treasury instead of bringing means into it, were considered with much sorrow, and some counsel was offered as to the best way of dealing with those who were proving unfaithful to their trust.

When other grave matters had been presented, I arose and said, For a long time I have been pressed under the burden of the fact that we are not elevating the standard as we should. New fields are continually opening, and the third angel's message must be proclaimed to all kindreds, nations, tongues, and peoples.

We must not feel that we are compelled to hover over churches who have received the truth. We are not to spend our time doing detail work, but are to educate others, teaching them how to labor in right lines. We must not encourage the people to depend on ministerial help and labor to preserve spiritual life. Everyone who has received the truth must go to God for his individual self, and decide to live by every word that proceedeth out of the mouth of God, and do true service for God. Those who have embraced the third angel's message must not make man their trust, depending upon the ministers to make their experience for them. They are to secure an individual experience by looking to God for themselves.

"Have Root in Yourselves"

Let the people of God have root in themselves, because they are planted in Jesus Christ. There must be no strife for supremacy. Let everyone seek God for himself, and know for himself that the truth of God is the sanctifier of soul, life, and character. Service to God is an individual responsibility. Let all feel that it is their duty and privilege to bear their testimony in the church, speaking of those things which will edify. No one should try to sermonize. No one should speak in a way that savors in the least of self-exaltation, or raise questions that will cause dissension. Let each one present lessons from the life of Christ, and reveal none of self but all of Jesus.

Let ministers and responsible men impress the individual members of the church that in order to grow in spirituality they must take the burden of the work which the Lord has laid upon them—the burden of leading souls into the truth. Let them teach the people that they should have a strong desire to see those not in the faith converted to the truth. Let those who have opportunity do their God-given work. Those who are not fulfilling their responsibility should be visited, prayed with, and labored for, that they may become faithful stewards of the grace of Christ. Do not lead the people to depend upon you as ministers, but teach every one who shall embrace the truth that he has a work to do in using the talents God has given him to save the souls of those who are nigh him. In thus working, the people will have the co-operation of the angels of God. They will obtain a valuable experience which will increase their faith and give them a strong hold of God.

Pray for the Laborers

Let everyone do all in his power to help both by his means and by his prayers to carry the burden for the souls for whom the ministers are laboring. Earnest prayer sent up to God for His blessing upon the laborers in the field will follow the laborers as sharp sickles into the harvest field. When the people thus pray for the work, they will not be selfish. They will seek to answer their own prayers by corresponding works. They will not hold the minister preaching to them, but will say to him, Go and carry the truth so precious to us to those who are in error, and our prayers will go with you. This will be a valuable experience to every member of the church.

In Humanity and Weakness

The messengers God sends to the people must not permit the people to attach themselves to them. They must ever keep Jesus Christ before their congregations as the One in whom all their hopes of eternal life are centered.

In every messenger whom the Lord uses there must be humility, meekness, and lowliness of mind.... Self must not seek for recognition. There should be no striving to be first. Self must be hid with Christ in God. Self must die, and Christ must live in the soul.

Call for Action

The laborers must learn to bear a firm, decided testimony, in humility of mind. The truth [must be] unadulterated with cheap matters which are never a help, but always a hindrance to the truth. Carry the people upward and forward positively, step by step, from strength to strength, to the firm foundation of sound Bible doctrine. The laborers should have an intense interest in their work, and as they advance, call for decided action. While the spirit of conviction rests upon the hearts of the people, fasten upon their minds the importance of deciding for and living out the truth. While they are obtaining gems of truth, lead them out to give practical expression to their faith and their gratitude for every ray of light. Let them see that the truth is a living reality to those who are holding forth the words of life. Impress upon them the importance of walking in the light that shines upon them from the Word of God.

The workers in the cause of God are to hold themselves continually under the bright rays of the Sun of Righteousness. They are to pray much, opening their hearts to receive the Holy Spirit into the life and character. Then they will manifest His holy influence in their life practice. They are not to feel that it is their prerogative to work the Holy Spirit. The Holy Spirit is to work them, mold them out of self, away from hereditary and cultivated tendencies, and fashion them into the image of Christ's mind and ways. The workers must present with long patience, line upon line, precept upon precept, the duty of the people to be earnest workers.

Religion in the Home

They are to point out the duty of parents to teach their little ones the truth as it is in Jesus, that in their simplicity the children may present to their associates that which they have learned.... The home is to be an educating school where parents are to do their work in perfecting the characters of their children. But parents are asleep. Their children are going to destruction before their eyes, and the Lord would have His messengers present before the people the necessity of home religion. Urge this matter home upon your congregation. Press the conviction of these solemn duties, so long neglected, upon the conscience. This will break up the spirit of Pharisaism and resistance to the truth as nothing else can. Religion in the home is our great hope, and makes the prospect bright for the conversion of the whole family to the truth of God.

Will not our ministers wrestle in earnest prayer for the holy unction, that they may not bring unimportant, unessential things into their labor at this important time? Let them not bring into their ministerial labors only that which can be heard in any of the denominational churches. Let them ever keep an uplifted Saviour before their hearers, in order to prevent their converts from attaching themselves to the man, to bear his mold, and copy his ways in their manner of conversation and conduct.

Workers in Many Lines to Blend

The Lord has a variety of workers who must impress the people in various lines. One man's mind and one man's manner or ways are not to be regarded as perfect, to be imitated exclusively. Christ is our model.

This Scripture is to be understood: "And He gave some, apostles; and some, prophets; and some, evangelists; and some, pastors and teachers." These different workers are each to do a special work; but are they to separate themselves from their fellow laborers, confining their labors to a few whom they think they have succeeded in bringing to a knowledge of the truth? Shall one say to another of the instrumentalities of God, Leave these souls to me to work with, and to bring to perfection of the faith? Let me work for them and train and educate them to perfection of faith and character?

No, this is not the way the Lord works. The one who thus thinks and thus acts is himself deficient in character. He has some strong points, and can work in certain lines; but in other lines he is weak. Other human agencies are needed whom the Holy Spirit shall guide to act their part in completing the work. No man is complete in or through any other man. It is not any one man's gift that accomplishes the work essential. It is the Holy Spirit that works the man. Human agents of diverse gifts are needed.

By the Power of the Spirit

One man cannot carry through any work and make it complete himself, unless no other worker is available; then the Holy Spirit supplies the deficiencies of the worker. But because a measure of success attends his labors, let him not suppose that it is his methods and capabilities which have done the work; for this idea will often bring defeat. Let not men flatter themselves and take to themselves the credit of doing wonderful things; for they are weak and feeble in doing even their best. The Holy Spirit is the worker, and if the human instrument is a close student of his Bible, seeking to know the light and to walk in it, thus learning daily of Jesus, the Holy Spirit will use him as a means of communicating the Word while the Holy Spirit Himself works the heart.

All those who hold forth the Word of Life, whether they be apostles, prophets, evangelists, pastors, or teachers, have a part to act in the work of the perfection of the saints, wherever they may be. They are all to work together harmoniously.

[Read Ephesians 4:12-16.]

Begin at the Heart

To every man is given his work. One man may not be able to do the work for which another man has been trained and educated. But the work of every man must begin at the heart, not resting in a theory of the truth. The work of him who surrenders the soul to God and co-operates with divine agencies will reveal an able, wise workman, who discerns how to adapt himself to the situation. The root must be holy, or there will be no holy fruit. All are to be workers together with God. Self must not become prominent. The Lord has entrusted talents and capabilities to every individual, and those who are most highly favored with opportunities and privileges to hear the Spirit's voice are under the heaviest responsibility to God.

Those who are represented as having but one talent have also their work to do. By trading, not with pounds, but with pence, they are diligently to employ their ability, determined not to fail or be discouraged. They are to ask in faith, and depend upon the Holy Spirit to work upon unbelieving hearts. If they depend upon their own capabilities, they will fail. Those who faithfully trade upon the one talent will hear the gracious commendations spoken to them with as much heartiness as to those who have been gifted with many talents, and who have wisely improved them, "Well done, thou good and faithful servant; thou hast been faithful over a few things, I will make thee ruler over many things."

It is the spirit of humility in which the work is done which God regards. He who had but one talent had an influence to exert, and his work was needed. In perfecting his own character, in learning in the school of Christ, he was exerting an influence that helped to perfect the character of those who had larger responsibilities, who were in danger of building themselves up, and of neglecting some important little things, which that faithful man with his one talent was regarding with diligent care....

God Honors the Humble Worker

There should be no murmuring or complaining among the workers, when one who moves in a humble position is appointed to work with them, who are looked upon as more capable. They may suppose this humble worker incapable of co-operating with them; but in this they may be greatly in error. It is essential that they learn the lesson of humility and contrition, and become capable of blending in unity with any of God's workers, doing their best under all circumstances, believing that God alone can water the seed sown. In thus doing they will double their influence; for when duty is done with fidelity, and faithful diligence is manifested by the worker, it is evident that he bears the test and pruning of God; and the Lord requires nothing more. That man who thinks himself least the Holy Spirit assists most.—Manuscript 21, 1894.

[131] **Chapter 41—A Perfect Service Required By God**

By Ellen G. White

Everything that God could do was done to save a perishing world. "God so loved the world, that He gave His only-begotten Son, that whosoever believeth in Him should not perish, but have everlasting life." God has made it impossible for it to be said that He could have done more than He has done for the fallen race. When He gave His Son, He gave Himself. In one great gift He poured out the whole treasure of heaven. He has revealed a love that defies all computation, a love that should fill our hearts and lives with gratitude.

Christ loves human beings, and He died to save them. At an infinite price He ransomed them from the power of the enemy. He invites them to become members of the royal family, children of the heavenly King. He desires to see them prepared to receive the crown of life. He longs to bestow on them the eternal riches. He came to restore in them the image of Divinity. He calls upon those who have accepted Him to join Him in this work. He has chosen us as His instruments. By us He desires to carry out His merciful purposes. He says, You are laborers together with Me. Shall we not co-operate with Him in His great plan, working earnestly to save His blood-bought heritage?

Proper Use of the Voice

He has given us grand and solemn truths to impart to those who are in darkness. Let us not mar these truths by imperfect utterance. God has given us voices that we may speak His truth. He desires that the music of the voice shall aid in impressing His word upon minds.

We should train ourselves to take deep, full inspirations, and to speak clearly and distinctly. The voice should not be dropped at the end of a sentence, so that the closing words are hardly audible.

Those who open the oracles of God to the people should improve in their manner of communicating the truth, that it may be presented to the world in an acceptable way. Place proper emphasis upon the words that should be made impressive. Speak slowly. Let the voice be as musical as possible.

Seek for Perfection

God desires His ministers to seek for perfection, that they may be vessels unto honor. They are to be controlled by the Holy Spirit; and when they speak, they are to show an energy proportionate to the importance of the subject they are presenting. They are to show that the power about which they speak has made a change in their lives. When they are truly united with Christ, they will give the heavenly invitation with an earnestness that will impress hearts. As they manifest zeal in proclaiming the gospel message, a corresponding earnestness will be produced in the hearers, and lasting impressions for good will be made.

The greater the influence of the truth upon us, the greater will be our earnestness in seeking for perfection in our manner of imparting truth.

An Increase of Vitality

Sin brings physical and spiritual disease and weakness. Christ has made it possible for us to free ourselves from this curse. The Lord promises, by the medium of truth, to renovate the soul. The Holy Spirit will make all who are willing to be educated able to communicate the truth with power. It will renew every organ of the body, that God's servants may work acceptably and successfully. Vitality increases under the influence of the Spirit's action. Let us, then, by this power lift ourselves into a higher, holier atmosphere, that we may do well our appointed work.

By constant obedience those who are born again are fitted for service. The entire being is to be placed under the molding, fashioning hand of God, that physical, mental, and spiritual perfection may be attained. Christians are to grow to the full stature of men and women in Christ.

Counsel Regarding Prayer

The Lord desires His servants to improve in their manner of praying. He inquires, Where is the vivifying influence of your prayers? He does not accept the tame, lifeless, lengthy prayers which are so destitute of His Spirit. He calls for a reformation, else He will remove the candlestick out of its place. He desires the candle to burn brightly, sending forth light to all parts of the world. When the church turns fully to the Lord, lifeless, spiritless prayers will no more be heard.

I urge my ministering brethren to improve in their manner of praying. This can and must be done. I must say to them, The shorter you make your spiritless prayers, the better will it be for the congregation. It is generally the case that the less of heaven's vitality there is in a prayer, the more lengthy it is. Do not spend a long time in prayer before a congregation unless you know that God is inditing the prayer. Let the prayers made in public be short and full of earnestness. The effectual, fervent prayer of a righteous man availeth much; but the prayer uttered in a low, monotonous tone and spiritless manner is not accepted by God. The voice of prayer should rise to God from hearts burdened by a sense of need. Let there be a revival of the Holy Spirit, that your prayers may be filled with the power of heaven.

Learn to seek the Lord most earnestly for power to reach sinners. Heed the message God has sent to His church of today. [Read Revelation 3:15-18.]

The Lord calls for those in His service to make all the improvement He has made it possible for them to make. The truth in our possession is of infinite importance. How essential, then, that it should lose none of its power in passing from us to those who are in darkness. It should not be bereft of its luster by our inefficiency. Our expression of God's wondrous loving-kindness, frame our words as we may, will be tame enough as it falls from our lips. But when, with sanctified lips, we offer praise for God's love, hearts are reached. Let us pray that the wondrous message of Christ's love may reach hearts. Let us watch for the Lord more earnestly than they that watch for the morning. Let us hope in Him and walk in His ways. He is well pleased when His servants work with implicit faith in Him, asking Him to supply all their needs.

Importunate, Prevailing Prayer

From the experience of Jacob we may learn the power of importunate prayer. [Read Patriarchs and Prophets, 196, 197.]

Jacob prevailed because he was persevering and determined. His experience testifies to the power of importunate prayer. It is now that we are to learn this lesson of prevailing prayer, of unyielding faith. The greatest victories to the church or to the individual Christian are not those that are gained by talents or education, by wealth, or the favor of men; they are those victories that are gained in the audience chamber with God, when earnest, agonizing faith lays hold upon the mighty arm of power.

We can do nothing of ourselves. In our helpless unworthiness we must trust in the merits of the crucified and risen Saviour. None will ever perish while they do this. The long, black catalog of our delinquencies is before the eye of the Infinite. The register is complete; none of our offenses are forgotten. But He who listened to the cries of His servants of old, will hear the prayer of faith, and pardon our transgressions. He has promised, and He will fulfill His word.—The Review and Herald, January 14, 1902.

* * * * *

Angels Are Amazed

Angels are amazed that men regard so lightly and indifferently the vital truths which mean so much to the sinner, and continue willing subjects under the captivity of Satan and sin, when so much has been endured in the divine person of the Son of God. O that we may cultivate habits of contemplation, of the self-denial and self-sacrifice of the life of Christ, until we shall have a deep sense of the aggravating character of sin; and hate it as the vile thing it is.

Let the mind awaken to gratitude that through Christ Jesus, the Father is faithful to fulfill the promise to forgive all sin. His mercy and His love are forever an assurance as we look upon Christ uplifted upon the cross of Calvary. Will we individually rise to the appreciation as far as we have capacity to comprehend the truth, that God Jehovah, loves and forgives us if we believe in and love Jesus?

O what a glorious truth! God is waiting to forgive all who come unto Him with repentance. Preach it. Lift up Jesus high that the people may behold Him. Let the salvation of the souls of men, women, and children be the great aim and purpose of our labor....

The Jews saw in the sacrificial offerings the symbol of Christ whose blood was shed for the salvation of the world. All these offerings were to typify Christ and to rivet the great truth in their hearts that the blood of Jesus Christ alone cleanseth from all sin, and without the shedding of blood there is no remission of sins. Some wonder why God desired so many sacrifices and appointed the offering of so many bleeding victims in the Jewish economy.

Every dying victim was a type of Christ, which lesson was impressed on mind and heart in the most solemn sacred ceremony, and explained definitely by the priests. Sacrifices were explicitly planned by God Himself to teach this great and momentous truth, that through the blood of Christ alone there is forgiveness of sins.

This grand and saving truth is oft repeated in the hearing of believers and unbelievers, and yet it is with amazement that angels behold the indifference on men to whom these truths mean so much. How little is evidenced that the church feels the force of the wonderful plan of redemption. How few make this truth, that only through faith in the cleansing blood of Jesus Christ there is forgiveness of the sins that cling to human beings like the foul leprosy, a living reality.

What depths of thought should this awaken in every mind. He needed no suffering to atone for Himself. His was a depth of suffering, proportionate to the dignity of His person, and His sinless exalted character.—Letter 43, 1892.

* * * * *

Spasmodic Repentance

"Behold, I stand at the door, and knock: if any man hear My voice, and open the door, I will come in to him, and will sup with him, and he with Me. To him that overcometh will I grant to sit with

Me in My throne, even as I also overcame, and am set down with My Father in His throne."

Some may say, Why is this message sounded so constantly in our ears? It is because you do not thoroughly repent. You do not live in Christ and have Christ abiding in you. When one idol is expelled from the soul, Satan has another prepared to supply its place. Unless you make an entire consecration to Christ and live in communion with Him, unless you make Him your Counselor, you will find that your heart, open to evil thoughts, is easily diverted from the service of God to the service of self.

As Morning Dew

At times you may have a desire to repent. But unless you decidedly reform and put into practice the truths you have learned, unless you have an active, working faith, a faith that is constantly increasing in strength, your repentance is as the morning dew. It will give no permanent relief to the soul. A repentance caused by a spasmodic exercise of the feelings is a repentance that needs to be repented of; for it is delusive. A violent exercise of the feelings, which does not produce in you the peaceable fruits of righteousness, leaves you in a worse state than you were in before.

Every day the tempter will be on your track with some delusive, plausible excuse for your self-serving, your self-pleasing, and you will fall back into your old practices, neglecting the work of serving God, by which you would gain hope and comfort and assurance.

God calls for willing service—a service inspired by the love of Jesus in the heart. God is never satisfied with halfhearted, selfish service. He requires the whole heart, the undivided affections, and a complete faith and trust in His power to save from sin....

God will honor and uphold every truehearted, earnest soul who is seeking to walk before Him in the perfection of the grace of Christ. The Lord Jesus will never leave nor forsake one humble, trembling soul. Shall we believe that God will work in our hearts? that if we allow Him to do so, He will make us pure and holy, by His rich grace qualifying us to be laborers together with Him. Can we with keen, sanctified perception appreciate the strength of the promises of God, and appropriate them to our individual selves, not because we are worthy, but because Christ is worthy, not because we are righteous, but because by living faith we claim the righteousness of Christ in our behalf?—Manuscript 125, 1901.

Chapter 42—Give the Medical Missionary Work Its Place*

By Ellen G. White

I have been given light all along the way in regard to the workings of the cause, and last night some things in regard to the medical missionary work were brought more especially before me.

When health reform was first brought to our notice, about thirty-five years ago, the light presented to me was contained in this scripture, "The Spirit of the Lord God is upon Me; because the Lord hath anointed Me to preach good tidings unto the meek; He hath sent Me to bind up the brokenhearted, to proclaim liberty to the captives, and the opening of the prison to them that are bound; to proclaim the acceptable year of the Lord, and the day of vengeance of our God; to comfort all that mourn; to appoint unto them that mourn in Zion, to give unto them beauty for ashes, the oil of joy for mourning, the garment of praise for the spirit of the heaviness; that they might be called trees of righteousness, the planting of the Lord, that He might be glorified. And they shall build the old wastes, they shall raise up the former desolations, and they shall repair the waste cities, the desolations of many generations."

In the light given me so long ago, I was shown that our own people, those who claimed to believe the present truth, should do this work. How were they to do it? In accordance with the directions Christ gave His twelve disciples, when He called them together, and sent them forth to preach the gospel. "When He had called unto Him His twelve disciples, He gave them power against unclean spirits,

---
*Remarks of Mrs. E. G. White before the General Conference in Battle Creek, April 11, 1901, speaking to a resolution that made provision for the selection of six members of the General Conference Committee, especially to represent the medical missionary work. It will be noted by those familiar with the Testimonies on this subject that several striking sentences or paragraphs were published in later compiled articles. Considering the occasion, these remarks are of interest in their original setting.

to cast them out, and to heal all manner of sickness, and all manner of disease.... These twelve Jesus sent forth, and commanded them, saying, Go not into the way of the Gentiles, and into any city of the Samaritans enter ye not. But go rather to the lost sheep of the house of Israel. And as ye go, preach, saying, The kingdom of heaven is at hand. Heal the sick, cleanse the lepers, raise the dead, cast out devils: freely ye have received, freely give."

The Call for Reform

In the light given me so long ago, I was shown that intemperance would prevail in the world to an alarming extent, and that every one of the people of God must take an elevated stand in regard to reformation in habits and practices. At that time I was eating meat two or three times a day, and I was fainting away two or three times a day. The Lord presented a general plan before me. I was shown that God would give to His commandment-keeping people a reform diet, and that as they received this, their disease and suffering would be greatly lessened. I was shown that this work would progress.

[136]

Teaching Health Principles

Then, in afteryears, the light was given that we should have a sanitarium, a health institution, which was to be established right among us. This was the means God was to use in bringing His people to a right understanding in regard to health reform. It was also to be the means by which we were to gain access to those not of our faith. We were to have an institution where the sick could be relieved of suffering, and that without drug medication. God declared that He Himself would go before His people in this work.

Well, the work has been steadily increasing. The way was opened for our churches to take hold of it. I proclaimed health reform everywhere I went. At our camp meetings I spoke on Sunday afternoons, and I proclaimed the message of temperance in eating, drinking, and dressing. This was the message I bore for years before I left for Australia.

But there were those who did not come up to the light God had given. There were those in attendance at our camp meetings who ate and drank improperly. Their diet was not in harmony with the light God had given, and it was impossible for them to appreciate the truth in its sacred, holy bearing.

So the light has been gradually coming in. Over and over again instruction was given that our health institutions were to reach all classes of people. The gospel of Jesus Christ includes the work of helping the sick. When I heard that Dr. Kellogg had taken up the medical missionary work, I encouraged him with heart and soul, because I knew that only by this work can the prejudice which exists in the world against our faith be broken down.

In Australia we have tried to do all we could in this line. We located in Cooranbong, and there, where the people have to send twenty-five miles for a doctor, and pay him twenty-five dollars a visit, we helped the sick and suffering all we could. Seeing that we understood something of disease, the people brought their sick to us, and we cared for them. Thus we entirely broke down the prejudice in that place.

Here is Battle Creek, with a large church, the members of which are called upon, in the name of the Lord, to go out into the field and help their fellow beings, to bring joy to those in sorrow, to heal the sick, to show men and women that they are destroying themselves.

A Pioneer Work

Medical missionary work is the pioneer work. It is to be connected with the gospel ministry. It is the gospel in practice, the gospel practically carried out. I have been made sorry to see that our people have not taken hold of this work as they should. They have not gone out into the places round about to see what they could do to help the suffering....

This is the work which is to interest the world, which is to break down prejudice, and force itself upon the attention of the world....

I have seen that all heaven is interested in the work of relieving suffering humanity. Satan is exerting all his powers to obtain control over the souls and bodies of men. He is trying to bind them to the wheels of his chariot. My heart is made sad as I look at our churches, which ought to be connected in heart and soul and practice with the medical missionary work.

In Australia we have been wrestling to get a sanitarium established, and a building is now in progress of erection, though not yet completed. The sanitarium work was started in a private dwelling house, and the one in charge of it devoted part of his time to conference work and part of his time to medical work. He was afraid that it would not be possible to pay the rent of the house which had been hired; so in order to help, I rented one room, and Brother Baker rented two. But these rooms were soon needed for patients, and the work has grown so that at the present time several houses are rented for the sanitarium patients and nurses.

[137]

Through this work many souls have accepted the truth. A minister from Tasmania, a wealthy and educated man, came to the sanitarium for treatment, and while there, became interested in the truth. He soon began keeping the Sabbath, and he at once began to help the work with his means.

Whole families have commenced keeping the Sabbath through some of the members coming to the sanitarium for treatment. But I need not say more about this; for you know it. You are not ignorant of it.

I wish to tell you that soon there will be no work done in ministerial lines but medical missionary work. The work of a minister is to minister. Our ministers are to work on the gospel plan of ministering. It has been presented to me that all through America there are barren fields.

Each Member to Work

As I traveled through the South on my way to the Conference, I saw city after city that was unworked. What is the matter? The ministers are hovering over churches which know the truth, while thousands are perishing out of Christ. If the proper instruction were given, if the proper methods were followed, every church member would do his work as a member of the body. He would do Christian missionary work. But the churches are dying, and they want a minister to preach to them. They should be taught to bring a faithful tithe to God, that He may strengthen and bless them. They should be brought into working order, that the breath of God may come to them. They should be taught that unless they can stand alone, without a minister, they need to be converted anew, and baptized anew. They need to be born again.

The barren fields in America have been presented to me. In every city in Michigan there should be a monument erected for God. You have been long in the truth. Had you carried the work forward in the lines in which God intended you to, had you done medical missionary work, trying to heal soul and body, you would have seen hundreds and thousands coming into the truth....

Practical Missionary Work

Go to places where the people have not heard the truth, and live before them the gospel of Jesus Christ. Do among them practical missionary work. Thus many souls will be brought to a knowledge of the truth.

You will never be ministers after the gospel order till you show a decided interest in medical missionary work, the gospel of healing and blessing and strengthening. Come up to the help of the Lord, to the help of the Lord against the mighty powers of darkness, that it be not said of you, "Curse ye Meroz, ... curse ye bitterly the inhabitants thereof; because they came not to the help of the Lord." ...

I knew that the ministers laboring with those who know the truth, tending them like sick sheep, should be out in the field, planting the standard of truth in new places, bringing the sick to their houses, and clothing the naked. Christ says that His righteousness will go before those who do this work, and that the glory of God will be their rereward. But this work is not done by our churches, and the ministers are preaching to those who know the truth, when there are thousands who know nothing of the third angel's message....

Come Into Line

It is because of the directions I have received from the Lord that I have the courage to stand among you and speak as I do, notwithstanding the way in which you may look at the medical missionary work. I wish to say that the medical missionary work is God's work. The Lord wants every one of His ministers to come into line. Take hold of the medical missionary work, and it will give you access to the people. Their hearts will be touched as you minister to their necessities. As you relieve their sufferings, you will find opportunity to speak to them of the love of Jesus....

God will work mightily with His ministers when their hearts are filled with love for the poor lost sheep of the house of Israel. Hunt up the backsliders, those who once knew what religion was, and give them the message of mercy. The story of Christ's love will touch a chord in their hearts. Christ draws human beings to Himself with the cord which God has let down from heaven to save the race. The love of Christ can be measured only when this cord is measured....

Medical missionary work, ministering to the sick and suffering, cannot be separated from the gospel. God help those whose attention has been aroused on this subject to have the mind of Christ, the sympathy of Christ. God help you to remember that Christ was a worker, that He went from place to place healing the sick. If we were as closely connected with Christ as were His disciples, God could work through us to heal many who are suffering.

The Lord bless His people, and enable them to come to a right understanding of His will.—*G. C. B., April 12, 1901.*

No Better Way

From talk given by Mrs. E. G. White, Sabbath, April 20, 1901—"His Wonderful Love."—From The General Conference Bulletin, April 23, 1901.

There is a great work to be done. How shall we reveal Christ? I know of no better way to reveal Him than to go forth as missionaries to our world. I know of no better way than to take hold of the medical missionary work in connection with the ministry. Wherever you go, there begin to work. Take an interest in those around you who need help and light. You may stand and preach to those here who know the truth, you may preach sermon after sermon to them, but they do not appreciate it. Why?—Because they are inactive. Everyone who is able to get out and work should bring to the foundation stone, not hay, wood, or stubble, but gold, silver, and precious stones.—Manuscript 150, 1901.

Chapter 43—How to Open Closed Doors [139]

By Ellen G. White

During the night season I was speaking in a large congregation. We have been instructed by the Lord that the medical missionary work is to be to the work of the third angel's message as the right hand to the body. The right hand is used to open doors through which the body may find entrance. This is the part the medical missionary work is to act. It is to largely prepare the way for the reception of the truth for this time. A body without hands is useless. In giving honor to the body, honor must also be given to the helping hands, which are agencies of such importance that without them the body can do nothing. Therefore the body which treats indifferently the right hand, refusing its aid, is able to accomplish nothing.

In Australia we found that the medical missionary work breaks down prejudice and opens the way for the truth to go with power. And I have now come to America to see if my words will have more power than my letters have had in leading my brethren to a proper appreciation of medical missionary work....

No Other Work So Successful

In new fields no work is so successful as medical missionary work. If our ministers would work earnestly to obtain an education in medical missionary lines, they would be far better fitted to do the work Christ did as a medical missionary. By diligent study and practice, they can become so well acquainted with the principles of health reform, that wherever they go they will be a great blessing to impart information so much needed to the people they meet....

"They shall build the old wastes, they shall raise up the former desolations, and they shall repair the waste cities, the desolations of many generations. And strangers shall stand and feed your flocks, and the sons of the alien shall be your plowmen and your vinedressers. But ye shall be named the Priests of the Lord: men shall call you the Ministers of our God: ye shall eat the riches of the Gentiles, and in their glory shall ye boast yourselves. For your shame ye shall have double; and for confusion they shall rejoice in their portion: therefore in their land they shall possess the double: everlasting joy shall be unto them." ...

A Revelation of Christ's Compassion

Medical missionary work brings to humanity the gospel of release from suffering. It is the pioneer work of the gospel. It is the gospel practiced, the compassion of Christ revealed. Of this work there is great need, and the world is open for it. God grant that the importance of medical missionary work shall be understood, and that new fields may be immediately entered. Then will the work of the ministry be after the Lord's order; the sick will be healed, and poor, suffering humanity will be blessed.

Begin to do medical missionary work with the conveniences which you have at hand. You will find that thus the way will open for you to hold Bible readings. The heavenly Father will place you in connection with those who need to know how to treat their sick ones. Put into practice what you know regarding the treatment of disease. Thus suffering will be relieved and you will have opportunity to break the bread of life to starving souls.

It is the duty of Christians to convince the world that the religion of Christ disrobes the soul of the garments of heaviness and mourning, and clothes it with joy and gladness. Those who receive Christ as a sin-pardoning Saviour are clothed with His garments of light. He takes away their sin and imparts to them His righteousness. Their joy is full.

Who have a better right than Christians to sing songs of rejoicing? Have they not the expectation of being members of the royal family, children of the heavenly King? Is not the gospel good tidings of great joy? When the promises of God are freely and fully accepted, heaven's brightness is brought into the life....

Brings Rays of Heavenly Brightness

The doing of medical missionary work brings rays of heavenly brightness to wearied, perplexed, suffering souls. It is as a fountain opened for the wayworn, thirsty traveler. At every work of mercy, every work of love, angels of God are present. Those who live nearest to heaven will reflect the brightness of the Sun of Righteousness....

This is True Ministry

Read the Scriptures carefully, and you will find that Christ spent the largest part of His ministry in restoring the suffering and afflicted to health. Thus He threw back upon Satan the reproach of the evil which the enemy of all good had originated. Satan is the destroyer; Christ is the restorer. And in our work as Christ's colaborers, we shall have success if we work on practical lines. Ministers, do not confine your work to giving Bible instruction. Do practical work. Seek to restore the sick to health. This is true ministry. Remember that the restoration of the body prepares the way for the restoration of the soul.—Manuscript 55, 1901.

The Right Hand of the Gospel

Medical missionary work is the right hand of the gospel. It is necessary to the advancement of the cause of God. As through it men and women are led to see the importance of right habits of living, the saving power of the truth will be made known. Every city is to be entered by workers trained to do medical missionary work. As the right hand of the third angel's message, God's methods of treating disease will open doors for the entrance of present truth. Health literature must be circulated in many lands. Our physicians in Europe and other countries should awake to the necessity of having health works prepared by men who are on the ground and who can meet the people where they are with the most essential instruction.—Testimonies for the Church 7:59.

* * * * *

Preparing for Service

So great are the world's needs, that not all who are called to be medical missionary evangelists can afford to spend years in preparation before beginning to do actual field work. Soon doors now open to the gospel messenger will be forever closed. God calls upon many who are prepared to do acceptable service, to carry the message now, not waiting for further preparation; for while some delay, the enemy may take possession of fields now open.

I have been instructed that little companies who have received a suitable training in evangelical and medical missionary lines, should go forth to do the work to which Christ appointed His disciples. Let them labor as evangelists, scattering our publications, talking of the truth to those they meet, praying for the sick, and, if need be, treating them, not with drugs, but with nature's remedies, ever realizing their dependence on God. As they unite in the work of teaching and healing, they will reap a rich harvest of souls.

And while God is calling upon young men and women who have already gained a practical knowledge of how to treat the sick, to labor as gospel medical missionaries in connection with experienced evangelical workers, He is also calling for many recruits to enter our medical missionary training schools to gain a speedy and thorough preparation for service. Some need not spend so long a time in these schools as do others. It is not in harmony with God's purpose that all should plan to spend exactly the same length of time, whether three, four, or five years in preparation, before beginning to engage in active field work. Some, after studying for a time, can develop more rapidly by working along practical lines in different places, under the supervision of experienced leaders, than they could by remaining in an institution. As they advance in knowledge and ability, some of these will find it much to their advantage to return to one of our sanitarium training schools for more instruction. Thus they will become efficient medical missionaries, prepared for trying emergencies.—Counsels to Parents, Teachers, and Students, 469, 470.

* * * * *

The stream of living water is to deepen and widen in its course. In all fields, nigh and afar off, men will be called from the plow and from the more common commercial business vocations that largely occupy the mind, and will be educated in connection with men of experience. As they learn to labor effectively, they will proclaim the truth with power.—Life Sketches of Ellen G. White, 415.

The Divine Plan

Our Saviour never used His power to make His own life less taxing. He went about doing good, healing the sick and preaching the gospel. In our work today the ministry of the Word and medical missionary work are to be combined.

Luke is called "the beloved physician." Paul heard of his skill as a physician, and he sought him out as one to whom the Lord had entrusted a special work. He secured his cooperation in his work. After a time he left him at Philippi. Here Luke continued to labor for several years, doing double service as a physician and a gospel minister. He was indeed a medical missionary. He did his part, and then besought the Lord to let His healing power rest upon the afflicted ones. His medical skill opened the way for the gospel message to find access to hearts. It opened many doors for him, giving him opportunity to preach the gospel among the heathen.

Christ's Instruction

Christ understood the work that needed to be done for suffering humanity. As He was sending out the twelve disciples on their first missionary tour, He said to them, "As ye go, preach, saying, The kingdom of heaven is at hand. Heal the sick, cleanse the lepers, raise the dead, cast out devils: freely ye have received, freely give." The fulfillment of this commission by the disciples made their message the power of God unto salvation.

It is the divine plan that we shall work as the disciples worked. Connected with the divine Healer, we may do great good in the world. The gospel is the only antidote for sin. As Christ's witnesses we are to bear testimony to its power. We are to bring the afflicted ones to the Saviour. His transforming grace and miracle-working

[142] power will win many souls to the truth. His healing power, united with the gospel message, will bring us success in emergencies. The Holy Spirit will work upon hearts, and we shall see the salvation of God.

In a special sense the healing of the sick is our work. But in order to do this work, we must have faith—that faith which works by love and purifies the soul.

The Great Teacher delegated power to His servants. "All power is given unto Me in heaven and in earth," He said. "Go ye therefore, and teach all nations, baptizing them in the name of the Father, and of the Son, and of the Holy Ghost: teaching them to observe all things whatsoever I have commanded you: and, lo, I am with you alway, even unto the end of the world."

The lapse of time has wrought no change in Christ's parting promise. He is with us today as He was with the disciples, and He will be with us "unto the end." Christ ordained that a succession of men should proclaim the gospel, deriving their authority from Him, the Great Teacher.

In our work we meet with many discouragements. But we shall not gain a particle of strength by dwelling on the discouragements. By beholding we become changed. As we look in faith to Jesus, His image is engraven on the heart. We are transformed in character.—Letter 134, 1903.

* * * * *

In Time of Persecution

As religious aggression subverts the liberties of our nation, those who would stand for freedom of conscience will be placed in unfavorable positions. For their own sake, they should, while they have opportunity, become intelligent in regard to disease, its causes, prevention, and cure. And those who do this will find a field of labor anywhere. There will be suffering ones, plenty of them, who will need help, not only among those of our own faith, but largely among those who know not the truth. The shortness of time demands an energy that has not been aroused among those who claim to believe the present truth.—Counsels on Health, 506.

* * * * *

Zeal and Perseverance In Medical Missionary Work

Could I arouse our people to Christian effort, could I lead them to engage in medical missionary work with holy zeal and divine perseverance, not in a few places, but in every place, putting forth personal effort for those out of the fold, how grateful I should be! This is true missionary work. In some places it is attended with little success, apparently; but again the Lord opens the way, and signal success attends the effort. Words are spoken which are as nails fastened in a sure place. Angels from heaven co-operate with human instrumentalities, and sinners are won to the Saviour....

Christ has placed upon His church a sacred charge, the fulfilling of which calls for self-denial at every step. When those who believe in Him are seen lifting the cross and bearing it after Him in the path of self-denial, willingly doing all in their power to bring blessing to those for whom Christ died, witness will be borne to the power of Christianity, and in the hearts of many now unbelievers will spring up faith in Him who gave His life to save a guilty world from eternal ruin.—Letter 43, 1903.

Notebook Leaflets from the Elmshaven Library Vol. 2

Ellen G. White

1985

Contents

"Preach the Word" 4
   Let Christ Appear 4
   Righteousness and Love of Christ 4
   The Holy Spirit 5
   Effect of Preaching the Second Advent 6
   Teach Steps in Conversion 6
   The Ministration of Angels 7
   Revival of Old Advent Truths 7
   Eloquent Sermons 7
   Argumentative Sermons 8
   Not Excitement, But Solid Work 8
   Present Truth in the Meekness and Love of Christ 8
   A Device of the Enemy 9
   Mingling Human Suppositions and Conjectures 10
   Our Faith Founded on Truth 10
   The Truths That Have Been Revealed 12
   Questions of Eternal Import 12
   Points Unnecessary for Faith 13
   Our Attitude Toward Doctrinal Controversy 13
   Not a Test Question 15
   No Compromise 17
   A Life and Death Question 18
   Conjectures Regarding the Future Life 19
   Preach the Word 20
   Invitation to the Banquet 21
   The One Hundred and Forty-Four Thousand 21
   Effect of Difference Among Ministers 22

"Preach the Word"

By Ellen G. White

Much valuable instruction pertaining to the work of the ministry has been published from the pen of Ellen G. White. For the benefit of leading evangelists, however, the following passages relating to the subject matter of their discourses has been compiled from the Manuscript and Letter file.—Trustees of the Ellen G. White Estate.

Let Christ Appear

The object of all ministry is to keep self out of sight, and to let Christ appear. The exaltation of Christ is the great truth that all who labor in word and doctrine are to reveal.—Manuscript 109, 1897.

Righteousness and Love of Christ

Laborers in the cause of truth should present the righteousness of Christ, not as new light, but as precious light that has for a time been lost sight of by the people. We are to accept of Christ as our personal Saviour, and He imputes unto us the righteousness of God in Christ. Let us repeat and make prominent the truth that John has portrayed, "Herein is love, not that we loved God, but that He loved us and sent His Son to be the propitiation for our sins." 1 John 4:10.

In the love of God has been opened the most marvelous vein of precious truth, and the treasures of the grace of Christ are laid open before the church and the world. "For God so loved the world that He gave His only begotten Son, that whosoever believeth in Him should not perish, but have everlasting life." John 3:16. What love is this, what marvelous, unfathomable love that would lead Christ to die for us while we were yet sinners. What a loss it is to the soul who understands the strong claims of the law, and who yet fails to understand the grace of Christ which doth much more abound.

It is true that the law of God reveals the love of God when it is preached as the truth in Jesus; for the gift of Christ to this guilty world must be largely dwelt upon in every discourse. It is no wonder that hearts have not been melted by the truth, when it has been presented in a cold and lifeless manner. No wonder faith has staggered at the promises of God, when ministers and workers have failed to present Jesus in His relation to the law of God. How often should they have assured the people that "He that spared not His own Son, but delivered him up for us all, how shall He not with Him also freely give us all things?" Romans 8:32.

Satan is determined that men shall not see the love of God which led Him to give His only begotten Son to save a lost race; for it is the goodness of God that leads men to repentance. O how shall we succeed in setting forth before the world the deep, precious love of God? In no other way can we compass it except by exclaiming "Behold what manner of love the Father hath bestowed upon us, that we should be called the sons of God." 1 John 3:1. Let us say to sinners, "Behold the Lamb of God, which taketh away the sins of the world." John 1:29. By presenting Jesus as the representative of the Father, we shall be able to dispel the shadow that Satan has cast upon our pathway, in order that we shall not see the mercy and inexpressible love of God as manifested in Jesus Christ. Look at the cross of Calvary. It is a standing pledge of the boundless love, the measureless mercy of the heavenly Father.—Manuscript 154, 1897.

[154]

The Holy Spirit

Christ, the great Teacher, had an infinite variety of subjects from which to choose, but the one upon which He dwelt most largely was the endowment of the Holy Spirit. What great things He predicted for the church because of this endowment. Yet what subject is less dwelt upon now? What promise is less fulfilled? An occasional discourse is given upon the Holy Spirit, and then the subject is left for after consideration.—Manuscript 20, 1891.

Effect of Preaching the Second Advent

The second coming of the Son of man is to be the wonderful theme kept before the people. Here is a subject that should not be left out of our discourses. Eternal realities must be kept before the mind's eye, and the attractions of the world will appear as they are, altogether profitless as vanity. What are we to do with the world's vanities, its praises, its riches, its honors, or its enjoyments?

We are pilgrims and strangers who are waiting, hoping and praying for that blessed hope, the glorious appearing of our Lord and Saviour Jesus Christ. If we believe this and bring it into our practical life, what vigorous action would this faith and hope inspire; what fervent love one for another; what careful holy living for the glory of God, and in our respect for the recompense of the reward, what distinct lines of demarcation would be evidenced between us and the world.—Manuscript 39, 1893.

Teach Steps in Conversion

Ministers need to have a more clear, simple manner in presenting the truth as it is in Jesus. Their own minds need to comprehend the great plan of salvation more fully. Then they can carry the minds of the hearers away from earthly things to the spiritual and eternal. There are many who want to know what they must do to be saved. They want a plain and clear explanation of the steps requisite in conversion, and there should not a sermon be given unless a portion of that discourse is to especially make plain the way that sinners may come to Christ and be saved. They should point them to Christ, as did John and with touching simplicity, their hearts aglow with the love of Christ, say, "Behold the Lamb of God, which taketh away the sins of the world." Strong and earnest appeals should be made to the sinner to repent and be converted.

Those who neglect this part of the work need to be converted themselves before venturing to give a discourse. Those whose hearts are filled with the love of Jesus, with the precious truths of His word, will be able to draw from the treasure-house of God things new and old. They will not find time to relate anecdotes; they will not strain to become orators, soaring so high that they cannot carry the people with them; but in simple language, with touching earnestness, they will present the truth as it is in Jesus.—*R. & H., Feb. 22, 1887.*

[155]

The Ministration of Angels

Over every man good and evil angels strive. It is the man himself who determines which shall win. I call upon the ministers of Christ to press home upon the understanding of all who come within the reach of their voice, the truth of the ministration of angels. Do not indulge in fanciful speculations. The written word is our only safety. We must pray as did Daniel, that we may be guarded by heavenly intelligences.—Letter 201, 1899.

Revival of Old Advent Truths

There is a work of sacred importance for ministers and people to do. They are to study the history of the cause and people of God. They are not to forget the past dealing of God with His people. They are to revive and recount the truths that have come to seem of little value to those who do not know by personal experience of the power and brightness that accompanied them when they were first seen and understood. In all their original freshness and power these truths are to be given to the world.—Manuscript Ms 22, 1890.

Eloquent Sermons

The minister may make a high range into the heavens, by poetical descriptions, and fanciful presentations which please the senses and feed the imagination, but which do not touch the common life experience, the daily necessities; bringing home to the heart the very truths which are of vital interest. The immediate requirements, the present trials, need present help and strength,—the faith that works by love and purifies the soul, not words which have no real influence upon the living daily walk in practical Christianity.

The minister may think that with his fanciful eloquence, he has done great things in feeding the flock of God; the hearers may suppose that they never before heard such beautiful themes, they have never seen the truth dressed up in such beautiful language, and as God was represented before them in His greatness, they felt a glow of emotion. But trace from cause to effect all this ecstasy of feeling caused by these fanciful representations. There may be truths, but too often they are not the food that will fortify them for the daily battles of life.—Manuscript 59, 1900.

Argumentative Sermons

The many argumentative sermons preached, seldom soften and subdue the soul.... It should be the burden of every messenger to set forth the fulness of Christ. When the free gift of Christ's righteousness is not presented, the discourses are dry and spiritless; the sheep and lambs are not fed. Said Paul, "My speech and my preaching was not with enticing words of man's wisdom, but in demonstration of the Spirit and of power." There is marrow and fatness in the gospel. Jesus is the living center of everything. Put Christ into every sermon. Let the preciousness, mercy and glory of Jesus Christ be dwelt upon; for Christ formed within is the hope of glory.—Letter 15, 1892.

Not Excitement, But Solid Work

Those who have the outpouring of the gospel of Christ which comes from the heart imbued by His Holy Spirit, will give light and comfort and hope to hearts that are hungering and thirsting for righteousness. It is not excitement we wish to create, but deep, earnest consideration that those who hear shall do solid work, real sound, genuine work that will be enduring as eternity. We hunger not for excitement, for the sensational; the less we have of this, the better. The calm, earnest reasoning from the Scriptures is precious and fruitful. Here is the secret of success, in preaching a living personal Saviour in so simple and earnest a manner that the people may be able to lay hold by faith of the power of the word of life.—Letter 102, 1894.

Present Truth in the Meekness and Love of Christ

Be careful messengers. Do not be anxious to hear and accept new theories; for often they are such as should never be presented before any congregation. Speak no boastful, self-exalting words.

Let the word of God come forth from lips that are sanctified by the truth. Every minister is to preach the truth as it is in Jesus. He should be assured of that which he affirms, and should handle the word of God under the direction of the Holy Spirit of God. Walk and work carefully before God, my brethren, that no soul may be led into deception by your example. It had been better for you never to have been born, than that you should lead one soul astray.

Those who profess to be servants of God need to make diligent work for the obtaining of that life where sin and sickness and sorrow cannot enter. They are to be instant in season and out of season.

God is calling for reformers who will speak strong, uplifting words from our pulpits. It is when men speak their own words in their own strength, instead of preaching the word of God in the power of the Spirit, that they are hurt and offended when their words are not received with enthusiasm. It is then that they are tempted to speak words that will arouse a spirit of bitterness and opposition in their hearers. My brethren, be advised. Such words are not to come from the lips of Christ's ambassadors. Sanctified lips will speak words that reform, but do not exasperate. The truth is to be presented in the meekness and love of Christ.—Letter 348, 1907.

A Device of the Enemy

We are to pray for divine enlightenment, but at the same time we should be careful how we receive everything termed new light. We must beware lest, under cover of searching for new truth, Satan shall divert our minds from Christ and the special truths for this time. I have been shown that it is the device of the enemy to lead minds to dwell upon some obscure or unimportant point, something that is not fully revealed or is not essential to our salvation. This is made the absorbing theme, the "present truth," when all their investigations and suppositions only serve to make matters more obscure than before, and to confuse the minds of some who ought to be seeking for oneness through sanctification of the truth.—Letter 7, 1891.

Mingling Human Suppositions and Conjectures

Let no one present beautiful, scientific sophistries to lull the people of God to sleep. Clothe not the solemn, sacred truth for this time in any fantastic dress of man's wisdom. Let those who have been doing this stop and cry unto God to save their souls from deceiving fables.

It is the living energy of the Holy Spirit that will move hearts, not pleasing, deceptive theories. Fanciful representations are not the bread of life; they can not save the soul from sin.

Christ was sent from heaven to redeem humanity. He taught the doctrines that God gave Him to teach. The truths that He proclaimed, as found in the Old Testament and the New, we today are to proclaim as the word of the living God.

Let those who want the bread of life go to the Scriptures, not to the teaching of finite, erring man. Give the people the bread of life that Christ came from heaven to bring to us. Do not mix with your teaching human suppositions and conjectures. Would that all knew how much they need to eat the flesh and drink the blood of the Son of God,—to make His words a part of their very lives.—Manuscript 44, 1904.

Our Faith Founded on Truth

I long daily to be able to do double duty. I have been pleading with the Lord for strength and wisdom to reproduce the writings of the witnesses who were confirmed in the faith and in the early history of the message. After the passing of the time in 1844, they received the light and walked in the light, and when the men claiming to have new light would come in with their wonderful messages regarding various points of Scripture, we had, through the moving of the Holy Spirit, testimonies right to the point, which cut off the influence of such messages as Elder ----- has been devoting his time to presenting....

When the power of God testifies as to what is truth, that truth is to stand forever as the truth. No after-suppositions, contrary to the light God has given are to be entertained. Men will arise with interpretations of Scripture which are to them truth, but which are not truth. The truth for this time, God has given us as a foundation for our faith. He Himself has taught us what is truth. One will arise, and still another with new light, which contradicts the light that God has given under the demonstration of His Holy Spirit. A few are still alive who passed through the experience gained in the establishment of this truth. God has graciously spared their lives to repeat and repeat till the close of their lives, the experience through which they passed even as did John the apostle till the very close of his life. And the standard bearers who have fallen in death, are to speak through the reprinting of their writings. I am instructed that thus their voices are to be heard. They are to bear their testimony as to what constitutes the truth for this time.

We are not to receive the words of those who come with a message that contradicts the special points of our faith. They gather together a mass of Scripture, and pile it as proof around their asserted theories. This has been done over and over again during the past fifty years. And while the Scriptures are God's Word, and are to be respected, the application of them, if such application moves one pillar from the foundation that God has sustained these fifty years, is a great mistake. He who makes such an application knows not the wonderful demonstration of the Holy Spirit that gave power and force to the past messages that have come to the people of God.

Elder -----'s proofs are not reliable. If received they would destroy the faith of God's people in the truth that has made us what we are.

We must be decided on this subject; for the points that he is trying to prove by Scripture, are not sound. They do not prove that the past experience of God's people was a fallacy. We had the truth; we were directed by the angels of God. It was under the guidance of the Holy Spirit that the presentation of the sanctuary question was given.... God never contradicts Himself. Scripture proofs are misapplied if forced to testify to that which is not true. Another and still another will arise and bring in supposedly great light, and make their assertions. But we stand by the old land marks.... We are hindered in our work by men who are not converted, who seek their own glory. They wish to be thought originators of new theories, which they present claiming that they are truth. But if these theories are received they will lead to a denial of the truth that for the past

[158]

fifty years God has been giving to His people, substantiating it by the demonstration of the Holy Spirit.—*Letter 329, 1905.*

The Truths That Have Been Revealed

"Study to show thyself approved unto God, a workman that needeth not to be ashamed, rightly dividing the word of truth." Learn to take the truths that have been revealed, and to handle them in such a way that they will be food for the flock of God.

We shall meet those who allow their minds to wander into idle speculations about things of which nothing is said in the word of God. God has spoken in the plainest language upon every subject that affects the salvation of the soul. But He desires us to avoid all day-dreaming, and He says, Go work today in my vineyard. The night cometh wherein no man can work. Cease all idle curiosity; watch, and work, and pray. Study the truths that have been revealed. Christ desires to break up all vacant reveries, and He points us to the fields ripe for the harvest. Unless we work earnestly, eternity will overwhelm us with its burden of responsibility....

In the days of the apostles the most foolish heresies were presented as truth. History has been and will be repeated. There will always be those who, though apparently conscientious, will grasp at the shadow, preferring it to the substance. They take error in the place of truth, because error is clothed with a new garment, which they think covers something wonderful. But let the covering be removed, and nothingness appears.—*R. and H., February 5, 1901.*

Questions of Eternal Import

Dwell upon the lessons that Christ dwelt upon. Present them to the people as He presented them. Dwell upon questions that concern our eternal welfare. Anything that the enemy can devise to divert the mind from God's word, anything new and strange that he can originate to create a diversity of sentiment, he will introduce as something wonderfully important. But those things that we cannot clearly comprehend are not a tenth as important to us as are the truths of God's word, that we can clearly comprehend and bring into our daily life. We are to teach the people the lessons that Christ brought into His teachings from the Old Testament Scriptures. The language of divine truth is exceedingly plain.—Letter 16, 1903.

Points Unnecessary for Faith

There are many questions treated upon that are not necessary for the perfection of the faith. We have no time for their study. Many things are above finite comprehension. *Truths are to be received not within the reach of our reason, and not for us to explain.* Revelation presents them to us to be implicitly received as the words of an infinite God. While every ingenious inquirer is to search out the truth as it is in Jesus, there are things not yet simplified, statements that human minds cannot grasp and reason out, without being liable to make human calculation and explanations, which will not prove a savor of life unto life.

[159]

But every truth which is essential for us to bring into our practical life, which concerns the salvation of the soul, is made very clear and positive.

—Letter 8, 1895.

Our Attitude Toward Doctrinal Controversy

I have words to speak to my brethren east and west, north and south. I request that my writings shall not be used as the leading argument to settle questions over which there is now so much controversy. I entreat of Elders -----, -----, -----, and others of our leading brethren, that they make no reference to my writings to sustain their views of "the daily."

It has been presented to me that this is not a subject of vital importance. I am instructed that our brethren are making a mistake in magnifying the importance of the difference in the views that are held. I can not consent that any of my writings shall be taken as settling this matter. The true meaning of "the daily" is not to be made a test question.

I now ask that my ministering brethren shall not make use of my writings in their arguments regarding this question ["the daily"]; for I have had no instruction on the point under discussion, and I see no need for the controversy. Regarding this matter under present conditions, silence is eloquence.

The enemy of our work is pleased when a subject of minor importance can be used to divert the minds of our brethren from the great questions that should be the burden of our message. As this is not a test question, I entreat of my brethren that they shall not allow the enemy to triumph by having it treated as such.

The work that the Lord has given us at this time is to present to the people the true light in regard to the testing questions of obedience and salvation,—the commandments of God and the testimony of Jesus Christ.

In some of our important books that have been in print for years, and which have brought many to a knowledge of the truth, there may be found matters of minor importance that call for careful study and correction. Let such matters be considered by those regularly appointed to have the oversight of our publications. Let not these brethren, nor our canvassers, nor our ministers magnify these matters in such a way as to lessen the influence of these good soul-saving books. Should we take up the work of discrediting our literature, we would place weapons in the hands of those who have departed from the faith, and confuse the minds of those who have newly embraced the message. The less that is done unnecessarily to change our publications, the better it will be.

In the night seasons I seem to be repeating to my brethren in responsible positions, words from the first epistle of John. [Chapter 1 is quoted.]

Our brethren should understand that self needs to be humbled, and brought under the control of the Holy Spirit. The Lord calls upon those of us who have had great light to be converted *daily*. This is the message I have to bear to our editors and to the presidents of all our conferences. We must walk in the light while we have the light, lest darkness come upon us.

All who are led by the Holy Spirit of God will have a message for this last time. With mind and heart they will be carrying a burden for souls, and they will bear the heavenly message of Christ to those with whom they associate. Those who in speech act as the Gentiles act, can not be introduced into the heavenly courts. My brethren, receive the light, redeeming the time because the days are evil.

Satan is busily working with all who will give him encouragement. Those who have the light, but refuse to walk in it, will become confused, until darkness pervades their souls, and shapes their whole course of action. But the spirit of wisdom and goodness of God as revealed in His word, will become brighter and brighter as they follow on in the path of true obedience. All the righteous demands of God will be met through sanctification of the Holy Spirit ....

There are great privileges and blessings for all who will humble themselves, and fully consecrate their hearts to God. Great light will be given to them. When men are willing to be transformed, then they will be exercised unto godliness.

"And of His fulness have all we received, and grace for grace." "My grace is sufficient for thee: for My strength is made perfect in weakness." Says the Saviour: "All power is given unto Me in heaven and in earth. Go ye therefore, and teach all nations, baptizing them in the name of the Father, and of the Son, and of the Holy Ghost: teaching them to observe all things whatsoever I have commanded you: and lo, I am with you alway, even unto the end of the world."

Shall this wealth of grace and power for service continue among us to be unappreciated and turned from, without relish or appetite?

The instruction I am bidden to give to our people now is the same as I gave while in Washington. The Lord calls for individual effort. One can not do the work of another. Great light has been shining, but it has not been fully comprehended and received.

If our brethren will now consecrate themselves, unreservedly to God, He will accept them. He will give them a transformation of mind, that they may be savors of life unto life. Wake up, brethren and sisters, that you may attain to your high calling through Christ Jesus our Lord.—Manuscript 11, 1910.

Not a Test Question

To My Brethren in the Ministry:
Dear Fellow-workers,

I have words to speak to...all who have been active in urging their views in regard to the meaning of "the daily" of Daniel 8. This is not to be made a test question, and the agitation that has resulted from its being treated as such has been very unfortunate. Confusion has resulted, and the minds of some of our brethren have been diverted from the thoughtful consideration that should have been given to the work that the Lord has directed should be done at this time in our cities. This has been pleasing to the great enemy of our work.

The light given me is that nothing should be done to increase the agitation upon this question. Let it not be brought into our discourses, and dwelt upon as a matter of great importance. We have a great work before us, and we have not an hour to lose from the essential work to be done. Let us confine our public efforts to the presentation of the important lines of truth on which we are united, and on which we have clear light.

[161] I would bring to your attention the last prayer of Christ, as recorded in John 17. There are many subjects upon which we can speak,—sacred, testing truths, beautiful in their simplicity. On these you may dwell with intense earnestness. But let not "the daily," or any other subject that will arouse controversy among brethren, be brought in at this time; for this will delay and hinder the work that the Lord would have the minds of our brethren centered upon just now. Let us not agitate questions that will reveal a marked difference of opinion, but rather let us bring from the Word the sacred truths regarding the binding claims of the law of God.

Our ministers should seek to make the most favorable presentation of truth. So far as possible, let all speak the same things. Let the discourses be simple, and treating upon vital subjects that can be easily understood. When all our ministers see the necessity of humbling themselves, then the Lord can work with them. We need now to be reconverted, that angels of God may cooperate with us, making a sacred impression upon the minds of those for whom we labor.

We must blend together in the bonds of Christ-like unity; then our labors will not be in vain. Draw in even cords, and let no contentions be brought in. Reveal the unifying power of truth, and this will make a powerful impression on human minds. In unity there is strength.

This is not a time to make prominent unimportant points of difference. If some who have not had a strong living connection with the Master, reveal to the world their weakness of Christian experience, the enemies of the truth who are watching us closely will make the most of it, and our work will be hindered. Let all cultivate meekness, and learn lessons from Him who is meek and lowly in heart.

The subject of "the daily" should not call forth such movements as have been made. As a result of the way this subject has been handled by men on both sides of the question, controversy has arisen and confusion has resulted.... While the present condition of difference of opinion regarding this subject exists, let it not be made prominent. Let all contention cease. At such a time silence is eloquence.

The duty of God's servants at this time is to preach the Word in the cities. Christ came from the heavenly courts to this earth in order to save souls, and we, as almoners of His grace, need to impart to the inhabitants of the great cities, a knowledge of His saving truth.—Letter 62, 1910.

No Compromise

I must bear a decided message to our brethren. Let there be no compromise with evil. Meet boldly the dangerous influences that arise. Do not fear for the results of resisting the powers of the enemy.

In these days many deceptions are being taught as truth. Some of our brethren have taught views which we cannot endorse. Fanciful ideas, strained and peculiar interpretations of the Scripture are coming in. Some of these teachings may seem to be but jots and tittles now, but they will grow and become snares to the inexperienced.

We have a decided work to do. Let not the enemy cause us to swerve from the proclamation of the definite truth for this time, and turn our attention to fanciful ideas.

Unless we are individually wide-awake to discern the workings of the Holy Spirit, we shall certainly stumble and fall into Satan's pitfalls of unbelief. I call upon our brethren to watch as faithful shepherds and guardians over the inexperienced, who are exposed to the wiles of seductive influences. Keep a continual lookout for rocks and quicksands that threaten to destroy faith in the messages that God has given for us at this time. Watch for souls as they that must give account....

We need to search the Scriptures daily, that we may know the way of the Lord, and that we be not deceived by religious fallacies.

The world is full of false theories and seductive spiritualistic ideas, which tend to destroy clear spiritual perception, and to lead away from truth and holiness. Especially at this time do we need to heed the warning, "Let no man deceive you with vain words." Ephesians 5:6.

We must be careful lest we misinterpret the Scriptures. The plain teachings of the word of God are not to be so spiritualized, that the reality is lost sight of. Do not overstrain the meaning of sentences in the Bible in an effort to bring forth something odd in order to please the fancy. Take the Scriptures as they read. Avoid idle speculation concerning what will be in the kingdom of heaven.—Manuscript 30, 1904.

A Life and Death Question

I would say to my brethren and sisters, Keep close to the instruction found in the word of God. Dwell upon the rich truths of the Scriptures. Thus only can you become one in Christ. You have no time to engage in controversy regarding the killing of insects. Jesus has not placed this burden upon you. "What is the chaff to the wheat?" These side issues which arise are as hay, wood, and stubble compared with the truth for these last days. Those who leave the great truths of God's word to speak of such matters are not preaching the gospel. They are dealing with the idle sophistry which the enemy brings forward to divert minds from the truths that concern their eternal welfare. They have no word from Christ to vindicate their suppositions.

Do not spend your time in the discussion of such matters. If you have any question as to what you should teach, any question as to the subjects upon which you should dwell, go right to the discourses of the Great Teacher, and follow his instructions....

Do not allow anything to draw your attention from the question, "What shall I do to inherit eternal life?" This is a life and death question, which we must each settle for eternity. Let the mind be weighted with the importance of the solemn truth which we possess. Those who allow the mind to wander in search of cheap, unimportant theories need to be converted.

Erroneous theories, with no authority from the word of God, will come in on the right hand and on the left, and to weaklings these theories will appear as truth which makes wise. But they are as nothingness. And yet many church members have become so well satisfied with cheap food that they have a dyspeptic religion. Why will men and women belittle their experience by gathering up idle tales and presenting them as matters worthy of attention? The people of God have no time to dwell on the indefinite, frivolous questions which have no bearing on God's requirements.

God desires men and women to think soberly and candidly. They are to ascend to a higher and still higher grade, commanding a wider and still wider horizon. Looking unto Jesus, they are to be changed into His image. They are to spend their time in searching for the deep, everlasting truths of heaven. Then there will be nothing frivolous in their religious experience. As they study the grand truths of God's word, they endure the seeing of Him who is invisible. They see that the most uplifting, ennobling truths are those most closely connected with the Source of all truth. And as they learn of Him, their motives and sympathies become firm and unchanging; for the impressions made by the All-Wise are substantial and enduring. The living water, which Christ gives, is not like a surface spring, which babbles for a short time, and then dries up. The living water springs up unto everlasting life. [163]

Let us follow the revealed will of God. Then we shall know that the light we receive comes from the divine source of all true light. Those who cooperate with Christ are on safe ground. God richly blesses them as they consecrate their energies to the work of rescuing the world from corruption. Christ is our example. By beholding Him we are to be changed into His image, from glory to glory, from character to character. This is our work. God help us rightly to represent the Saviour to the world.—*R. and H., August 13, 1901.*

Conjectures Regarding the Future Life

There are men today who express their belief that there will be marriages and births in the new earth; but those who believe the Scriptures cannot accept such doctrines. The doctrine that children will be born in the new earth is not a part of the "sure word of prophecy." The words of Christ are too plain to be misunderstood. They should forever settle the question of marriages and births in the new earth. Neither those who shall be raised from the dead, nor those who shall be translated without seeing death, will marry or be given in marriage. They will be as the angels of God, members of the royal family.

Preach the Word

I would say to those who hold views contrary to this plain declaration of Christ, Upon such matters silence is eloquence. It is presumption to indulge in suppositions and theories regarding matters that God has not made known to us in His word. We need not enter into speculation regarding our future state.

To my ministering brethren, I would say, "Preach the Word. Be instant in season and out of season." Do not bring to the foundation wood, and hay, and stubble,—your own surmisings and speculations, which can benefit no one.

Christ withheld no truths essential to our salvation. Those things that are revealed are for us and our children, but we are not to allow our imagination to frame doctrines concerning things not revealed.

The Lord has made every provision for our happiness in the future life, but He has made no revelations regarding these plans, and we are not to speculate concerning them. Neither are we to measure the conditions of the future life by the conditions of this life.

Matters of vital importance have been plainly revealed in the word of God. These subjects are worthy of our deepest thought. But we are not to search into matters on which God has been silent. Some have put forth the speculation that the redeemed will not have gray hair. Other foolish suppositions have been put forward, as though these were matters of importance. May God help His people to think rationally. When questions arise upon which we are uncertain, we should ask, "What saith the Scripture?"

Let those who wish for something new seek for that newness of life resulting from the new birth. Let them purify their souls by obeying the truth, and act in harmony with the instruction Christ gave to the lawyer who asked what he must do in order to inherit eternal life:

"Thou shalt love the Lord thy God with all thy heart, and with all thy soul, and with all thy strength and with all thy mind; and thy neighbor as thyself." "This do and thou shalt live." Luke 10:27, 28. All who will conform their lives to the plain requirements of God's word will inherit eternal life.—Manuscript 28, 1904.

Invitation to the Banquet

In this work there is danger of bringing before the people theories, which, while they may be all truth, will create controversy, and will not lead men to the great supper prepared for them. We want the love of God formed within to subdue and soften our human nature, and to bring us into conformity to His holy character. Then we shall spread before the people the unsearchable riches of Christ in all their abundance. The invitation is given by Christ Himself, and it is the work of all His followers to call attention to the board of provisions that has been made accessible to all. Then let not subjects difficult to be understood come first. Christ is calling men to the banquet, and let all who will, come.—Letter 89, 1898.

The One Hundred and Forty-Four Thousand

Christ says that there will be those in the church who will present fables and suppositions, when God has given grand, elevating, ennobling truths, which should ever be kept in the treasure-house of the mind. When men pick up this theory and that theory, when they are curious to know something it is not necessary for them to know, God is not leading them. It is not His plan that His people shall present something which they have to suppose, which is not taught in the Word. It is not His will that they shall get into controversy over questions which will not help them spiritually, such as, Who is to compose the hundred and forty-four thousand. This those who are the elect of God will in a short time know without question.

My brethren and sisters, appreciate and study the truths God has given for you and your children. Spend not your time in seeking to know that which will be no spiritual help. "What shall I do to inherit eternal life?" This is the all-important question, and it has been clearly answered. "What is written in the law? how readest thou?"—Manuscript 26, 1901.

Effect of Difference Among Ministers

Our church members see that there are differences of opinion among the leading men, and they themselves enter into controversy regarding the subjects under dispute. Christ calls for unity. But He does not call for us to unify on wrong practices. The God of heaven draws a sharp contrast between pure, elevating, ennobling truth and false, misleading doctrines. He calls sin and impenitence by the right name. He does not gloss over wrongdoing with a coat of untempered mortar. I urge our brethren to unify upon a true, Scriptural basis.—Manuscript 10, 1905.

"I write from fifteen to twenty pages each day. It is now 11 o'clock and I have written fourteen pages of manuscript for Volume IV.... As I write upon my book I feel intensely moved. I want to get it out as soon as possible, for our people need it so much. I shall complete it next month if the Lord gives me health as He has done. I have been unable to sleep nights, for thinking of the important things to take place. Three hours and sometimes five is the most sleep I get. My mind is stirred so deeply I cannot rest. Write, write, write, I feel that I must and not delay.

"Great things are before us, and we want to call the people from their indifference to get ready. Things that are eternal crowd upon my vision day and night. The things that are temporal fade from my sight."—Letter 11a, 1884.

"I regard this new edition with great satisfaction." "The book 'Great Controversy' I appreciate above silver or gold, and I greatly desire that it shall come before the people. While writing the manuscript of 'Great Controversy' I was often conscious of the presence of the angels of God. And many times the scenes about which I was writing were presented to me anew in visions of the night, so that they were fresh and vivid in my mind."—Letter 56, 1911.

"I walk with trembling before God, I know not how to speak or trace with pen the large subjects of the atoning sacrifice. I know not how to present subjects in the living power in which they stand before me. I tremble for fear lest I shall belittle the great plan of salvation by cheap words. I bow my soul in awe and reverence before God and say, 'Who is sufficient for these things?"—Letter 40, 1892.

"Now after I have been in this country nearly three years, there is still much to be done before the book will be ready for publication. Many branches of work have demanded my attention. I am pressed beyond measure with the work of writing out testimonies, caring for the poor, and traveling with my own conveyance, 8, 11 and 13 miles to meet with the churches."—Letter 69, 1894.

"My time for writing usually commences at three o'clock in the morning," she says, "when all in the house are asleep. Often I am awakened at half past twelve; one or two o'clock."—Letter 114, 1896.

"I awaken at half past two, and offer up my prayer to God in the name of Jesus. I am weak in physical strength; my head is not free from pain; my left eye troubles me. In writing upon the life of Christ, I am deeply wrought upon. I forget to breathe as I should. I cannot endure the intensity of feeling that comes over me as I think of what Christ has suffered in our world.

"He was a man of sorrows and acquainted with grief; He was wounded for our transgressions; He was bruised for our iniquities; the chastisement of our peace was upon Him, and with His stripes we are healed, if we receive Him by faith as our personal Saviour."—Manuscript 70, 1897.

"I have been passing through great trial in pain and suffering and helplessness, but through it all I have obtained a precious experience more valuable to me than gold."

"This unreconciliation was at the beginning of my sufferings and helplessness, but it was not long until I felt that my affliction was a part of God's plan. I found that by partly lying and partly sitting I could place myself in position to use my crippled hands, and although suffering much pain, I could do considerable writing. Since coming to this country, I have written sixteen hundred pages....

"Many nights during the past nine months, I was enabled to sleep but two hours a night, and then at times darkness would gather about me; but I prayed and realized much sweet comfort in drawing nigh

[192]

to God.... I was all light in the Lord. Jesus was sacredly near and I found the grace given sufficient."—Letter 7, 1892.

"I have about decided to ... devote all my time to writing for the books that ought to be prepared without further delay. I would like to write on the Life of Christ, on Christian Temperance ["Ministry of Healing"] and prepare testimony Number 34 [Volume 6], for it is very much needed....

"You know that my whole theme both in the pulpit and in private, by voice and pen, is the life of Christ."—Letter 41, 1895.

"The books are not Marian's productions, but my own, gathered from all my writings. Marian has a large field from which to draw, and her ability to arrange the matter is of great value to me. It saves my poring over a mass of matter, which I have no time to do."—Letter 61a, 1900.

"My work on the book, 'The Acts of the Apostles,' is completed. In a few weeks you shall have a copy. I have had excellent help in preparing this work for the press. There are other writings that I desire to get before our people, that they may speak when my voice is silent. The book on Old Testament History, ['Prophets and Kings'], which we hope to bring out next, will call for earnest effort. I am grateful for the help the Lord is giving me in the labors of faithful, trained workers, and that these workers are ready to carry forward this work as fast as it is possible."—Letter 88, 1911.

www.ingramcontent.com/pod-product-compliance
Lightning Source LLC
Chambersburg PA
CBHW080858010526
44118CB00015B/2190